Ken Bell

101 DAYS
IN THE
EPISTLES
WITH
OSWALD
CHAMBERS

Also available from Victor Books:

101 Days in the Gospels with Oswald Chambers / compiled by James R. Adair and Harry Verploegh

Plus:

A Time to Be Renewed (365 daily readings from the writings of Warren Wiersbe, compiled by James R. Adair)

Other available books compiled by Harry Verploegh:

A.W. Tozer: An Anthology, Christian Publications
The Set of the Sail, A.W. Tozer editorials, Christian Publications
We Travel an Appointed Way, A.W. Tozer editorials, Christian Publications
This World: Playground or Battleground? A.W. Tozer editorials, Christian Publications
The Price of Neglect, A.W. Tozer editorials, Christian Publications
The Warfare of the Spirit, A.W. Tozer editorials, Christian Publications
The Size of the Soul, A.W. Tozer editorials, Christian Publications
The Draper Book of Quotations for the Christian World, with Edythe Draper, Tyndale House Publishers
Prayer: A Holy Occupation, Oswald Chambers quotations on prayer, Discovery House

101 DAYS
IN THE
EPISTLES
WITH
OSWALD
CHAMBERS

including daily readings in
the Epistles in the words of
the *Holy Bible, New International Version*

Compiled by James R. Adair
and Harry Verploegh

VICTOR BOOKS

A DIVISION OF SCRIPTURE PRESS PUBLICATIONS INC.
USA CANADA ENGLAND

Editor: James Radford
Designer: Joe DeLeon

Library of Congress Cataloging-in-Publication Data

Chambers, Oswald, 1874–1917.
    101 days in the Epistles with Oswald Chambers / edited by James R. Adair and Harry Verploegh.
        p.   cm.
    Includes bibliographical references.
        1. Bible. N.T. Epistles—Meditations. 2. Devotional calendars.
I. Adair, James R., 1923– . II. Verploegh, Harry, 1909– . III. Bible. N.T. Epistles. English. New International. Selections. 1994. IV. Title. V. Title: One hundred one days in the Epistles with Oswald Chambers. VI. Title: One hundred and one days in the Epistles with Oswald Chambers.
    BS2635.4.C48 1994
    227'.06—dc20   94-8903
                                                                                   CIP

CONTENTS

FOREWORD

I first "met" Oswald Chambers when I was in prep school. The campus librarian, a grandmotherly type, knew my love for books, and for a birthday gift, she gave me a copy of the daily devotional *My Utmost for His Highest,* Chambers' most renowned work.

The man, of course, had been dead for forty years at that point, so you must understand that our introduction was a matter of my engaging him through his writings. When my friend the librarian brought us together, I had no clue that Chambers would become someone who would nourish me through the best and worst days of my life. So attached to him would I become that I would later refer to him as simply OC when I reflected on his words in my journal.

I must be candid to say that I was disappointed in the first encounters I had with OC because his words, which often challenged one to wait in silence upon God, were so adverse to my activist, make-it-all-happen-yourself mind-set. I neglected him for many months at a time and got back in touch only when I felt a surge of spiritual hunger or curiosity.

A second copy of Chamber's best-selling book came to me years later as a wedding gift. For the first months of our married life, Gail and I frequently looked into *My Utmost*, and I discovered that my friend was making more and more sense to me. OC tends to make that happen in the life of one who is getting older and feeling more and more beat up by the realities of life.

Since then I have received many more copies of Chambers' *Utmost* as gifts. And I have enjoyed using each one, marking the pages, underlining phrases, and writing blunt little notes to myself such as "he's sure got your number on this one."

Then there came the day when I spent several hours in delightful conversation with an aged woman, Dorothy Docking, who had known Oswald Chambers when she was a small girl. "Tell me everything you remember," I asked. And she did.

From her I learned that OC was a highly artistic man who could become consumed with the beauties of creation. Indeed, a reading of his journals (which I pursued much later) reveals this side of him when he goes to great lengths to describe the shadows and colors of a sunset on the Egyptian desert.

I learned that Chambers was a man with a brilliant mind and wit, and that he could seize and mold the minds and spirits of

9

tough men when he gave lectures on the Bible and on the classics. I learned that Chambers was a mentor to young people, a lover of children, and a shepherd to soldiers. Having heard all that, I returned to his writings and began to read far and wide everything that had been put into print under his name.

But this friendship with Oswald Chambers never reached its peak until I went through a deep personal trough in my life and was in great need of God's mercy. My sense of loss and shame was indescribable. Turning to my old friend, I began to realize that he must have known some deep personal losses of his own. No man could ever have written with the sensitivity and understanding of the restorative grace and kindness of Christ as he did unless he had somehow one day drawn upon those losses. That was a part of Chambers I'd not seen until I was in great need.

At that time I heard Chambers say (and I am paraphrasing), "When God permits you to be stripped of everything to do with your exterior life and work, He desires that you enhance the activities of your interior." I heard my friend encouraging me to seek silence, an enhanced intercessory life, and a deeper sense of the majesty of God. In just a sentence or two, OC had revitalized me with a sense of purpose and mission that no one could deny. There would be others swift to judge, quick to provide answers, and sharp to think that they understood causes and consequences. But Chambers understood that a persons' worst moments can be (in some cases) God's greatest opportunity to develop a person after His own heart. Themes of God's redeeming love began to leap out at me from all over Chamber's books, and I came to consider this man—even though he died more than twenty years before I was born—as among my closest friends.

I am delighted, therefore, to commend to you my "friend" Oswald Chambers and this book containing many of his insightful comments. He speaks to you and me out of his years among students and fighting men. He speaks from his days on the North African desert, which he loved, where he clearly derived many of his metaphors and appreciations of God's grandeur. He speaks from pain, from silence, from disciplined thought, and from a highly intimate journey with Jesus. In your desert moments, and in your spiritually curious hours, drink deeply from his well.

Gordon MacDonald

10

PREFACE

In this book you will enjoy readings in the Epistles of Paul, James, Peter, and John, portions of Scripture that you can comfortably read and assimilate in a devotional time. Combined with enlightening comments by Oswald Chambers, these readings will nurture you and give you a deeper understanding of the truths of God's Word.

Most of the comments by Chambers are from a collection of more than 10,000 excerpts that my longtime friend Harry Verploegh (pronounced Ver-ploo) chose from the author's more than thirty books, including his classic devotional, *My Utmost for His Highest.* Some excerpts not found in his books are from articles that Chambers wrote in the early 1900s for *God's Revivalist and Bible Advocate,* published by God's Bible School, Cincinnati, where Chambers taught for a time.

101 Days in the Epistles follows *101 Days in the Gospels with Oswald Chambers,* published in 1992 by Victor Books. Both books grew out of a desire on the part of the compilers to assemble a devotional book containing daily selections of Scripture of reasonable length, in contrast to a devotional volume with an overwhelming amount of Scripture or with only a verse or two for each reading.

In this book, the incisive comments by Oswald Chambers cast light on one key thought in each of the 101 readings and in a few instances illuminate the entire Scripture reading.

Why Chambers and not someone else? I can vividly recall Harry's excitement when in the mid-1980s he "discovered" Oswald Chambers and his uncanny knack for expressing Christian truth. More than once I heard Harry say, "Nobody says it quite like Chambers." Both of us had had a brushing acquaintance with Chambers long before Harry became a devotee of the beloved minister of the late 1800s and early 1900s. Harry gained his intense admiration for Chambers after he retired from the business world in the late '70s and began avidly reading "the saints and sages of the ages." Often reading and clipping quotations into the early morning hours and mounting them by subject on cards, he eventually had file drawers bulging with more than 100,000 quotations. Included were the thousands of excerpts from the writings of Chambers.

At times as I visited him, Harry enthusiastically shared some of the quotations he had dug out of Chamber's books. And since we had been talking about working together on a devotional book, I agreed with him that more readers should be exposed to the thinking of the great English preacher. The result: this book and our first, *101 Days in the Gospels with Oswald Chambers.*

We are indebted to Discovery House, Grand Rapids, Michigan, the U.S. representative of the Oswald Chambers Publications Association, South Croydon, Surrey, England, and to the Association itself for permission to include the excerpts from the books of Chambers.

The quotations have been edited from the standpoint of modern punctuation and spelling. Pronouns referring to deity in quotations are capitalized, whereas in the NIV text they are rendered in lowercase per NIV style. Bible quotations in excerpts are from a version of the *King James Bible* in use in the early 1900s.

Harry and I hope and pray that God will use this book to deepen your walk with Him, and that you will enjoy it enough to share the book with others.

James R. Adair

GOD'S UTMOST MAN

Oswald Chambers was remembered as a child for his readiness to pray and his confidence that God would answer his prayers, but it was not until his teenage years that prayer became the working of the miracle of redemption in him. Chambers was born on July 24, 1874 in Aberdeen, the fourth son of Clarence and Hannah Chambers. Hannah had been raised an Irvingite but became a Baptist under Spurgeon. Oswald's father was pastor of the Crown Terrace Baptist Church in Aberdeen, and later ministered in Stoke-on-Trent, Perth, and London.

After hearing Spurgeon preach in Dulwich, the city where his father retired, as a teenager Chambers professed faith in Christ and asked to be baptized and began visiting men in the YMCA lodging house. Later, he began teaching Sunday School and taking the Gospel to men—many of them ex-convicts—in lodging houses and missions. As a boy Chambers studied drawing at Sharp's Institute in Perth. He won an arts scholarship to study abroad from the Art School in South Kensington, but instead took the Arts Course at the University of Edinburgh until he decided at twenty-three to follow the counsel of a number of Scottish men of God who were aware of his spiritual gifts and to accept God's call to the ministry.

He attended the Dunoon Training School, founded by Duncan MacGregor, and within a year became a tutor in philosophy and psychology, taught art, and formed a Browning Society chapter. Chambers became known at Dunoon as a man of prayer who relied unequivocally on God to supply his needs. He was admired for his love of art and poetry, his radiant disposition, and his generosity to others. At this time he began to speak in open air meetings.

After seven years of study and teaching, Chambers left Dunoon in 1905. In that same year he met Bishop Juji Nakada, a Japanese evangelist, at a Pentecostal League meeting in Perth. Together, these two men—Chambers, "long like a poker," and Nakada, "short like a shovel"—planned to stir up the Spirit of God among the Holiness people in an evangelistic tour of America and Japan. Of this tour in 1906–1907, Chambers wrote in his diary that he felt a perfect sense of God's call and leading. In America he was one of "the Lord's spoilt bairns" who was being introduced in Brooklyn, Providence, Cincinnati, and Seattle to "choice souls." During his tour of Japan, Chambers visited the Oriental Mission Bible Society in Tokyo and several interior mission stations. He preached, and he witnessed the mighty preaching of Nakada.

Upon returning to London via Hong Kong, the Suez, Rome, and Paris, Chambers continued evangelistic work with the League of Prayer and made the acquaintance of the family of the Rev. David Lambert, then a junior minister of Sunderland. He wrote of Chambers during this period of evangelistic preaching:

> At the big London meetings he would find an odd corner to be alone with God before speaking in public. Now I know how much preparation there had been in years of discipline, and Christ-following, and strenuous thinking. I did not know it then, yet felt that there was insight and authority and spiritual power far above that of the average minister or missioner.

In the years 1911–1915, preceding his principleship of the Bible Training School near Clapham Common, London, Chambers preached and taught many missions for the League of Prayer in England, Scotland, and Ireland. He began to develop some of the characteristic emphases of his ministry. He stressed the artificiality of man-made religion. He insisted on God's high intention of blessing toward the lowliest and most ordinary Christian who abandons himself or herself in faith to Jesus Christ and makes an absolute commitment to the Word of God. He believed in disciplined study of the humanities as well as of the Bible lest the student learn no method to study God's Word and be forced, in Chambers' terms, to wander aimlessly in it as in a cultivated park. He stressed the importance of seeking a means of applying the experience of sanctification in practical Christian service.

Chambers' own characteristic readiness for God's use is demonstrated in a comment he made to H. Stark upon arriving in Plymouth for meetings: "I hope we shall have a very blessed weekend, Mr. Chambers," said Stark. Chambers replied, "If we behave ourselves, the Lord will help Himself to all He wants from us."

In the spring of 1910 Chambers married Gertrude Hobbs

("Biddy"), the woman who would later use her language skills to publish after his death Oswald Chambers' manuscripts and her notes of his lectures, sermons, and talks, including the devotional classic, *My Utmost for His Highest,* which she compiled.

After their marriage, Mrs. Chambers accompanied her husband on a four-month mission to the United States. On their return, Chambers settled into his work as principal of the new nondenominational Bible Training College for the education of home and foreign workers founded in Battersea, London, the center of the League of Prayer. After Chambers' death, student after student wrote of the special features of Chambers' leadership of the school in the five years before he went to the Eastern front as a chaplain for the YMCA. As a teacher, Chambers knew instinctively which students could not be forced to change their pet theories and required only his listening ear and patience to develop new understanding, and which students needed a devastating but salutary blow to their prejudices and pettinesses. Chambers was a beloved example to them of childlike trust in God and self-discipline ("Get out of bed and think about it afterwards," he would advise) and of a rare balance between flexibility and strength in both spiritual and practical matters.

At the outbreak of World War I, Chambers felt a deep and urgent need to exercise his ministry among the British forces but waited patiently for almost nine months for the details to fall into place. Between the fall of 1915 and his death in November 1917, Chambers established desert mission camps for British troops in Egypt at Zeitoun, nine miles from Cairo and at Ismailia, on the banks of the Suez Canal.

These places of peace in the midst of war preparation were built of native rush mats. The Zeitoun camp included a refreshment marquee for soldiers, a devotional hut for worship services, a smaller hut where Chambers and his assistants conducted Bible classes, a tiny "items" hut where stationery and books were sold, and a dugout. The Chambers family, which now included the tiny Kathleen and their devoted helper, Mary Riley, lived in a bungalow built for them. There they entertained a constant stream of guests. Former students from the Bible Training College assisted Chambers with the administration of the camp activities and the care of souls.

During his two-year ministry in Egypt, Chambers kept a diary where he recorded his early morning thoughts, activities of the day, plans for Bible studies or talks, the responses of his audiences, and encounters with individuals. Sixteen years after his death, extracts from this diary were published with many tributes to his influence on the Mediterranean Expeditionary Forces in *Oswald Chambers: His Life and Work.* With a painter's eye, Chambers repeatedly described the sunrise on the desert, sublime and dazzling with praise to God, a "sealing witness of peace," and at other times a scene of desperate turmoil about which he could be equally delighted:

> This morning is thick with Khamseen wind. As I write, the sky is a most formidable color, dense lurid copper, and the wind is rampaging with the old antique heat of leagues of desert, not a heat like the sun's heat, but the heat of blinding devastation. . . .

Chambers found his work among the men and the activity of the desert camps constantly invigorating. Of the sunrise near the Suez, he wrote:

> The splendor of these sunrises is unique. . . . All the noises of the camp are stirring and fine, the men are astir at 4 A.M., the stir, the movement of horses, the bugles, the whirr of aeroplanes, all makes this life a real delight to me somehow.

And of an Egyptian noon in July, Chambers noted:

> Sun! I have been considering it. One cannot conceive of such sun unless one has summered in Egypt. It is the only power that makes this land possibly habitable. It is fierce, appallingly so, but fascinating; my own experience is that desert life is productive of intense vitality and energy, not of languor.

Boundless energy and vitality is precisely what Chambers gave to thousands of soldiers from all parts of the Commonwealth who passed through the YMCA mission camps. Living in the discomfort of military bases, their futures uncertain, many afterward

gave tribute to the eloquence and spiritual influence of this gifted man of God. Douglas Downes described Chambers at work in
Egypt:

> One of my early memories of Oswald Chambers is that of a
> lithe figure in khaki, with the eyes of a prophet and the
> profile of a Savaronola, seated with a group of younger men
> at a table in the Central YMCA in Cairo. He is telling them
> in his delightful, sparkling, humorous way that he cannot
> see the need of so much entertainment stuff to keep the
> men together for an evening. Out there in his hut at
> Zeitoun, he can get a crowd of Australians night after night
> attracted by nothing but the message of redemption.
>   I went over to Zeitoun, and found the unheard-of thing
> had come to pass. Men whom no one could accuse of being
> religious turned up in large numbers on a weeknight to hear
> a religious talk. But it is no ordinary talk, and the man who
> gives it is no ordinary man. There is no appeal to the emo-
> tions, no cant religious phrases, no anecdotes, just a flow of
> clear, convincing reasoning — stark sincerity, speaking with
> the authority of deep personal experience; you are brought
> to the point where the natural man breaks down and where
> the supernatural must come in to carry you with its confi-
> dence right into the presence of God.

Men who visited the mission huts used similar words to describe Chambers' discernment of biblical truth as well as of human need. They mentioned his "penetrating gaze," his keen and
alert face, his "canny" understanding of individual men. Many
remembered the personal words of comfort Chambers gave them
on their departure for front lines in Palestine or France. Others
were visited by him while laid aside in hot canvas hospitals. He
was for more than one soldier a "detective of the soul, one who
has been in intimate fellowship with the unseen." With others
who have written of the heightened intensity that war brings to
the experience of life, Chambers knew that for many men bound
for the front, irresponsible pleasure-seeking would end and stern
issues would confront them. He relished the opportunity to speak
to them at a time when they would be more open to talk about
God and the soul, when the faith of many would be strained. He

insisted that in the midst of life-threatening circumstances, a soldier could maintain an unchanging relationship to God through the redemptive work of Christ.

Throughout the period of his chaplaincy, Chambers would not allow the disruption, devastation, and death that impringed on his consciousness, and crippled many spirits working near the front, to undermind his natural buoyancy and confidence in God's sovereignty. He was steadfast in his belief that "the lack of ability and master-mindedness to conduct the war" was an occasion for men to cast themselves on God and find His order in the "haphazard" of ordinary experience or in the midst of an appalling war when hundreds of thousands of men would be battered into eternity.

Chambers was aware, however, that his confidence in God's ends could seem like indifference to the senses of others assaulted by the horror and the contradictions of war. Together with the soldiers who visited the YMCA camps, he probed the meaning of war to men of faith, lecturing boldly on such topics as "Religious Problems Raised by War," "Is Human Sacrifice Redemptive?", "Has History Disproved the Song of the Angels?" (a Christmas talk), and "Does War Create or Reveal Wickedness?" Chambers read other men's attempts to sustain a Christian hope in wartime and was particularly helped by Denny's *War and the Fear of God* and Forsyth's *The Christian Ethics of War.*

At one point in his diary, Chambers recorded his mistaken intuition that the war would end by late 1916. Chambers found that his miscalculation was an indication that "the Holy Spirit must be recognized as the sagacious Ruler in all affairs, and not our astute common sense." In his own experience and in his detailed study of the Old Testament prophets in the last months of his life, Chambers found God's ways inscrutable, but that in the mystery of redemption:

God is prepared to run the risk of evil, so to speak, and the Cross is the proof that He Himself has taken the responsibility of its removal.

With many Christians of the Great War period, Chambers looked with amazement, wonder, and tears at the great bravery of the young men who, made of "grand human stuff," withstood the wrath and chaos of war. He prayed that the sacrifices would be acts of worship mirroring the obedience of Christ's painful sacrifice as the means of God's redeeming work. In the last weeks of his life, Chambers meditated on Israel's history as seen through the eyes of the prophets Hosea, Joel, and Amos, and considered the spectacle of human evil in his own time. He noted that Amos ascribes to God the power to effect "blasting and mildew and disease and pestilence and error and wrong." He concluded with Amos that all these occurrences are beyond the control of man, that all the consequences are in the "powerful hand of God, and not of blind cause and effect." Again and again, Chambers recorded his "joyful detection of God's ruling in the haphazard" in his diary. A month before his death, on a glorious morning when the East was "like a celestial scheme of shot silk," Chambers' heart sprang up to the call of the Prophet Amos:

Seek Him that maketh the Pleiades and Orion, and maketh the day dark with night, and turneth the shadow of death into the morning (Amos 4:8).

In the entries for October 1917, one senses that Chambers had extended himself to the limit of God's requirement. Twice he had to lump diary entries together for lack of opportunity to write. He persuaded Swan, a colleague in the YMCA mission, to lecture on Islam for him. Then, in preparation for a mission to Palestine to minister to the wounded and dying for General Allenby, he asked his wife to conduct services and rejoiced in the "lift" of inspiration he felt at those she led. Soon Mrs. Chambers would be called upon to carry Chambers' work, for by November 15, 1917 Oswald Chambers was at rest from the intense labor of biblical interpretation and spiritual counsel he fulfilled for the church in the period of the Great War.

It is hoped that this new book containing excerpts from the Chambers' publications will introduce a rising generation of Christians to the profound themes this gifted and faithful teacher explored during his vital ministry in God's joy and under His hand in the second decade of this century.

Virginia Verploegh Steinmetz
Durham, North Carolina

KEY TO SOURCES

The sources of Oswald Chambers' quotations appearing with daily Gospel readings in this volume are indicated in each instance by the abbreviation of the title of the Chambers' book from which the extract was taken. Page numbers shown relate to editions of Chambers' books published and copyrighted by Marshall, Morgan & Scott, London, England and/or Christian Literature Crusade, Fort Washington, Pennsylvania.

In the source list, the word *Discovery* following titles and dates indicates Oswald Chambers' titles more recently published and copyrighted by Discovery House Publishers, Grand Rapids, Michigan. *Zondervan* indicates titles now published and copyrighted by Zondervan Publishing House, Grand Rapids. *Chosen* indicates books now published and copyrighted by Chosen Books, Grand Rapids. In all cases, rights have been granted by the Oswald Chambers Publications Association.

AUG	*Approved unto God,* 1946, 1948
BFB	*Baffled to Fight Better,* 1931, 1990, Discovery
BE	*Biblical Ethics,* 1947
BP	*Biblical Psychology,* 1962
BSG	*Bringing Sons unto Glory,* 1943, 1990, Discovery (combined with *Making All Things New*)
CD VOL. 1	*Christian Discipline,* vol. I, 1935, 1936, 1985, Zondervan
CD VOL. 2	*Christian Discipline,* vol. II, 1935, 1936, 1986, Zondervan
CHI	*Conformed to His Image,* 1950, 1985, Chosen
DDL	*Devotions for a Deeper Life,* edited by Glenn D. Black (Grand Rapids: Frances Asbury Press, © 1986, God's Bible School)
DI	*Disciples Indeed,* 1955
GR	*God's Revivalist and Bible Advocate*
GW	*God's Workmanship,* 1953
HGM	*He Shall Glorify Me,* 1946
HG	*The Highest Good,* 1937, 1938, 1940, 1992, Discovery
HRL	*His Resurrection and Our Life,* 1930 by Oswald Chambers Publications Assoc., com-

	bined with *Bringing Sons unto Glory, Making All Things New* © 1990, Discovery
IWP	*If Thou Wilt Be Perfect,* 1941
IYA	*If Ye Shall Ask,* 1958, 1985, Chosen (*If You Will Ask,* revised title, 1989, Discovery)
LG	*The Love of God,* 1973, 1985, Chosen (Discovery, 1988)
MFL	*Moral Foundations of Life,* 1966
MUH	*My Utmost for His Highest,* © 1935, Dodd, Mead & Co., 1935; © renewed by Oswald Chambers Publications Association, 1963 (Discovery, 1989)
MUH-UE	*My Utmost for His Highest* (updated edition), © 1992 by Oswald Chambers Publications Assoc. Original edition © 1935 by Dodd, Mead & Co., Inc. Published by Discovery.
NKW	*Not Knowing Whither,* 1934, 1989, Discovery (combined with *Our Portrait in Genesis* under title *Not Knowing Where*)
OBH	*Our Brilliant Heritage,* 1929, 1930, 1931, 1975
OPG	*Our Portrait in Genesis,* 1957, 1989, Discovery (combined with *Not Knowing Where*)
PS	*The Philosophy of Sin,* 1960
PH	*The Place of Help,* 1935, 1989, Discovery
PR	*The Psychology of Redemption,* 1930, 1990, Discovery (under the title *Making All Things New,* combined with *Bringing Sons Unto Glory*)
RTR	*Run Today's Race,* 1968
SHL	*The Servant as His Lord,* 1957
SHH	*The Shade of His Hand,* 1936, 1991, Discovery
SA	*The Shadow of an Agony,* 1934, 1992, Discovery (combined with *The Highest Good*)
SSY	*So Send I You,* 1930
SH	*Still Higher for His Highest* (Grand Rapids: Zondervan, by special arrangement with Marshall, Morgan & Scott; © 1970, D.W. Lambert)
SSM	*Studies in the Sermon on the Mount,* 1960
WG	*Workmen of God,* 1937

1

To All Loved by God

Paul, a servant of Christ Jesus, called to be an apostle and set apart for the gospel of God – the gospel he promised beforehand through his prophets in the Holy Scriptures regarding his Son, who as to his human nature was a descendant of David, and who through the Spirit[a] of holiness was declared with power to be the Son of God by his resurrection from the dead: Jesus Christ our Lord. Through him and for his name's sake, we received grace and apostleship to call people from among all the Gentiles to the obedience that comes from faith. And you also are among those who are called to belong to Jesus Christ.

To all in Rome who are loved by God and called to be saints:

Grace and peace to you from God our Father and from the Lord Jesus Christ.

Paul's Longing to Visit Rome

First, I thank my God through Jesus Christ for all of you, because your faith is being reported all over the world. God, whom I serve with my whole heart in preaching the gospel of his Son, is my witness how constantly I remember you in my prayers at all times; and I pray that now at last by God's will the way may be opened for me to come to you.

I long to see you so that I may impart to you some spiritual gift to make you strong – that is, that you and I may be mutually encouraged by each other's faith. I do not want you to be unaware, brothers, that I planned many times to come to you (but have been prevented from doing so until now) in order that I might have a harvest among you, just as I have had among the other Gentiles.

23

I am obligated both to Greeks and non-Greeks, both to the wise and the foolish. That is why I am so eager to preach the gospel also to you who are at Rome.

I am not ashamed of the gospel, because it is the power of God for the salvation of everyone who believes: first for the Jew, then for the Gentile. For in the gospel a righteousness from God is revealed, a righteousness that is by faith from first to last,[b] just as it is written: "The righteous will live by faith."[c]

GOD'S WRATH AGAINST MANKIND

The wrath of God is being revealed from heaven against all the godlessness and wickedness of men who suppress the truth by their wickedness, since what may be known about God is plain to them, because God has made it plain to them. For since the creation of the world God's invisible qualities—his eternal power and divine nature—have been clearly seen, being understood from what has been made, so that men are without excuse.

For although they knew God, they neither glorified him as God nor gave thanks to him, but their thinking became futile and their foolish hearts were darkened. Although they claimed to be wise, they became fools and exchanged the glory of the immortal God for images made to look like mortal man and birds and animals and reptiles.

Therefore God gave them over in the sinful desires of their hearts to sexual impurity for the degrading of their bodies with one another. They exchanged the truth of God for a lie, and worshiped and served created things rather than the Creator—who is forever praised. Amen.

Because of this, God gave them over to shameful lusts. Even their women exchanged natural relations for unnatural ones. In the same way the men also abandoned natural relations with women and were inflamed with lust for one another. Men committed indecent acts with other men, and received in themselves the due penalty for their perversion.

Furthermore, since they did not think it worthwhile to retain the knowledge of God, he gave them over to a depraved mind, to do what ought not to be done. They have become filled with every kind of wickedness, evil, greed and depravity. They are full of envy, murder, strife, deceit and malice. They are gossips, slanderers, God-haters, insolent, arrogant and boastful; they invent ways of doing evil; they disobey their parents; they are senseless, faithless, heartless, ruthless. Although they know God's righteous decree that those who do such things deserve death, they not only continue to do these very things but also approve of those who practice them.

"I am not ashamed of the gospel, because it is the power of God
for the salvation of everyone who believes:
first for the Jew, then for the Gentile. . . .
Just as it is written: 'The righteous will live by faith.' "

From Oswald Chambers

꿀 We have no right to preach unless we present the Gospel; we should not advocate a cause or a creed or an experience but present the Gospel, and we cannot do that unless we have a personal testimony based on the Gospel. That is why so many preach what is merely the outcome of a higher form of culture. Until men get into a right relationship with God, the Gospel is always in bad taste. There is a feeling of silent resentment: "Don't talk about being born again and being sanctified; be vague." "Do remember the people you are talking to." "Preach the simple Gospel. . . ." If you take the people as a standard, you will never preach the Gospel; it is too positive. Our obligation to the Gospel is to preach it. AUG 39

꿀 "Yea, woe is unto me, if I preach not the Gospel!" (1 Cor. 9:16) An orator rouses human nature to do what it is asleep over; the New Testament preacher has to move men to do what they are dead-set against doing, viz., giving up the right to themselves to Jesus Christ. Consequently, the preaching of the Gospel awakens a terrific longing, but an equally intense resentment. The aspect of the Gospel that awakens desire in a man is the message of peace and good-will — but I must give up my right to myself to get there. The basis of human life has been put on redemption, and on the ground of that redemption any man can be lifted into right relationship with God. The Gospel is "the power of God unto salvation to everyone that believeth." There is no room for despair on the part of any man if he will only believe what the New Testament preacher proclaims — but it takes some believing. No thinking will ever make me a Christian; I can become a Christian only through listening to what is preached and accepting salvation as a gift; but I must think after I am a Christian. BE 52

ᴥ That the natural heart of man does not want the Gospel of God is proved by the resentment of the heart against the working of the Spirit of God: "No, I don't object to being forgiven; I don't mind being guided and blessed, but it is too much of a radical surrender to ask me to give up my right to myself and allow the Spirit of God to have absolute control of my heart." BP 135

ᴥ The Bible never gives definitions; the Bible states facts, and the Gospel that Jesus brought of good news about God is the most astounding thing the world ever heard, but it must be the Gospel that Jesus brought. HG 51

ᴥ Belief in Jesus is a miracle produced only by the effectiveness of redemption, not by impressive speech, nor by wooing and persuading, but only by the sheer unaided power of God. The creative power of redemption comes through the preaching of the Gospel, but never because of the personality of the preacher. MUH-UE 7/17

a. Or *who as to his spirit of holiness*
b. Or *is from faith to faith*
c. Hab. 2:4

2

ROMANS 2

GOD'S RIGHTEOUS JUDGMENT

Y ou, therefore, have no excuse, you who pass judgment on someone else, for at whatever point you judge the other, you are condemning yourself, because you who pass judgment do the same things. Now we know that God's judgment against those who do such things is based on truth. So when you, a mere man, pass judgment on them and yet do the same things, do you think you will escape God's judgment? Or do you show contempt for the riches of his kindness, tolerance and patience, not realizing that God's kindness leads you toward repentance?

But because of your stubbornness and your unrepentant heart, you are storing up wrath against yourself for the day of God's wrath, when his righteous judgment will be revealed. God "will give to each person according to what he has done."[a] To those who by persistence in doing good seek glory, honor and immortality, he will give eternal life. But for those who are self-seeking and who reject the truth and follow evil, there will be wrath and anger. There will be trouble and distress for every human being who does evil: first for the Jew, then for the Gentile; but glory, honor and peace for everyone who does good: first for the Jew, then for the Gentile. For God does not show favoritism.

All who sin apart from the law will also perish apart from the law, and all who sin under the law will be judged by the law. For it is not those who hear the law who are righteous in God's sight, but it is those who obey the law who will be declared righteous. (Indeed, when Gentiles, who do not have the law, do by nature things required by the law, they are a law for themselves, even though they do not have the law, since they show that the requirements of the law are written on their hearts, their con-

27

sciences also bearing witness, and their thoughts now accusing, now even defending them.) This will take place on the day when God will judge men's secrets through Jesus Christ, as my gospel declares.

THE JEWS AND THE LAW

Now you, if you call yourself a Jew; if you rely on the law and brag about your relationship to God; if you know his will and approve of what is superior because you are instructed by the law; if you are convinced that you are a guide for the blind, a light for those who are in the dark, an instructor of the foolish, a teacher of infants, because you have in the law the embodiment of knowledge and truth—you, then, who teach others, do you not teach yourself? You who preach against stealing, do you steal? You who say that people should not commit adultery, do you commit adultery? You who abhor idols, do you rob temples? You who brag about the law, do you dishonor God by breaking the law? As it is written: "God's name is blasphemed among the Gentiles because of you."[b]

Circumcision has value if you observe the law, but if you break the law, you have become as though you had not been circumcised. If those who are not circumcised keep the law's requirements, will they not be regarded as though they were circumcised? The one who is not circumcised physically and yet obeys the law will condemn you who, even though you have the[c] written code and circumcision, are a lawbreaker.

A man is not a Jew if he is only one outwardly, nor is circumcision merely outward and physical. No, a man is a Jew if he is one inwardly; and circumcision is circumcision of the heart, by the Spirit, not by the written code. Such a man's praise is not from men, but from God.

"Do you show contempt for the riches of His [God's]
kindness, tolerance and patience,
not realizing that God's kindness leads you toward repentance?"

FROM OSWALD CHAMBERS

❧ Because a man has altered his life, it does not necessarily mean that he has repented. A man may have lived a bad life and suddenly stops being bad—not because he has repented—but because he is like an exhausted volcano. The fact that he has become good is no sign of his having become a Christian. BFB 103

❧ Repentance brings us to the place where we are willing to receive any punishment under heaven so long as the law we have broken is justified. That is repentance, and I think I am right in saying that very few of us know anything at all about it. We have the idea that because God is so loving and gentle and kind, all we need do is to say we feel sorry for the wrong we have done and we will try to be better. That is not repentance; repentance means that I am remade on a plane which justifies God in forgiving me. CHI 27

❧ The last delusion God delivers us from is the idea that we don't deserve what we get. Once we see ourselves under the canopy of God's overflowing mercy, we are dissolved in wonder, love, and praise. That is the meaning of repentance, which is the greatest gift God ever gives a man. CHI 70

❧ Repentance means that we recognize the need for forgiveness— "Hands up, I know it." HGM 101

❧ It is not repentance that saves me; repentance is the sign that I realize what God has done in Christ Jesus. The danger is to put the emphasis on the effect instead of on the cause: It is my obedience that puts me right with God, my consecration. Never! I am put right with God because prior to all, Christ died. When I turn to God and by belief accept what God reveals, instantly the stupendous atonement of Jesus Christ rushes me into a right relationship with God; and by the supernatural miracle of God's grace I stand justified, not because I am sorry for my sin, not because I have repented, but because of what Jesus has done. The Spirit of God brings it with a breaking, all-over light, and I know, though I do not know how, that I am saved. MUH 302

❧ Repentance means that I estimate exactly what I am in God's sight, and I am sorry for it, and on the basis of redemption I become the opposite. SA 121

a. Psalm 62:12; Prov. 24:12
b. Isaiah 52:5; Ezek. 36:22
c. Or *who, by means of a*

29

3

ROMANS 3

GOD'S FAITHFULNESS

hat advantage, then, is there in being a Jew, or what value is there in circumcision? Much in every way! First of all, they have been entrusted with the very words of God.

What if some did not have faith? Will their lack of faith nullify God's faithfulness? Not at all! Let God be true, and every man a liar. As it is written:

"So that you may be proved right when you speak
   and prevail when you judge."[a]

But if our unrighteousness brings out God's righteousness more clearly, what shall we say? That God is unjust in bringing his wrath on us? (I am using a human argument.) Certainly not! If that were so, how could God judge the world? Someone might argue, "If my falsehood enhances God's truthfulness and so increases his glory, why am I still condemned as a sinner?" Why not say—as we are being slanderously reported as saying and as some claim that we say—"Let us do evil that good may result"? Their condemnation is deserved.

NO ONE IS RIGHTEOUS

What shall we conclude then? Are we any better?[b] Not at all! We have already made the charge that Jews and Gentiles alike are all under sin. As it is written:

"There is no one righteous, not even one;
   there is no one who understands,

no one who seeks God.
All have turned away,
 they have together become worthless;
there is no one who does good, not even one."ᶜ
"Their throats are open graves;
 their tongues practice deceit."ᵈ
"The poison of vipers is on their lips."ᵉ
"Their mouths are full of cursing and bitterness."ᶠ
"Their feet are swift to shed blood;
 ruin and misery mark their ways,
and the way of peace they do not know."ᵍ
 "There is no fear of God before their eyes." ʰ

Now we know that whatever the law says, it says to those who are under the law, so that every mouth may be silenced and the whole world held accountable to God. Therefore no one will be declared righteous in his sight by observing the law; rather, through the law we become conscious of sin.

RIGHTEOUSNESS THROUGH FAITH

But now a righteousness from God, apart from law, has been made known, to which the Law and the Prophets testify. This righteousness from God comes through faith in Jesus Christ to all who believe. There is no difference, for all have sinned and fall short of the glory of God, and are justified freely by his grace through the redemption that came by Christ Jesus. God presented him as a sacrifice of atonement,ⁱ through faith in his blood. He did this to demonstrate his justice, because in his forbearance he had left the sins committed beforehand unpunished — he did it to demonstrate his justice at the present time, so as to be just and the one who justifies those who have faith in Jesus.

Where, then, is boasting? It is excluded. On what principle? On that of observing the law? No, but on that of faith. For we maintain that a man is justified by faith apart from observing the law. Is God the God of Jews only? Is he not the God of Gentiles too? Yes, of Gentiles too, since there is only one God, who will justify the circumcised by faith and the uncircumcised through that same faith. Do we, then, nullify the law by this faith? Not at all! Rather, we uphold the law.

"No one will be declared righteous . . . by observing the law; rather, through the law we become conscious of sin. But now a righteousness from God . . . has been made known. . . . This righteousness from God comes through faith in Jesus Christ.

FROM OSWALD CHAMBERS

ॐ Imputed righteousness must never be made to mean that God puts the robe of His righteousness over our moral wrong, like a snow-drift over a rubbish heap; that He pretends we are all right when we are not. The revelation is that "Christ Jesus is made unto us righteousness" (see 2 Cor. 5:21); it is the distinct impartation of the very life of Jesus on the ground of the Atonement, enabling me to walk in the light as God is in the light, and as long as I remain in the light, God sees only the perfections of His Son. We are "accepted in the Beloved" (Eph. 1:6). CHI 81

ॐ No one is ever united with Jesus Christ until he is willing to relinquish not sin only, but his whole way of looking at things. To be born from above of the Spirit of God means that we must let go before we lay hold, and in the first stages it is the relinquishing of all pretense. What our Lord wants us to present to Him is not goodness, nor honesty, nor endeavor, but real solid sin; that is all He can take from us. And what does He give in exchange for our sin? Real solid righteousness. But we must relinquish all pretense of being anything, all claim of being worthy of God's consideration. MUH 68

ॐ The righteousness of God must be the foundation of our life as Christians. It is easy to talk about God's righteousness and His justice, but too often we banish the revelation of His character into the limbo of the abstract; we accept His righteousness as a theological doctrine, but we do not believe it practically. GW 44

ॐ If I try to be right, it is a sure sign I am wrong; the only way to be right is by stopping the humbug of trying to be and remaining steadfast in faith in Jesus Christ. "He that doeth righteousness is righteous, even as He is righteous" (1 John 3:7). GW 46

ॐ Righteousness must never be made to mean less than a guiltless position in the presence of justice and right. God justifies me by my

33

supernatural faith in Him, but it is my just walk that proves Him just in saving me; if I do not walk in the life of faith, I am a slander to God. NKW 46

❧ All our righteousness is "as filthy rags," unless it is the blazing holiness of Jesus in uniting us with Him until we see nothing but Jesus first, Jesus second, and Jesus third. SSM 54

---

a. Psalm 51:4
b. Or *worse*
c. Psalms 14:1-3; 53:1-3; Eccles. 7:20
d. Psalm 5:9
e. Psalm 140:3
f. Psalm 10:7
g. Isaiah 59:7-8
h. Psalm 36:1
i. Or *as the one who would turn aside his wrath, taking away sin*

4

ABRAHAM JUSTIFIED BY FAITH

 hat then shall we say that Abraham, our forefather, discovered in this matter? If, in fact, Abraham was justified by works, he had something to boast about — but not before God. What does the Scripture say? "Abraham believed God, and it was credited to him as righteousness."[a]

Now when a man works, his wages are not credited to him as a gift, but as an obligation. However, to the man who does not work but trusts God who justifies the wicked, his faith is credited as righteousness. David says the same thing when he speaks of the blessedness of the man to whom God credits righteousness apart from works:

"Blessed are they
　whose transgressions are forgiven,
　whose sins are covered.
Blessed is the man
　whose sin the Lord will never count against him."[b]

Is this blessedness only for the circumcised, or also for the uncircumcised? We have been saying that Abraham's faith was credited to him as righteousness. Under what circumstances was it credited? Was it after he was circumcised, or before? It was not after, but before! And he received the sign of circumcision, a seal of the righteousness that he had by faith while he was still uncircumcised. So then, he is the father of all who believe but have not been circumcised, in order that righteousness might be credited to them. And he is also the father of the circumcised who not only are circumcised but who also walk in the footsteps of the faith that our father Abraham had before he was circumcised.

It was not through law that Abraham and his offspring received the promise that he would be heir of the world, but through the righteousness that comes by faith. For if those who live by law are heirs, faith has no value and the promise is worthless, because law brings wrath. And where there is no law there is no transgression.

Therefore, the promise comes by faith, so that it may be by grace and may be guaranteed to all Abraham's offspring—not only to those who are of the law but also to those who are of the faith of Abraham. He is the father of us all. As it is written: "I have made you a father of many nations."[c] He is our father in the sight of God, in whom he believed—the God who gives life to the dead and calls things that are not as though they were.

Against all hope, Abraham in hope believed and so became the father of many nations, just as it had been said to him, "So shall your offspring be."[d] Without weakening in his faith, he faced the fact that his body was as good as dead—since he was about a hundred years old—and that Sarah's womb was also dead. Yet he did not waver through unbelief regarding the promise of God, but was strengthened in his faith and gave glory to God, being fully persuaded that God had power to do what he had promised. This is why "it was credited to him as righteousness." The words "it was credited to him" were written not for him alone, but also for us, to whom God will credit righteousness—for us who believe in him who raised Jesus our Lord from the dead. He was delivered over to death for our sins and was raised to life for our justification.

> *"He [Jesus] was delivered over to death for our sins*
> *and was raised to life for our justification."*

FROM OSWALD CHAMBERS

ও True justification can only result in sanctification. By justification God anticipates that we are holy in His sight, and if we will obey the Holy Spirit we will prove in our actual lives that God is justified in justifying us. Ask yourself—Is God justified in my justification?

Do I prove by the way I live and talk and do my work that God has made me holy? Am I converting God's purpose in justifying me into actual experience, or only delighting in God's anticipation? There is a great snare, especially in evangelical circles, of knowing the will of God as expressed in the Bible without the slightest practical working of it out in life. The Christian religion is the most practical thing on earth. CHI 58

❧ The meaning of the redemption is that God can justify the unjust and remain righteous, and He does it through the cross of Christ. It is not a thing to reason out, but a thing to have resolute faith in. GW 45

❧ Justification means two things—first, that God's Law is just, and second, that every sinner is unjust; therefore, if God is to justify a man, He can only do it by vindicating the Law, and by destroying the sinner out of him. GW 85

❧ In the cross of Calvary, our Lord is revealed as the Just One, making men just before God. God never justifies men outside Christ. No man can stand for one second on any right or justice of his own; but as he abides in Christ, Jesus Christ is made righteousness unto him. HG 108

❧ The justification of every sinner is by faith and by faith alone, and when a man walks in that faith, his justification appears in his flesh and justifies God. NKW 46

❧ We may be consciously free of sin, but we are not justified on that account; we may be walking in the light of our conscience, but we are not justified on that account either; we are only justified in the sight of God through the Atonement at work in our inner life. SHL 52

❧ We should battle through our moods, feelings, and emotions into absolute devotion to the Lord Jesus. We must break out of our own little world of experience into abandoned devotion to Him. Think who the New Testament says Jesus Christ is, and then think of the despicable meagerness of the miserable faith we exhibit by saying, "I haven't had this experience or that experience"! Think what faith in Jesus Christ claims and provides—He can present us faultless before the throne of God, inexpressibly pure, absolutely righteous, and profoundly justified. Stand in absolute adoring faith "in Christ Jesus, who became for us wisdom from God—and righteousness and sanctification and redemption . . ." (1 Cor. 1:30). How dare we talk of making a sacrifice for the Son of God! We are saved from hell and total destruction, and then we talk about making sacrifices! MUH-UE 11/13

---

a. Gen. 15:6; also in verse 22
b. Psalm 32:1-2
c. Gen. 17:5
d. Gen. 15:5

5

Peace and Joy through Christ

Therefore, since we have been justified through faith, we[a] have peace with God through our Lord Jesus Christ, through whom we have gained access by faith into this grace in which we now stand. And we rejoice in the hope of the glory of God. Not only so, but we also rejoice in our sufferings, because we know that suffering produces perseverance; perseverance, character; and character, hope. And hope does not disappoint us, because God has poured out his love into our hearts by the Holy Spirit, whom he has given us.

You see, at just the right time, when we were still powerless, Christ died for the ungodly. Very rarely will anyone die for a righteous man, though for a good man someone might possibly dare to die. But God demonstrates his own love for us in this: While we were still sinners, Christ died for us.

Since we have now been justified by his blood, how much more shall we be saved from God's wrath through him! For if, when we were God's enemies, we were reconciled to him through the death of his Son, how much more, having been reconciled, shall we be saved through his life! Not only is this so, but we also rejoice in God through our Lord Jesus Christ, through whom we have now received reconciliation.

Death through Adam,
Life through Christ

Therefore, just as sin entered the world through one man, and death through sin, and in this way death came to all men, because all sinned—for before the law was given, sin was in the world. But sin is not taken into account when there is no law.

39

Nevertheless, death reigned from the time of Adam to the time of Moses, even over those who did not sin by breaking a command, as did Adam, who was a pattern of the one to come.

But the gift is not like the trespass. For if the many died by the trespass of the one man, how much more did God's grace and the gift that came by the grace of the one man, Jesus Christ, overflow to the many! Again, the gift of God is not like the result of the one man's sin: The judgment followed one sin and brought condemnation, but the gift followed many trespasses and brought justification. For if, by the trespass of the one man, death reigned through that one man, how much more will those who receive God's abundant provision of grace and of the gift of righteousness reign in life through the one man, Jesus Christ.

Consequently, just as the result of one trespass was condemnation for all men, so also the result of one act of righteousness was justification that brings life for all men. For just as through the disobedience of the one man the many were made sinners, so also through the obedience of the one man the many will be made righteous.

The law was added so that the trespass might increase. But where sin increased, grace increased all the more, so that, just as sin reigned in death, so also grace might reign through righteousness to bring eternal life through Jesus Christ our Lord.

"Therefore, since we have been justified through faith,
we have peace with God through our Lord Jesus Christ,
through whom we have gained access by faith
into this grace in which we now stand."

FROM OSWALD CHAMBERS

❧ The path of peace for us is to hand ourselves over to God and ask Him to search us and reveal not what we think we are, or what other people think we are, or what we persuade ourselves we are or would like to be, but "Search *me* out, O God, explore *me* as I really am in Thy sight." BP 158

❧ The new creation is not something you can hold in your hand and say, "What a wonderful thing God has done for me"; the one indelible sign of the new creation is *"my* [Christ's] *peace."* It is never safe to trust in manifestations and experiences; where the miracle of the new creation touches the shores of our individual lives, it is always on the line of "My peace I give unto you." That is the meaning of, "And all things are of God, who hath reconciled us to Himself by Jesus Christ" (2 Cor. 5:18). GW 66

⁊ᵂ The redemption at work in my actual life means the nature of God garrisoning me round; it is the God of peace who sanctifies wholly; the security is almighty. The gift of the peace of Christ on the inside; the garrison of God on the outside. Then I have to see that I allow the peace of God to regulate all that I do, that is where my responsibility comes in — "and let the peace of Christ rule" (Col. 3:5), i.e., arbitrate, "in your hearts" and life will be full of praise all the time. HG 113

⁊ᵂ Whenever you obey God, His seal is always that of peace, the witness of an unfathomable peace, which is not natural, but the peace of Jesus. Whenever peace does not come, tarry till it does or find out the reason why it does not. MUH 349

⁊ᵂ "My help cometh from the Lord, who made heaven and earth" (Ps. 121:2). He will take you up, He will re-make you, He will make your soul young and will restore to you the years that the cankerworm hath eaten, and place you higher than the loftiest mountain peak, safe in the arms of the Lord Himself, secure from all alarms, and with an imperturbable peace that the world cannot take away. PH 5

⁊ᵂ The surest sign that God has done a work of grace in my heart is that I love Jesus Christ best, not weakly and faintly, not intellectually, but passionately, personally, and devotedly, overwhelming every other love of my life. SP 134

⁊ᵂ The essence of the Gospel of God working through conscience and conduct is that it shows itself at once in action. God can make simple, guileless people out of cunning, crafty people; that is the marvel of the grace of God. It can take the strands of evil and twistedness out of a man's mind and imagination and make him simple toward God, so that his life becomes radiantly beautiful by the miracle of God's grace. BP 206

⁊ᵂ *Grace* is a theological word and is unfortunately used, because we usually mean by theology something remote that has to do with

41

controversy, something whereby our mind is tied up in knots and our practical life left alone. In the Bible, theology is immensely practical. *Grace* means the overflowing nature of God; we see it in nature; we have no words to describe the lavishness of God. "The grace of our Lord Jesus Christ" is the overflowing of God's nature in entire and absolute forgiveness through His own sacrifice. BSG 47

≈ Purity in God's children is not the outcome of obedience to His Law, but the result of the supernatural work of His grace. "*I* will cleanse you"; "*I* will give you a new heart"; "*I* will put My Spirit within you, and cause you to walk in My statutes"; "*I* will do it all." GW 75

≈ The grace of God makes us honest with ourselves. We must be humorous enough to see the shallow tricks we all have, no matter what our profession of Christianity. We are so altogether perverse that God Almighty had to come and save us! NKW 89

≈ The grace of God is absolute, but your obedience must prove that you do not receive it in vain. OBH 111

≈ Grace is the overflowing immeasurable favor of God; God cannot withhold; the only thing that keeps back His grace and favor is our sin and perversity. OPG 18

≈ The phrase "a sinner saved by grace" means that a man is no longer a sinner; if he is, he is not saved. PS 25

---

a. Or *let us;* also in verses 2 and 3

6

ROMANS 6

DEAD TO SIN, ALIVE IN CHRIST

hat shall we say, then? Shall we go on sinning so that grace may increase? By no means! We died to sin; how can we live in it any longer? Or don't you know that all of us who were baptized into Christ Jesus were baptized into his death? We were therefore buried with him through baptism into death in order that, just as Christ was raised from the dead through the glory of the Father, we too may live a new life.

If we have been united with him like this in his death, we will certainly also be united with him in his resurrection. For we know that our old self was crucified with him so that the body of sin might be done away with, that we should no longer be slaves to sin—because anyone who has died has been freed from sin.

Now if we died with Christ, we believe that we will also live with him. For we know that since Christ was raised from the dead, he cannot die again; death no longer has mastery over him. The death he died, he died to sin once for all; but the life he lives, he lives to God.

In the same way, count yourselves dead to sin but alive to God in Christ Jesus. Therefore do not let sin reign in your mortal body so that you obey its evil desires. Do not offer the parts of your body to sin, as instruments of wickedness, but rather offer yourselves to God, as those who have been brought from death to life; and offer the parts of your body to him as instruments of righteousness. For sin shall not be your master, because you are not under law, but under grace.

SLAVES TO RIGHTEOUSNESS

What then? Shall we sin because we are not under law but under grace? By no means! Don't you know that when you offer yourselves to someone to obey him as slaves, you are slaves to the one

43

whom you obey—whether you are slaves to sin, which leads to death, or to obedience, which leads to righteousness? But thanks be to God that, though you used to be slaves to sin, you whole-heartedly obeyed the form of teaching to which you were entrusted. You have been set free from sin and have become slaves to righteousness.

I put this in human terms because you are weak in your natural selves. Just as you used to offer the parts of your body in slavery to impurity and to ever-increasing wickedness, so now offer them in slavery to righteousness leading to holiness. When you were slaves to sin, you were free from the control of righteousness. What benefit did you reap at that time from the things you are now ashamed of? Those things result in death! But now that you have been set free from sin and have become slaves to God, the benefit you reap leads to holiness, and the result is eternal life. For the wages of sin is death, but the gift of God is eternal life in[a] Christ Jesus our Lord.

> *"For we know that our old self was crucified with Him*
> *so that the body of sin might be rendered powerless,*
> *that we should no longer be slaves to sin —*
> *because anyone who has died has been freed from sin."*

FROM OSWALD CHAMBERS

- Sin is the outcome of a relationship set up between man and the devil whereby man becomes "boss" over himself, his own god. BE 52

- Sin is not wrong doing; it is wrong being, independence from God. God has undertaken the responsibility for its removal on the ground of the redemption. BE 62

- Knowledge of what sin is is in inverse ratio to its presence; only as sin goes do you realize what it is. When it is present, you do not realize what it is because the nature of sin is that it destroys the capacity to know that you sin. BE 78

- If we have light views about sin, we are not students in the school of Christ. The fact of sin is the secret of Jesus Christ's Cross; its removal is the secret of His risen and ascended life. BE 114 ɤ We express our character through our body; you cannot express a character without a body. When we speak of character, we think of a flesh-and-blood thing; when we speak of disposition, we think of something that is not flesh and blood. Through the Atonement, God gives us the right disposition; that disposition is inside our body, and we have to manifest it in character through our body and by means of our body. BP 167

ɤ The body we have is not sinful in itself; if it were, it would be untrue to say that Jesus Christ was sinless. IWP 55

ɤ Our spiritual life does not grow in spite of the body, but because of the body. "Of the earth, earthy" is man's glory, not his shame; and it is in the "earth, earthy" that the full regenerating work of Jesus Christ has its ultimate reach. MFL 39

ɤ Many put Romans 6:11 before Romans 6:6; i.e., they try to reckon themselves dead unto sin, before the old man has been crucified, and they find him very much alive. Supposing I [a slight-built person] should say, "I am going to reckon that I am enormously fat; that I weigh 253 pounds." That would be no more absurd than some people's reckoning that the old man is dead before entire sanctification. How do you know that he is not dead? Because you have to provide breakfast for him. You have to look after him. No man ever got through to sanctification without a tragedy; crucifixion is a cruel, ghastly death, and I have got to be willing to sign the death warrant. When you bring the old man to the cross for execution, he will do anything you like. He will say, "I will give all my money; I will give my gifts." But Christ has just one word for him — "GET!" He may plead, he may cry, but our Lord is merciless to sin. Your religion is becoming a vain farce, unless you have signed the death warrant. GR/ND

---

a. Or *through*

7

ROMANS 7

AN ILLUSTRATION FROM MARRIAGE

Do you not know, brothers—for I am speaking to men who know the law—that the law has authority over a man only as long as he lives? For example, by law a married woman is bound to her husband as long as he is alive, but if her husband dies, she is released from the law of marriage. So then, if she marries another man while her husband is still alive, she is called an adulteress. But if her husband dies, she is released from that law and is not an adulteress, even though she marries another man.

So, my brothers, you also died to the law through the body of Christ, that you might belong to another, to him who was raised from the dead, in order that we might bear fruit to God. For when we were controlled by the sinful nature,[a] the sinful passions aroused by the law were at work in our bodies, so that we bore fruit for death. But now, by dying to what once bound us, we have been released from the law so that we serve in the new way of the Spirit, and not in the old way of the written code.

STRUGGLING WITH SIN

What shall we say, then? Is the law sin? Certainly not! Indeed I would not have known what sin was except through the law. For I would not have known what coveting really was if the law had not said, "Do not covet."[b] But sin, seizing the opportunity afforded by the commandment, produced in me every kind of covetous desire. For apart from law, sin is dead. Once I was alive apart from law; but when the commandment came, sin sprang to life and I died. I found that the very commandment that was intended to bring life actually brought death. For sin, seizing the opportunity afforded by the commandment, deceived me, and through the commandment put me to death. So then, the law is holy, and the commandment is holy, righteous and good.

Did that which is good, then, become death to me? By no means! But in order that sin might be recognized as sin, it produced death in me through what was good, so that through the commandment sin might become utterly sinful.

We know that the law is spiritual; but I am unspiritual, sold as a slave to sin. I do not understand what I do. For what I want to do I do not do, but what I hate I do. And if I do what I do not want to do, I agree that the law is good. As it is, it is no longer I myself who do it, but it is sin living in me. I know that nothing good lives in me, that is, in my sinful nature.[c] For I have the desire to do what is good, but I cannot carry it out. For what I do is not the good I want to do; no, the evil I do not want to do — this I keep on doing. Now if I do what I do not want to do, it is no longer I who do it, but it is sin living in me that does it.

So I find this law at work: When I want to do good, evil is right there with me. For in my inner being I delight in God's law; but I see another law at work in the members of my body, waging war against the law of my mind and making me a prisoner of the law of sin at work within my members. What a wretched man I am! Who will rescue me from this body of death? Thanks be to God — through Jesus Christ our Lord!

So then, I myself in my mind am a slave to God's law, but in the sinful nature a slave to the law of sin.

> *"Who will rescue me from this body of death?*
> *Thanks be to God — through Jesus Christ our Lord."*

FROM OSWALD CHAMBERS

❧ When a person cries out who shall deliver him from the body of this death, he is not referring so much to the "old man" as he is referring to the whole man taken as a natural man. He therefore cries, "Where can I be delivered from this body that is now cleaving to me as a corpse? Nevermore can I live in peace. Where is the peace and the contentment that I used to know once? Where is the peace that I used to know before I ever knew these enormous truths of God?"

When Christ meets a man with the dark disposition, He disturbs him, then He *Delivers* him. "I thank God," says Paul, "through Jesus Christ." Christ divorces the two dispositions and gives the man victory. He puts the "old man" under and the "new man" over. Now we have the experience described in Galatians 5. Paul says, "The Spirit lusteth against the flesh (the old disposition), and the flesh lusteth against the Spirit," but the Spirit triumphs. Every man born again experiences glorious victory. The regenerated life is not an "up and down" life; it is a life of "up and up" until he gets to the place of sanctification. This is the first work of grace, *Salvation,* the experience of men and women who have been awakened by God, and have been born of the Spirit. Hundreds who have been born again believe they are sanctified, and when they find they are not, they go after the gift of tongues or something else, and say that Pentecost does not satisfy. The baptism with the Holy Ghost does satisfy, and puts a man where he can begin to satisfy Jesus. Regeneration divorces the two dispositions, then produces a wonderful thing in man's human nature, viz., 1 John 3:9: "Whosoever is born of God doth not commit sin." This is not sanctification; this is salvation. Sanctification makes little difference in a man's external life, but it makes all the difference inside. The man who is born again of the Spirit of God has victory all along the line. GR 4/14/10

ɤ The Bible reveals that death is inevitable — "and so death passed upon all men" (Rom. 5:12). "It is appointed unto men once to die" (Heb. 9:27). Repeat that over to yourself. It is appointed to every one of us that we are going to cease to be as we are now, and the place that knows us now shall know us no more. We may shirk it, we may ignore it, we may be so full of robust health and spirits that the thought of death never enters, but it is inevitable. SHL 35

ɤ The Bible says there are those who are intimidated by death, "That through death He might bring to nought him that had the power of death, that is, the devil; and might deliver them who through fear of death were all their lifetime subject to bondage" (Heb. 2:14-15). The thought of death is never away from them; it terrorizes their days, it alarms their nights. Now read very reverently Hebrews 5:7: "Who . . . having offered up prayers and supplications with strong crying and tears unto Him that was able to save Him from death . . . ? Who is that? The Lord Jesus Christ. SHL 25

---

a. Or *the flesh;* also in verse 25
b. Ex. 20:17; Deut. 5:21
c. Or *my flesh*

8

ROMANS 8

───────────◆───────────

LIFE THROUGH THE SPIRIT

T herefore, there is now no condemnation for those who are in Christ Jesus,[a] because through Christ Jesus the law of the Spirit of life set me free from the law of sin and death. For what the law was powerless to do in that it was weakened by the sinful nature,[b] God did by sending his own Son in the likeness of sinful man to be a sin offering.[c] And so he condemned sin in sinful man,[d] in order that the righteous requirements of the law might be fully met in us, who do not live according to the sinful nature but according to the Spirit.

Those who live according to the sinful nature have their minds set on what that nature desires; but those who live in accordance with the Spirit have their minds set on what the Spirit desires. The mind of sinful man[e] is death, but the mind controlled by the Spirit is life and peace; the sinful mind[f] is hostile to God. It does not submit to God's law, nor can it do so. Those controlled by the sinful nature cannot please God.

You, however, are controlled not by the sinful nature but by the Spirit, if the Spirit of God lives in you. And if anyone does not have the Spirit of Christ, he does not belong to Christ. But if Christ is in you, your body is dead because of sin, yet your spirit is alive because of righteousness. And if the Spirit of him who raised Jesus from the dead is living in you, he who raised Christ from the dead will also give life to your mortal bodies through his Spirit, who lives in you.

Therefore, brothers, we have an obligation—but it is not to the sinful nature, to live according to it. For if you live according to the sinful nature, you will die; but if by the Spirit you put to death the misdeeds of the body, you will live, because those who are led by the Spirit of God are sons of God. For you did not receive a spirit that makes you a slave again to fear, but you received the Spirit of sonship.[g] And by him we cry, "Abba,[h] Father." The Spirit himself testifies with our spirit that we are God's children. Now if we are children, then we are heirs—heirs of God and co-heirs with Christ, if indeed we share in his sufferings in order that we may also share in his glory.

FUTURE GLORY

I consider that our present sufferings are not worth comparing with the glory that will be revealed in us. The creation waits in eager expectation for the sons of God to be revealed. For the creation was subjected to frustration, not by its own choice, but by the will of the one who subjected it, in hope that[i] the creation itself will be liberated from its bondage to decay and brought into the glorious freedom of the children of God.

We know that the whole creation has been groaning as in the pains of childbirth right up to the present time. Not only so, but we ourselves, who have the firstfruits of the Spirit, groan inwardly as we wait eagerly for our adoption as sons, the redemption of our bodies. For in this hope we were saved. But hope that is seen is no hope at all. Who hopes for what he already has? But if we hope for what we do not yet have, we wait for it patiently.

In the same way, the Spirit helps us in our weakness. We do not know what[j] we ought to pray for, but the Spirit himself intercedes for us with groans that words cannot express. And he who searches our hearts knows the mind of the Spirit, because the Spirit intercedes for the saints in accordance with God's will.

MORE THAN CONQUERORS

And we know that in all things God works for the good of those who love him,[k] who[l] have been called according to his purpose. For those God foreknew he also predestined to be conformed to the likeness of his Son, that he might be the firstborn among many brothers. And those he predestined, he also called; those he called, he also justified; those he justified, he also glorified.

What, then, shall we say in response to this? If God is for us, who can be against us? He who did not spare his own Son, but gave him up for us all—how will he not also, along with him, graciously give us all things? Who will bring any charge against those whom God has chosen? It is God who justifies. Who is he that condemns? Christ Jesus, who died—more than that, who was raised to life—is at the right hand of God and is also interceding for us. Who shall separate us from the love of Christ? Shall trouble or hardship or persecution or famine or nakedness or danger or sword? As it is written:

"For your sake we face death all day long;
we are considered as sheep to be slaughtered."[m]

No, in all these things we are more than conquerors through him who loved us. For I am convinced that neither death nor life, neither angels nor demons,[n] neither the present nor the future, nor any powers, neither height nor depth, nor anything else in all creation, will be able to separate us from the love of God that is in Christ Jesus our Lord.

*"Those who live according to the sinful nature
have their minds set on what that nature desires;
but those who live in accordance with the Spirit
have their minds set on what the Spirit desires."*

FROM OSWALD CHAMBERS

୬ The Holy Ghost is seeking to awaken men and women out of lethargy; He is pleading, yearning, blessing, pouring benedictions on them, convicting and drawing them nearer, for one purpose only, that they may receive Him so that He may make them holy men and women exhibiting the life of Jesus Christ. BE 99

୬ The Holy Spirit alone makes Jesus real; the Holy Spirit alone expounds His Cross; the Holy Spirit alone convicts of sin; the Holy Spirit alone does in us what Jesus did for us. BE 99

୬ The thought is unspeakably full of glory that God the Holy Ghost can come into my heart and fill it so full that the life of God will manifest itself all through this body which used to manifest exactly the opposite. If I am willing and determined to keep in the light and obey the Spirit, then the characteristics of the indwelling Christ will manifest themselves. BP 146

℘ When the Holy Spirit comes in, unbelief is turned out and the energy of God is put into us, and we are enabled to will and to do of His good pleasure. When the Holy Spirit comes in, He sheds abroad the love of God in our hearts, so that we are able to show our fellows the same love that God has shown to us. When the Holy Spirit comes in, He makes us as "light," and our righteousness will exceed the righteousness of the most moral, upright, natural man because the supernatural has been made natural in us. BP 222

℘ Our great need is to ask for and receive the Holy Ghost in simple faith in the marvelous Atonement of Jesus Christ, and He will turn us into passionate lovers of the Lord. It is this passion for Christ worked out in us that makes us witnesses to Jesus wherever we are, men and women in whom He delights, upon whom He can look down with approval; men and women whom He can put in the shadow or the sun; men and women whom He can put upon their beds or on their feet; men and women whom He can send anywhere He chooses PH 33

℘ The Holy Spirit does in us what Jesus Christ did for us. PR 14

---

a. Some later manuscripts *Jesus, who do not live according to the sinful nature but according to the Spirit,*
b. Or *the flesh;* also in verses 4, 5, 8, 9, 12 and 13
c. Or *man, for sin*
d. Or *in the flesh*
e. Or *mind set on the flesh*
f. Or *the mind set on the flesh*
g. Or *adoption*
h. Aramaic for *Father*
i. Or *subjected it in hope.* [21]*For*
j. Some manuscripts *And we know that all things work together for good to those who love God*
k. Or *works together with those who love him to bring about what is good — with those who*
l. Psalm 44:22
m. Or *nor heavenly rulers*

9

━━━━━ ✤ ━━━━━

GOD'S SOVEREIGN CHOICE

I speak the truth in Christ—I am not lying, my conscience confirms it in the Holy Spirit—I have great sorrow and unceasing anguish in my heart. For I could wish that I myself were cursed and cut off from Christ for the sake of my brothers, those of my own race, the people of Israel. Theirs is the adoption as sons; theirs the divine glory, the covenants, the receiving of the law, the temple worship and the promises. Theirs are the patriarchs, and from them is traced the human ancestry of Christ, who is God over all, forever praised!ᵃ Amen.

It is not as though God's word had failed. For not all who are descended from Israel are Israel. Nor because they are his descendants are they all Abraham's children. On the contrary, "It is through Isaac that your offspring will be reckoned."ᵇ In other words, it is not the natural children who are God's children, but it is the children of the promise who are regarded as Abraham's offspring. For this was how the promise was stated: "At the appointed time I will return, and Sarah will have a son."ᶜ

Not only that, but Rebekah's children had one and the same father, our father Isaac. Yet, before the twins were born or had done anything good or bad—in order that God's purpose in election might stand: not by works but by him who calls—she was told, "The older will serve the younger."ᵈ Just as it is written: "Jacob I loved, but Esau I hated."ᵉ

What then shall we say? Is God unjust? Not at all! For he says to Moses,

"I will have mercy on whom I have mercy,
  and I will have compassion on whom I
    have compassion."ᶠ

It does not, therefore, depend on man's desire or effort, but on God's mercy. For the Scripture says to Pharaoh: "I raised you up for this very purpose, that I might display my power in you and that my name might be proclaimed in all the earth."[g] Therefore God has mercy on whom he wants to have mercy, and he hardens whom he wants to harden.

One of you will say to me: "Then why does God still blame us? For who resists his will?" But who are you, O man, to talk back to God? "Shall what is formed say to him who formed it, 'Why did you make me like this?' "[h] Does not the potter have the right to make out of the same lump of clay some pottery for noble purposes and some for common use?

What if God, choosing to show his wrath and make his power known, bore with great patience the objects of his wrath—prepared for destruction? What if he did this to make the riches of his glory known to the objects of his mercy, whom he prepared in advance for glory—even us, whom he also called, not only from the Jews but also from the Gentiles? As he says in Hosea:

"I will call them 'my people' who are not my people;
    and I will call her 'my loved one' who is not my loved one,"[i]

and,

"It will happen that in the very place where it was said
        to them,
    'You are not my people,'
they will be called 'sons of the living God.' "[j]

Isaiah cries out concerning Israel:

"Though the number of the Israelites be like the sand by
        the sea,
    only the remnant will be saved.
For the Lord will carry out
    his sentence on earth with speed and finality."[k]

It is just as Isaiah said previously:

"Unless the Lord Almighty
    had left us descendants,

we would have become like Sodom,
    we would have been like Gomorrah."[l]

ISRAEL'S UNBELIEF

What then shall we say? That the Gentiles, who did not pursue righteousness, have obtained it, a righteousness that is by faith; but Israel, who pursued a law of righteousness, has not attained it. Why not? Because they pursued it not by faith but as if it were by works. They stumbled over the "stumbling stone." As it is written:

"See, I lay in Zion a stone that causes men to stumble
    and a rock that makes them fall,
and the one who trusts in him will never be put
    to shame."[m]

Brothers, my heart's desire and prayer to God for the Israelites is that they may be saved. For I can testify about them that they are zealous for God, but their zeal is not based on knowledge. Since they did not know the righteousness that comes from God and sought to establish their own, they did not submit to God's righteousness. Christ is the end of the law so that there may be righteousness for everyone who believes.

Moses describes in this way the righteousness that is by the law: "The man who does these things will live by them."[n] But the righteousness that is by faith says: "Do not say in your heart, 'Who will ascend into heaven?' "[o] (that is, to bring Christ down) "or 'Who will descend into the deep?' "[p] (that is, to bring Christ up from the dead). But what does it say? "The word is near you; it is in your mouth and in your heart,"[q] that is, the word of faith we are proclaiming: That if you confess with your mouth, "Jesus is Lord," and believe in your heart that God raised him from the dead, you will be saved. For it is with your heart that you believe and are justified, and it is with your mouth that you confess and are saved. As the Scripture says, "Anyone who trusts in him will never be put to shame."[r] For there is no difference between Jew and Gentile — the same Lord is Lord of all and richly blesses all who call on him, for, "Everyone who calls on the name of the Lord will be saved."[s]

How, then, can they call on the one they have not believed in? And how can they believe in the one of whom they have not heard? And how can they hear without someone preaching to them? And how can they preach unless they are sent? As it is written, "How beautiful are the feet of those who bring good news!"ᵗ

But not all the Israelites accepted the good news. For Isaiah says, "Lord, who has believed our message?"ᵘ Consequently, faith comes from hearing the message, and the message is heard through the word of Christ. But I ask: Did they not hear? Of course they did:

"Their voice has gone out into all the earth,
their words to the ends of the world."ᵛ

Again I ask: Did Israel not understand? First, Moses says,

"I will make you envious by those who are not a nation;
I will make you angry by a nation that has no
understanding."ʷ

And Isaiah boldly says,

"I was found by those who did not seek me;
I revealed myself to those who did not ask for me."ˣ

But concerning Israel he says,

"All day long I have held out my hands
to a disobedient and obstinate people."ʸ

"If you confess with your mouth, 'Jesus is Lord,'
and believe in your heart
that God raised Him from the dead,
you will be saved."

FROM OSWALD CHAMBERS

❧ Salvation is an immense marvel to me—I, a sinner, can be made into a saint; but it is only possible because of what Jesus Christ did.
BSG 53

58

❧ No man can be saved by praying, by believing, by obeying, or by consecration; salvation is a free gift of God's almighty grace. We have the sneaking idea that we earn things and get into God's favor by what we do — by our praying, by our repentance; the only way we get into God's favor is by the sheer gift of His grace. GW 11

❧ There is nothing so secure as the salvation of God; it is as eternal as the mountains, and it is our trust in God that brings us the conscious realization of this. HG 28

❧ Salvation is not merely deliverance from sin, nor the experience of personal holiness; the salvation of God is deliverance out of self entirely into union with Himself. My experimental knowledge of salvation will be along the line of deliverance from sin and of personal holiness; but salvation means that the Spirit of God has brought me into touch with God's personality, and I am thrilled with something infinitely greater than myself; I am caught up into the abandonment of God. MUH 73

❧ "Work out your salvation. . . ." We have not to work out that which tells for our salvation, but to work out in the expression of our lives the salvation which God has worked in. What does my tongue say? What things do my ears like to listen to? What kind of bodily associates do I like to be with? OBH 131

❧ It is God who is the architect of salvation; therefore salvation is not a commonsense design; what we have to do is to get inside that salvation. If I put my faith in any erection of my own, my vows and decisions, my consecration, I am building something for myself; I must cooperate with God in His plan of salvation. OPG 20

---

a. Or *Christ, who is over all. God be forever praised!* Or *Christ. God who is over all be forever praised!*
b. Gen. 21:12
c. Gen. 18: 10, 14
d. Gen. 25:23
e. Mal. 1:2-3
f. Exodus 33:19
g. Exodus 9:16
h. Isaiah 29:16; 45:9
i. Hosea 2:23
j. Hosea 1:10
k. Isaiah 10:22-23
l. Isaiah 1:9

m. Isaiah 8:14; 28:16
n. Lev. 18:5
o. Deut. 30:12
p. Deut. 30:13
q. Deut. 30:14
r. Isaiah 28:16
s. Joel 2:32
t. Isaiah 52:7
u. Isaiah 53:1
v. Psalm 19:4
w. Deut. 32:21
x. Isaiah 65:1
y. Isaiah 65:2

10

ROMANS 11

THE REMNANT OF ISRAEL

I ask then: Did God reject his people? By no means! I am an Israelite myself, a descendant of Abraham, from the tribe of Benjamin. God did not reject his people, whom he foreknew. Don't you know what the Scripture says in the passage about Elijah—how he appealed to God against Israel: "Lord, they have killed your prophets and torn down your altars; I am the only one left, and they are trying to kill me"?[a] And what was God's answer to him? "I have reserved for myself seven thousand who have not bowed the knee to Baal."[b] So too, at the present time there is a remnant chosen by grace. And if by grace, then it is no longer by works; if it were, grace would no longer be grace.[c]

What then? What Israel sought so earnestly it did not obtain, but the elect did. The others were hardened, as it is written:

"God gave them a spirit of stupor,
  eyes so that they could not see
  and ears so that they could not hear,
to this very day."[d]

And David says:

"May their table become a snare and a trap,
  a stumbling block and a retribution for them.
May their eyes be darkened so they cannot see,
  and their backs be bent forever."[e]

INGRAFTED BRANCHES

Again I ask: Did they stumble so as to fall beyond recovery? Not at all! Rather, because of their transgression, salvation has come to the Gentiles to make Israel envious. But if their transgression means riches for the world, and their loss means riches for the Gentiles, how much greater riches will their fullness bring!

I am talking to you Gentiles. Inasmuch as I am the apostle to the Gentiles, I make much of my ministry in the hope that I may somehow arouse my own people to envy and save some of them. For if their rejection is the reconciliation of the world, what will their acceptance be but life from the dead? If the part of the dough offered as firstfruits is holy, then the whole batch is holy; if the root is holy, so are the branches.

If some of the branches have been broken off, and you, though a wild olive shoot, have been grafted in among the others and now share in the nourishing sap from the olive root, do not boast over those branches. If you do, consider this: You do not support the root, but the root supports you. You will say then, "Branches were broken off so that I could be grafted in." Granted. But they were broken off because of unbelief, and you stand by faith. Do not be arrogant, but be afraid. For if God did not spare the natural branches, he will not spare you either.

Consider therefore the kindness and sternness of God: sternness to those who fell, but kindness to you, provided that you continue in his kindness. Otherwise, you also will be cut off. And if they do not persist in unbelief, they will be grafted in, for God is able to graft them in again. After all, if you were cut out of an olive tree that is wild by nature, and contrary to nature were grafted into a cultivated olive tree, how much more readily will these, the natural branches, be grafted into their own olive tree!

ALL ISRAEL WILL BE SAVED

I do not want you to be ignorant of this mystery, brothers, so that you may not be conceited: Israel has experienced a hardening in part until the full number of the Gentiles has come in. And so all Israel will be saved, as it is written:

"The deliverer will come from Zion;
  he will turn godlessness away from Jacob.
And this is my[f] covenant with them
  when I take away their sins."[g]

As far as the gospel is concerned, they are enemies on your account; but as far as election is concerned, they are loved on account of the patriarchs, for God's gifts and his call are irrevocable. Just as you who were at one time disobedient to God have now received mercy as a result of their disobedience, so they too have now become disobedient in order that they too may now[h] receive mercy as a result of God's mercy to you. For God has bound all men over to disobedience so that he may have mercy on them all.

DOXOLOGY

Oh, the depth of the riches of the wisdom and[i] knowledge
   of God!
How unsearchable his judgments,
  and his paths beyond tracing out!
"Who has known the mind of the Lord?
  Or who has been his counselor?"[j]
"Who has ever given to God,
  that God should repay him?"[k]
For from him and through him and to him are all things.
  To him be the glory forever! Amen.

"Some of the branches have been broken off, and you . . .
have been grafted in among the others and now share
in the nourishing sap from the olive root."

FROM OSWALD CHAMBERS

🙠 God created them [Jews] from Abraham to be His servants until through them every nation came to know who Jehovah was. They mistook the election of God's purpose to be the election of God's favoritism, and the story of their distress is due to their determination to use themselves for purposes other than God's. To this day they survive miraculously; the reason for their survival is the purpose of God to be fulfilled through them. OPG 39

🙠 God created the people known as Israel for one purpose, to be the servant of Jehovah until through them every nation came to knowwho Jehovah was. The nation created for the service of Jehovah failed to fulfill God's predestination for it; then God called out a remnant, and the remnant failed; then out of the remnant came One who succeeded, the One whom we know as the Lord Jesus Christ. The Savior of the world came of this nation. He is called "the Servant of God" because He expresses exactly the creative purpose of God for the historic people of God. Through that one Man, the purpose of God for the individual, for the chosen nation, and for the whole world is to be fulfilled. It is through Him that we are made "a royal priesthood." SSY 101

❧ There were no nations until after the Flood. After the Flood the human race was split up into nations, and God called off one stream of the human race in Abraham, and created a nation out of that one man. The Old Testament is not a history of the nations of the world, but the history of that one nation. In secular history Israel is disregarded as being merely a miserable horde of slaves, and justly so from the standpoint of the historian. The nations to which the Bible pays little attention are much finer to read about, but they have no importance in the redemptive purpose of God. His purpose was the creation of a nation to be His bondslave, that through that nation all the other nations should come to know Him.

The idea that Israel was a magnificently developed type of nation is a mistaken one. Israel was a despised, and a despisable nation, continually turning away from God into idolatry; but nothing ever altered the purpose of God for the nation. The despised element is always a noticeable element in the purpose of God. When the Savior of the world came, He came of that despised nation; He Himself was "despised and rejected of men" (Isa. 53:3), and in all Christian enterprise there is this same despised element, "things that are despised hath God chosen" (1 Cor. 1:28). SSY 104

❧ The essential pride of Israel and Judah (and of the Pharisees in our Lord's day) was that God was obliged to select them because of their superiority to other nations. God did not select them: God created them for one purpose, to be His bondslaves. SSY 103

❧ Israel is still in the shadow of God's hand, in spite of all her wickedness. God's purposes are always fulfilled, no matter how wide a compass He may permit to be taken first. SSY 108

---

a. 1 Kings 19:10, 14
b. 1 Kings 19:18
c. Some manuscripts *by grace. But if by works, then it is no longer grace; if it were, work would no longer be work.*
d. Deut. 29:4; Isaiah 29:10
e. Psalm 69:22-23

f. Or *will be*
g. Isaiah 59:20-21; 27:9; Jer. 31:33-34
h. Some manuscripts do not have *now.*
i. Or *riches and the wisdom and the*
j. Isaiah 40:13
k. Job 41:11

11

LIVING SACRIFICES

T herefore, I urge you, brothers, in view of God's mercy, to offer your bodies as living sacrifices, holy and pleasing to God—this is your spiritual[a] act of worship. Do not conform any longer to the pattern of this world, but be transformed by the renewing of your mind. Then you will be able to test and approve what God's will is—his good, pleasing and perfect will.

For by the grace given me I say to every one of you: Do not think of yourself more highly than you ought, but rather think of yourself with sober judgment, in accordance with the measure of faith God has given you. Just as each of us has one body with many members, and these members do not all have the same function, so in Christ we who are many form one body, and each member belongs to all the others. We have different gifts, according to the grace given us. If a man's gift is prophesying, let him use it in proportion to his[b] faith. If it is serving, let him serve; if it is teaching, let him teach; if it is encouraging, let him encourage; if it is contributing to the needs of others, let him give generously; if it is leadership, let him govern diligently; if it is showing mercy, let him do it cheerfully.

LOVE

Love must be sincere. Hate what is evil; cling to what is good. Be devoted to one another in brotherly love. Honor one another above yourselves. Never be lacking in zeal, but keep your spiritual fervor, serving the Lord. Be joyful in hope, patient in affliction, faithful in prayer. Share with God's people who are in need. Practice hospitality.

Bless those who persecute you; bless and do not curse. Rejoice with those who rejoice; mourn with those who mourn. Live in harmony with one another. Do not be proud, but be willing to associate with people of low position.[c] Do not be conceited.

Do not repay anyone evil for evil. Be careful to do what is right in the eyes of everybody. If it is possible, as far as it depends on you, live at peace with everyone. Do not take revenge, my friends, but leave room for God's wrath, for it is written: "It is mine to avenge; I will repay,"[d] says the Lord. On the contrary:

"If your enemy is hungry, feed him;
if he is thirsty, give him something to drink.
In doing this, you will heap burning coals on his head."[e]

Do not be overcome by evil, but overcome evil with good.

SUBMISSION TO THE AUTHORITIES

Everyone must submit himself to the governing authorities, for there is no authority except that which God has established. The authorities that exist have been established by God. Consequently, he who rebels against the authority is rebelling against what God has instituted, and those who do so will bring judgment on themselves. For rulers hold no terror for those who do right, but for those who do wrong. Do you want to be free from fear of the one in authority? Then do what is right and he will commend you. For he is God's servant to do you good. But if you do wrong, be afraid, for he does not bear the sword for nothing. He is God's servant, an agent of wrath to bring punishment on the wrongdoer. Therefore, it is necessary to submit to the author-ities, not only because of possible punishment but also because of conscience.

This is also why you pay taxes, for the authorities are God's servants, who give their full time to governing. Give everyone what you owe him: If you owe taxes, pay taxes; if revenue, then revenue; if respect, then respect; if honor, then honor.

LOVE, FOR THE DAY IS NEAR

Let no debt remain outstanding, except the continuing debt to love one another, for he who loves his fellowman has fulfilled the law. The commandments, "Do not commit adultery," "Do not murder," "Do not steal," "Do not covet,"[f] and whatever other commandment there may be, are summed up in this one rule: "Love your neighbor as yourself."[g] Love does no harm to its neighbor. Therefore love is the fulfillment of the law.

And do this, understanding the present time. The hour has come for you to wake up from your slumber, because our salvation is nearer now than when we first believed. The night is nearly over; the day is almost here. So let us put aside the deeds of darkness and put on the armor of light. Let us behave decently, as in the daytime, not in orgies and drunkenness, not in sexual immorality and debauchery, not in dissension and jealousy. Rather, clothe yourselves with the Lord Jesus Christ, and do not think about how to gratify the desires of the sinful nature.[h]

"In view of God's mercy . . . offer your bodies as living sacrifices,
holy and pleasing to God — which is your spiritual worship.
Do not conform any longer to the pattern of this world,
but be transformed by the renewing of your mind.
Then you will be able to test and approve what God's will is."

FROM OSWALD CHAMBERS

☙ Do you understand what you have to put on the altar before you are sanctified? Your whole body, your whole soul, and your whole spirit. Why people who claim to be Christians have to be preached to about smoking and chewing tobacco and all these sort of things is to me an amazement. There is a big mistake somewhere, and it is either in you or God, and I would rather make out man a liar and God be true, especially when I know what He has done for me. Bless my soul, if you stop all these things that is no sign that you are regenerated, much less sanctified! Not one bit of it. Scores of people who have not a spark of salvation live a cleaner life than some folks who say they are sanctified. Entire sanctification is not mere outward cleanness or moral living. That is your definition, not God's. Spirituality is based on the intensest morality. Christianity is not the annulling of the Ten Commandments. It is a transfiguration of the will. Why cannot you let God get you where Jesus Christ can be manifested in your flesh, in every fiber of your being? Jesus walking through your feet, talking through your mouth, and soothing with your hands. GR 4/30/08

❧ Continual renewal of mind is the only healthy state for a Christian. Beware of the ban of finality about your present views. BE 40

❧ When we receive the Spirit of God, we are lifted into a totally new realm. If we will bring our minds into harmony with what the Spirit of God reveals, begin to discipline ourselves and bring every thought into captivity, we shall not only begin to discern God's order in the Bible but our eyes will be opened and the secrets of the world will be understood and grasped. BP 235

❧ The particular forms of nature, i.e., rocks and trees, animals and men, are all the outcome of the breathing of the Spirit of God. There is a true law of correspondence between the things which we see, and the mind that is behind them. When we have in us the mind behind the things we see, we begin to understand how these things manifest that mind, but if we have not that mind we shall never understand them. BP 247

❧ A man's mental belief will show sooner or later in his practical living. DI 79

❧ Never submit to the tyrannous idea that you cannot look after your mind; you can. If a man lets his garden alone, it very soon ceases to be a garden; and if a saint lets his mind alone, it will soon become a rubbish heap for Satan to make use of. MFL 49

❧ Our minds are apt to be all abroad, like an octopus with its tentacles out to catch everything that comes along—newspaper garbage, spiritualistic garbage, advertisement garbage; we let them all come and make a dumping ground of our heads, and then sigh and mourn and say we cannot think right thoughts. MFL 86

---

a. Or *reasonable*
b. Or *in agreement with the*
c. Or *willing to do menial work*
d. Deut. 32:35
e. Prov. 25:21-22
f. Exodus 20:13-15, 17; Deut. 5:17-19, 21
g. Lev. 19:18
h. Or *the flesh*

12

ROMANS 14

THE WEAK AND THE STRONG

A ccept him whose faith is weak, without passing judgment on disputable matters. One man's faith allows him to eat everything, but another man, whose faith is weak, eats only vegetables. The man who eats everything must not look down on him who does not, and the man who does not eat everything must not condemn the man who does, for God has accepted him. Who are you to judge someone else's servant? To his own master he stands or falls. And he will stand, for the Lord is able to make him stand.

One man considers one day more sacred than another; another man considers every day alike. Each one should be fully convinced in his own mind. He who regards one day as special, does so to the Lord. He who eats meat, eats to the Lord, for he gives thanks to God; and he who abstains, does so to the Lord and gives thanks to God. For none of us lives to himself alone and none of us dies to himself alone. If we live, we live to the Lord; and if we die, we die to the Lord. So, whether we live or die, we belong to the Lord.

For this very reason, Christ died and returned to life so that he might be the Lord of both the dead and the living. You, then, why do you judge your brother? Or why do you look down on your brother? For we will all stand before God's judgment seat. It is written:

" 'As surely as I live,' says the Lord,
'every knee will bow before me;
    every tongue will confess to God.' "[a]

So then, each of us will give an account of himself to God.

Therefore let us stop passing judgment on one another. Instead, make up your mind not to put any stumbling block or obstacle in your brother's way. As one who is in the Lord Jesus, I am fully convinced that no food[b] is unclean in itself. But if anyone regards something as unclean, then for him it is unclean. If your brother is distressed because of what you eat, you are no longer acting in love. Do not by your eating destroy your brother for whom Christ died. Do not allow what you consider good to be spoken of as evil. For the kingdom of God is not a matter of eating and drinking, but of righteousness, peace and joy in the Holy Spirit, because anyone who serves Christ in this way is pleasing to God and approved by men.

Let us therefore make every effort to do what leads to peace and to mutual edification. Do not destroy the work of God for the sake of food. All food is clean, but it is wrong for a man to eat anything that causes someone else to stumble. It is better not to eat meat or drink wine or to do anything else that will cause your brother to fall.

So whatever you believe about these things keep between yourself and God. Blessed is the man who does not condemn himself by what he approves. But the man who has doubts is condemned if he eats, because his eating is not from faith; and everything that does not come from faith is sin.

> *"For the kingdom of God is not a matter of eating and drinking,*
> *but of righteousness, peace and joy in the Holy Spirit,*
> *because anyone who serves Christ in this way*
> *is pleasing to God and approved by men."*

FROM OSWALD CHAMBERS

ঌ The prevailing characteristics of the kingdom that Jesus represents are moral characteristics. There must be an alteration in me before I can be in the kingdom, or the kingdom can be in me, and that can be only by means of an inner crisis, viz., regeneration. There must be something outside me which will alter me on the inside. GW 53

ঌ The kingdom of God in this dispensation is the rule of God discerned by individuals alone. "Unless you are born from above," Jesus says, "you will never see the rule of God" (John 3:3). It is not seen by the intellect. The rule of God which individual saints see and recognize is "without observation" in this dispensation. There is another dispensation coming when the whole world will see it as individuals have seen it. HG 51

ϩ The majority of us know nothing whatever about the righteousness that is gifted to us in Jesus Christ. We are still trying to bring human nature up to a pitch it cannot reach, because there is something wrong with human nature. The old Puritanism which we are apt to ridicule did the same service for men that Pharisaism did for Saul, and that Roman Catholicism did for Luther; but nowadays we have no "iron" in us anywhere; we have no idea of righteousness; we do not care whether we are righteous or not. We have not only lost Jesus Christ's idea of righteousness, but we laugh at the Bible idea of righteousness; our god is the conventional righteousness of the society to which we belong. HG 12

ϩ Righteousness cannot be imitated. If I abide in Jesus, His righteousness is done through me. Nowadays the tendency is to switch away from abiding in Christ; it is—"Do this," and "Do that." You cannot do anything at all that does not become, in the rugged language of Isaiah, "as filthy rags" (Isa. 64:6); no matter how right it looks, if it is divorced from abiding in Christ. Haul yourself up a hundred times a day till you learn to abide. GW 46

ϩ The peace of Jesus is not a cherished piece of property that I possess; it is a direct impartation from Him, and my enjoying His peace depends on my recognizing this. CD VOL. 1, 153

ϩ The source of peace is God, not myself; it never is my peace but always His, and if once He withdraws, it is not there. CD VOL. 1, 152

ϩ Nothing else is in the least like His peace. It is the peace of God, which passeth all understanding. CD VOL. 1, 152

ϩ Joy is different from happiness, because happiness depends on what happens. There are elements in our circumstances we cannot help; joy is independent of them all. HGM 48

ϩ A man is only joyful when he fulfills the design of God's creation of him, and that is a joy that can never be quenched. HGM 48

---

a. Isaiah 45:23
b. Or *that nothing*

13

ROMANS 15

ACCEPT ONE ANOTHER

e who are strong ought to bear with the failings of the weak and not to please ourselves. Each of us should please his neighbor for his good, to build him up. For even Christ did not please himself but, as it is written: "The insults of those who insult you have fallen on me."[a] For everything that was written in the past was written to teach us, so that through endurance and the encouragement of the Scriptures we might have hope.

May the God who gives endurance and encouragement give you a spirit of unity among yourselves as you follow Christ Jesus, so that with one heart and mouth you may glorify the God and Father of our Lord Jesus Christ.

Accept one another, then, just as Christ accepted you, in order to bring praise to God. For I tell you that Christ has become a servant of the Jews[b] on behalf of God's truth, to confirm the promises made to the patriarchs so that the Gentiles may glorify God for his mercy, as it is written:

"Therefore I will praise you among the Gentiles;
  I will sing hymns to your name."[c]

Again, it says,

"Rejoice, O Gentiles, with his people."[d]

And again,

"Praise the Lord, all you Gentiles,
  and sing praises to him, all you peoples."[e]

And again, Isaiah says,

"The Root of Jesse will spring up,
  one who will arise to rule over the nations;
the Gentiles will hope in him."[f]

May the God of hope fill you with all joy and peace as you trust in him, so that you may overflow with hope by the power of the Holy Spirit.

PAUL THE MINISTER TO THE GENTILES

I myself am convinced, my brothers, that you yourselves are full of goodness, complete in knowledge and competent to instruct one another. I have written you quite boldly on some points, as if to remind you of them again, because of the grace God gave me to be a minister of Christ Jesus to the Gentiles with the priestly duty of proclaiming the gospel of God, so that the Gentiles might become an offering acceptable to God, sanctified by the Holy Spirit.

Therefore I glory in Christ Jesus in my service to God. I will not venture to speak of anything except what Christ has accomplished through me in leading the Gentiles to obey God by what I have said and done—by the power of signs and miracles, through the power of the Spirit. So from Jerusalem all the way around to Illyricum, I have fully proclaimed the gospel of Christ. It has always been my ambition to preach the gospel where Christ was not known, so that I would not be building on someone else's foundation. Rather, as it is written:

"Those who were not told about him will see,
  and those who have not heard will understand."[g]

This is why I have often been hindered from coming to you.

PAUL'S PLAN TO VISIT ROME

But now that there is no more place for me to work in these regions, and since I have been longing for many years to see you, I plan to do so when I go to Spain. I hope to visit you while passing through and to have you assist me on my journey there, after I have enjoyed your company for a while. Now, however, I am on my way to Jerusalem in the service of the saints there. For Macedonia and Achaia were pleased to make a contribution for the poor among the saints in Jerusalem. They were pleased to do it, and indeed they owe it to them. For if the Gentiles have shared in the Jews' spiritual blessings, they owe it to the Jews to share with them their material blessings. So after I have completed this task and have made sure that they have received this fruit, I will go to Spain and visit you on the way. I know that when I come to you, I will come in the full measure of the blessing of Christ.

I urge you, brothers, by our Lord Jesus Christ and by the love of the Spirit, to join me in my struggle by praying to God for me. Pray that I may be rescued from the unbelievers in Judea and that my service in Jerusalem may be acceptable to the saints there, so that by God's will I may come to you with joy and together with you be refreshed. The God of peace be with you all. Amen.

"May the God of hope fill you with all joy and peace
as you trust in him, so that you may overflow with hope
by the power of the Holy Spirit."

FROM OSWALD CHAMBERS

➣ Jesus Christ did not preach a gospel of hope: He came to reorganize humanity from the inside through a tremendous tragedy in His own life called the Cross, and through that Cross every member of the human race can be reinstated in God's favor and enter into a conscious inheritance of the Atonement. BSG 64

➣ Hope without faith loses itself in vague speculation, but the hope of the saints transfigured by faith grows not faint, but endures "as seeing Him who is invisible." CD VOL. 2, 152

➣ The hope of the saint is the expectation and certainty of human nature transfigured by faith. Let it be borne in mind that hope not transfigured by faith dies. CD VOL. 2, 152

75

❧ The hope of the saint gives the true value to the things seen and temporal—in fact the real enjoyment of things seen and temporal is alone possible to the saint because he sees them in their true relationship to God, and the sickening emptiness of the worldly minded who grasp the things seen and temporal as though they were eternal, is unknown to him. CD VOL. 2, 153

❧ When we meet extra goodness, we feel amazingly hopeful about everybody, and when we meet extra badness we feel exactly the opposite. But Jesus "knew what was in man"; He knew exactly what human beings were like and what they needed. And He saw in them something no one else ever saw—hope for the most degraded. Jesus had a tremendous hopefulness about man. CHI 96

❧ The only hope for a man lies not in giving him an example of how to behave, but in the preaching of Jesus Christ as the Savior from sin. The heart of every man gets hope when he hears that. DI 64

❧ To give an answer concerning the hope that is in us is not the same thing as convincing by reasonable argument why that hope is in us. A line we are continually likely to be caught by is that of argumentatively reasoning out why we are what we are; we cannot argue that out. There is not a saint among us who can give explicit reasonings concerning the hope that is in us, but we can always give this reason: We have received the Holy Spirit, and He has witnessed that the truths of Jesus are the truths for us. When we give that answer, anyone who hears it and refuses to try the same way of getting at the truth is condemned. IWP 72

❧ People who believe in an omnipotence with no character are shut up in a destiny of hopelessness; Jesus Christ can open the door of release and let them right out. There is no door that man or devil has closed but Jesus Christ can open it; but remember, there is the other side, the door He closes no man can open. IWP 128

❧ There is no such thing as dull despair anywhere in the Bible; there is tragedy of the most appalling order, but an equally amazing hopefulness—always a door deeper down than hell which opens into heaven. OPG 55

---

a. Psalm 69:9
b. Greek *circumcision*
c. 2 Samuel 22:50; Psalm 18:49
d. Deut. 32:43

e. Psalm 117:1
f. Isaiah 11:10
g. Isaiah 52:15

14

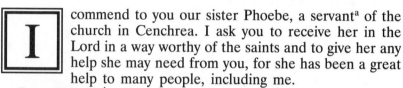

PAUL GREETS FELLOW WORKERS

I commend to you our sister Phoebe, a servant[a] of the church in Cenchrea. I ask you to receive her in the Lord in a way worthy of the saints and to give her any help she may need from you, for she has been a great help to many people, including me.

Greet Priscilla[b] and Aquila, my fellow workers in Christ Jesus. They risked their lives for me. Not only I but all the churches of the Gentiles are grateful to them.

Greet also the church that meets at their house.

Greet my dear friend Epenetus, who was the first convert to Christ in the province of Asia.

Greet Mary, who worked very hard for you.

Greet Andronicus and Junias, my relatives who have been in prison with me. They are outstanding among the apostles, and they were in Christ before I was.

Greet Ampliatus, whom I love in the Lord.

Greet Urbanus, our fellow worker in Christ, and my dear friend Stachys.

Greet Apelles, tested and approved in Christ. Greet those who belong to the household of Aristobulus.

Greet Herodion, my relative. Greet those in the household of Narcissus who are in the Lord.

Greet Tryphena and Tryphosa, those women who work hard in the Lord. Greet my dear friend Persis, another woman who has worked very hard in the Lord.

Greet Rufus, chosen in the Lord, and his mother, who has been a mother to me, too.

Greet Asyncritus, Phlegon, Hermes, Patrobas, Hermas and the brothers with them.

Greet Philologus, Julia, Nereus and his sister, and Olympas and all the saints with them.

Greet one another with a holy kiss. All the churches of Christ send greetings. I urge you, brothers, to watch out for those who cause divisions and put obstacles in your way that are contrary to the teaching you have learned. Keep away from them. For such people are not serving our Lord Christ, but their own appetites. By smooth talk and flattery they deceive the minds of naive people. Everyone has heard about your obedience, so I am full of joy over you; but I want you to be wise about what is good, and innocent about what is evil.

The God of peace will soon crush Satan under your feet.

The grace of our Lord Jesus be with you.

Timothy, my fellow worker, sends his greetings to you, as do Lucius, Jason and Sosipater, my relatives.

I, Tertius, who wrote down this letter, greet you in the Lord.

Gaius, whose hospitality I and the whole church here enjoy, sends you his greetings.

Erastus, who is the city's director of public works, and our brother Quartus send you their greetings.[c]

Now to him who is able to establish you by my gospel and the proclamation of Jesus Christ, according to the revelation of the mystery hidden for long ages past, but now revealed and made known through the prophetic writings by the command of the eternal God, so that all nations might believe and obey him — to the only wise God be glory forever through Jesus Christ! Amen.

"Be wise about what is good,
and innocent about what is evil."

FROM OSWALD CHAMBERS

> Human beings know human beings too well to mistake where goodness comes from; when they see certain characteristics, they will know they come only from the indwelling of Jesus. It is not the manifestation of noble human wits, but of a real family likeness to Jesus. It is *His* gentleness, *His* patience, *His* purity, never mine.
> CHI 21

❧ It has been a favorite belief in all ages that if only men were taught what good is, everyone would choose it; but history and human experience prove that that is not so. To know what good is is not to be good. DI 26

❧ One might almost say that our every effort to be good and our every effort to be holy is a sure sign that we are neither good nor holy. A child makes no effort to be the daughter or son of its parents, and a child of God born of the Spirit makes no conscious effort to be good or to be holy; but just as a child trying to imitate someone else's mother is bound to fail, so the natural man trying to imitate God is bound to fail. GW 67

❧ The best of men and women are but the best of men and women; the only good is God, and Jesus Christ always brings the soul face to face with God, and that is the one great thought we have to be soaked with. IWP 31

❧ The expression of Christian character is not good doing, but God-likeness. If the Spirit of God has transformed you within, you will exhibit divine characteristics in your life, not good human characteristics. God's life in us expresses itself as God's life, not as human life trying to be godly. MUH 264

❧ Very few of us debate with the sordid and evil and wrong, but we do debate with the good. It is good that hates the best, and the higher up you get in the scale of the natural virtues, the more intense is the opposition to Jesus Christ. MUH 344

❧ Get rid of the idea that you must do good things, and remember what Jesus says, "If you believe on Me, out of you will flow rivers of living water" (John 7:38). PH 67

❧ God cannot accept goodness from me. He can only accept my badness, and He will give me the solid goodness of the Lord Jesus in exchange for it. SSM 28

---

a. Or *deaconess*
b. Greek *Prisca,* a variant of *Priscilla*
c. Some manuscripts *their greetings. May the grace of our Lord Jesus Christ be with all of you. Amen.*

15

1 CORINTHIANS 1-2

TO THE CHURCH IN CORINTH

Paul, called to be an apostle of Christ Jesus by the will of God, and our brother Sosthenes,

To the church of God in Corinth, to those sanctified in Christ Jesus and called to be holy, together with all those everywhere who call on the name of our Lord Jesus Christ—their Lord and ours:

Grace and peace to you from God our Father and the Lord Jesus Christ.

THANKSGIVING

I always thank God for you because of his grace given you in Christ Jesus. For in him you have been enriched in every way—in all your speaking and in all your knowledge—because our testimony about Christ was confirmed in you. Therefore you do not lack any spiritual gift as you eagerly wait for our Lord Jesus Christ to be revealed. He will keep you strong to the end, so that you will be blameless on the day of our Lord Jesus Christ. God, who has called you into fellowship with his Son Jesus Christ our Lord, is faithful.

DIVISIONS IN THE CHURCH

I appeal to you, brothers, in the name of our Lord Jesus Christ, that all of you agree with one another so that there may be no divisions among you and that you may be perfectly united in mind and thought. My brothers, some from Chloe's household have informed me that there are quarrels among you. What I mean is this: One of you says, "I follow Paul"; another, "I follow Apollos"; another, "I follow Cephas";ª still another, "I follow Christ."

Is Christ divided? Was Paul crucified for you? Were you baptized into[b] the name of Paul? I am thankful that I did not baptize any of you except Crispus and Gaius, so no one can say that you were baptized into my name. (Yes, I also baptized the household of Stephanas; beyond that, I don't remember if I baptized anyone else.) For Christ did not send me to baptize, but to preach the gospel—not with words of human wisdom, lest the cross of Christ be emptied of its power.

CHRIST THE WISDOM AND POWER OF GOD

For the message of the cross is foolishness to those who are perishing, but to us who are being saved it is the power of God. For it is written:

"I will destroy the wisdom of the wise;
    the intelligence of the intelligent I will frustrate."[c]

Where is the wise man? Where is the scholar? Where is the philosopher of this age? Has not God made foolish the wisdom of the world? For since in the wisdom of God the world through its wisdom did not know him, God was pleased through the foolishness of what was preached to save those who believe. Jews demand miraculous signs and Greeks look for wisdom, but we preach Christ crucified: a stumbling block to Jews and foolishness to Gentiles, but to those whom God has called, both Jews and Greeks, Christ the power of God and the wisdom of God. For the foolishness of God is wiser than man's wisdom, and the weakness of God is stronger than man's strength.

Brothers, think of what you were when you were called. Not many of you were wise by human standards; not many were influential; not many were of noble birth. But God chose the foolish things of the world to shame the wise; God chose the weak things of the world to shame the strong. He chose the lowly things of this world and the despised things—and the things that are not—to nullify the things that are, so that no one may boast before him. It is because of him that you are in Christ Jesus, who has become for us wisdom from God—that is, our righteousness, holiness and redemption. Therefore, as it is written: "Let him who boasts boast in the Lord."[d]

When I came to you, brothers, I did not come with eloquence or superior wisdom as I proclaimed to you the testimony about God.[e] For I resolved to know nothing while I was with you except Jesus Christ and him crucified. I came to you in weakness and fear, and with much trembling. My message and my preaching were not with wise and persuasive words, but with a demonstration of the Spirit's power, so that your faith might not rest on men's wisdom, but on God's power.

WISDOM FROM THE SPIRIT

We do, however, speak a message of wisdom among the mature, but not the wisdom of this age or of the rulers of this age, who are coming to nothing. No, we speak of God's secret wisdom, a wisdom that has been hidden and that God destined for our glory before time began. None of the rulers of this age understood it, for if they had, they would not have crucified the Lord of glory. However, as it is written:

"No eye has seen,
no ear has heard,
no mind has conceived
what God has prepared for those who love him"[f] —

but God has revealed it to us by his Spirit.

The Spirit searches all things, even the deep things of God. For who among men knows the thoughts of a man except the man's spirit within him? In the same way no one knows the thoughts of God except the Spirit of God. We have not received the spirit of the world but the Spirit who is from God, that we may understand what God has freely given us. This is what we speak, not in words taught us by human wisdom but in words taught by the Spirit, expressing spiritual truths in spiritual words.[g] The man without the Spirit does not accept the things that come from the Spirit of God, for they are foolishness to him, and he cannot understand them, because they are spiritually discerned. The spiritual man makes judgments about all things, but he himself is not subject to any man's judgment:

"For who has known the mind of the Lord
that he may instruct him?"[h]

But we have the mind of Christ.

*"For the message of the cross is foolishness
to those who are perishing, but to us who are being
saved it is the power of God."*

FROM OSWALD CHAMBERS

ॐ The aspect of the cross in discipleship is lost altogether in the present-day view of following Jesus. The cross is looked upon as something beautiful and simple instead of a stern heroism. Our Lord never said it was easy to be a Christian; He warned men that they would have to face a variety of hardships, which He termed "bearing the cross." AUG 49

ॐ Either the Cross is the only way there is of explaining God, the only way of explaining Jesus Christ, and of explaining the human race, or there is nothing in it at all. BE 61

ॐ There is nothing more certain in time or eternity than what Jesus Christ did on the cross: He switched the whole human race back into right relationship to God and made the basis of human life redemptive; consequently, any member of the human race can get into touch with God *now*. BE 61

ॐ The Cross is a tragedy to man, but a tremendous triumph to God, an absolute triumph. BSG 52

ॐ The Bible says that God Himself accepted the responsibility for sin; the Cross is the proof that He did. It cost Jesus Christ to the last drop of blood to deal with "the vast evil of the world." CHI 45

a. That is, Peter
b. Or *in;* also in verse 15
c. Isaiah 29:14
d. Jer. 9:24
e. Some manuscripts *as I proclaimed to you God's mystery*
f. Isaiah 64:4
g. Or *Spirit, interpreting spiritual truths to spiritual men*
h. Isaiah 40:13

16

1 CORINTHIANS 3

ON DIVISIONS IN THE CHURCH

Brothers, I could not address you as spiritual but as worldly—mere infants in Christ. I gave you milk, not solid food, for you were not yet ready or it. Indeed, you are still not ready. You are still worldly. For since there is jealousy and quarreling among you, are you not worldly? Are you not acting like mere men? For when one says, "I follow Paul," and another, "I follow Apollos," are you not mere men?

What, after all, is Apollos? And what is Paul? Only servants, through whom you came to believe—as the Lord has assigned to each his task. I planted the seed, Apollos watered it, but God made it grow. So neither he who plants nor he who waters is anything, but only God, who makes things grow. The man who plants and the man who waters have one purpose, and each will be rewarded according to his own labor. For we are God's fellow workers; you are God's field, God's building.

By the grace God has given me, I laid a foundation as an expert builder, and someone else is building on it. But each one should be careful how he builds. For no one can lay any foundation other than the one already laid, which is Jesus Christ. If any man builds on this foundation using gold, silver, costly stones, wood, hay or straw, his work will be shown for what it is, because the Day will bring it to light. It will be revealed with fire, and the fire will test the quality of each man's work. If what he has built survives, he will receive his reward. If it is burned up, he will suffer loss; he himself will be saved, but only as one escaping through the flames.

Don't you know that you yourselves are God's temple and that God's Spirit lives in you? If anyone destroys God's temple, God will destroy him; for God's temple is sacred, and you are that temple.

Do not deceive yourselves. If any one of you thinks he is wise by the standards of this age, he should become a "fool" so that he may become wise. For the wisdom of this world is foolishness in God's sight. As it is written: "He catches the wise in their craftiness";[a] and again, "The Lord knows that the thoughts of the wise are futile."[b] So then, no more boasting about men! All things are yours, whether Paul or Apollos or Cephas[c] or the world or life or death or the present or the future — all are yours, and you are of Christ, and Christ is of God.

> *"The wisdom of this world*
> *is foolishness in God's sight."*

FROM OSWALD CHAMBERS

ॐ The wisdom of God is shown in that Jesus Christ is "made unto us . . . righteousness" (1 Cor. 1:30). GW 45

ॐ The wisdom of the Hebrews is based on an accepted belief in God; that is, it does not try to find out whether or not God exists; all its beliefs are based on God, and in the actual whirl of things as they are, all its mental energy is bent on practical living. The wisdom of the Greeks, which is the wisdom of our day, is speculative; that is, it is concerned with the origin of things, with the riddle of the universe, etc., consequently, the best of our wits is not given to practical living. SHH 1

ॐ The amazing simplicity of the nature of God is foolish judged by human wisdom; but "the foolishness of God is wiser than men." SSY 146

ॐ The wisdom of today concerns itself chiefly with the origin of things and not with God; consequently, neither the philosopher nor the mystic has time for actual life. The wisdom of the Hebrews concerns itself with practical life, and recognizes that the basis of things is tragic. The Bible attitude to practical life is [foreign to] most of us because we are far away from the rooted and grounded confidence in God of the Hebrews. We do not think on Bible lines; we think on pagan lines, and only in our emotional life do we

dabble in spirituality. Consequently, when we are hard hit, our religion finds us dumb; or if we do talk, we talk as pagans.
SHH 58

⁊ The wisdom of God is arrant stupidity to the wisdom of the world, until all of a sudden God makes the wisdom of the world foolish (1 Cor. 1:23-25). If you stand true to your faith in God, there will be situations in which you will come across extortioners, cunning, crafty people, who use their wits instead of worshiping God, and you will appear a fool. Are you prepared to appear a fool for Christ's sake? Very few of us know anything about suffering for Christ's sake. A man who knows nothing about Christ will suffer for the sake of conscience or conviction. To suffer for Christ's sake is to suffer because of being personally related to Him. SHH 83

⁊ If you are going to be true to God, you will appear a fool among those who do not believe in God, and you must lay your account with this. Jesus said, "Everyone therefore who shall confess Me before men" (Matt. 10:32), and it tests a man for all he is worth to confess Jesus Christ, because the confession has to be made in the set he belongs to and esteems. The "shame" of the Gospel. "I am not ashamed of the Gospel of Christ," says Paul (Rom. 1:36). SHH 83

---

a. Job 5:13
b. Psalm 94:11
c. That is, Peter

87

17

1 CORINTHIANS 4–5

APOSTLES OF CHRIST

S o then, men ought to regard us as servants of Christ and as those entrusted with the secret things of God. Now it is required that those who have been given a trust must prove faithful. I care very little if I am judged by you or by any human court; indeed, I do not even judge myself. My conscience is clear, but that does not make me innocent. It is the Lord who judges me. Therefore judge nothing before the appointed time; wait till the Lord comes. He will bring to light what is hidden in darkness and will expose the motives of men's hearts. At that time each will receive his praise from God.

Now, brothers, I have applied these things to myself and Apollos for your benefit, so that you may learn from us the meaning of the saying, "Do not go beyond what is written." Then you will not take pride in one man over against another. For who makes you different from anyone else? What do you have that you did not receive? And if you did receive it, why do you boast as though you did not?

Already you have all you want! Already you have become rich! You have become kings—and that without us! How I wish that you really had become kings so that we might be kings with you! For it seems to me that God has put us apostles on display at the end of the procession, like men condemned to die in the arena. We have been made a spectacle to the whole universe, to angels as well as to men. We are fools for Christ, but you are so wise in Christ! We are weak, but you are strong! You are honored, we are dishonored! To this very hour we go hungry and thirsty, we are in rags, we are brutally treated, we are homeless. We work hard with our own hands. When we are cursed, we bless; when we are persecuted, we endure it; when we are slandered, we answer kindly. Up to this moment we have become the scum of the earth, the refuse of the world.

I am not writing this to shame you, but to warn you, as my dear children. Even though you have ten thousand guardians in Christ, you do not have many fathers, for in Christ Jesus I became your father through the gospel. Therefore I urge you to imitate me. For this reason I am sending to you Timothy, my son whom I love, who is faithful in the Lord. He will remind you of my way of life in Christ Jesus, which agrees with what I teach everywhere in every church.

Some of you have become arrogant, as if I were not coming to you. But I will come to you very soon, if the Lord is willing, and then I will find out not only how these arrogant people are talking, but what power they have. For the kingdom of God is not a matter of talk but of power. What do you prefer? Shall I come to you with a whip, or in love and with a gentle spirit?

EXPEL THE IMMORAL BROTHER!

It is actually reported that there is sexual immorality among you, and of a kind that does not occur even among pagans: A man has his father's wife. And you are proud! Shouldn't you rather have been filled with grief and have put out of your fellowship the man who did this? Even though I am not physically present, I am with you in spirit. And I have already passed judgment on the one who did this, just as if I were present. When you are assembled in the name of our Lord Jesus and I am with you in spirit, and the power of our Lord Jesus is present, hand this man over to Satan, so that the sinful nature[a] may be destroyed and his spirit saved on the day of the Lord.

Your boasting is not good. Don't you know that a little yeast works through the whole batch of dough? Get rid of the old yeast that you may be a new batch without yeast — as you really are. For Christ, our Passover lamb, has been sacrificed. Therefore let us keep the Festival, not with the old yeast, the yeast of malice and wickedness, but with bread without yeast, the bread of sincerity and truth.

I have written you in my letter not to associate with sexually immoral people — not at all meaning the people of this world who are immoral, or the greedy and swindlers, or idolaters. In that case you would have to leave this world. But now I am writing you that you must not associate with anyone who calls himself a brother but is sexually immoral or greedy, an idolater or a slanderer, a drunkard or a swindler. With such a man do not even eat.

What business is it of mine to judge those outside the church? Are you not to judge those inside? God will judge those outside. "Expel the wicked man from among you."[b]

> *"It is required that those who have been given a trust must prove faithful."*

FROM OSWALD CHAMBERS

ॐ Watch where Jesus went. The one dominant note in His life was to do His Father's will. His is not the way of wisdom or of success, but the way of faithfulness. LG 156

ॐ Eliezer in many respects stands as a picture of a disciple of the Lord (Gen. 24:48), because the whole molding of his life is his devotion to another, not to a sense of right or duty, but to his master (cf. John 13:13-14). We know very little about devotion to Jesus Christ. We know devotion to right and to duty, but none of that is saintly, it is purely natural. The Sermon on the Mount nowhere tells us what our duty is; it tells us the things a saint will do— the things that are not his duty, e.g. Matthew 5:39-42. Be renewed in the spirit of your mind, says Paul, not that you may do your duty, but that you may make out what God's will is (see Rom. 12:2).

All the reward Eliezer seeks is the happiness of his master; self-remembrance in him is dead. He is shrewd and practical yet as guileless as a child, the exact embodiment of 1 Corinthians 4:2 — "It is required in stewards, that a man be found faithful." DDL 38

ॐ We have to be so faithful to God that through us may come the awakening of those who have not yet realized that they are redeemed. CHI 9

ॐ Being faithful to Jesus Christ is the most difficult thing we try to do today. We will be faithful to our work, to serving others, or to anything else; just don't ask us to be faithful to Jesus Christ. Many

Christians become very impatient when we talk about faithfulness to Jesus. Our Lord is dethroned more deliberately by Christian workers than by the world. We treat God as if He were a machine designed only to bless us, and we think of Jesus as just another one of the workers.

The goal of faithfulness is not that we will do work for God, but that He will be free to do His work through us. God calls us to His service and places tremendous responsibilities on us. He expects no complaining on our part and offers no explanation on His part. God wants to use us as He used His own Son. MUH-UE 12/19

---

a. Or *that his body;* or *that the flesh*
b. Deut. 17:7; 19:19; 21:21; 22:21, 24; 24:7

18

1 CORINTHIANS 6

LAWSUITS AMONG BELIEVERS

I f any of you has a dispute with another, dare he take it before the ungodly for judgment instead of before the saints? Do you not know that the saints will judge the world? And if you are to judge the world, are you not competent to judge trivial cases? Do you not know that we will judge angels? How much more the things of this life! Therefore, if you have disputes about such matters, appoint as judges even men of little account in the church![a] I say this to shame you. Is it possible that there is nobody among you wise enough to judge a dispute between believers? But instead, one brother goes to law against another—and this in front of unbelievers!

The very fact that you have lawsuits among you means you have been completely defeated already. Why not rather be wronged? Why not rather be cheated? Instead, you yourselves cheat and do wrong, and you do this to your brothers.

Do you not know that the wicked will not inherit the kingdom of God? Do not be deceived: Neither the sexually immoral nor idolaters nor adulterers nor male prostitutes nor homosexual offenders nor thieves nor the greedy nor drunkards nor slanderers nor swindlers will inherit the kingdom of God. And that is what some of you were. But you were washed, you were sanctified, you were justified in the name of the Lord Jesus Christ and by the Spirit of our God.

SEXUAL IMMORALITY

"Everything is permissible for me"—but not everything is beneficial. "Everything is permissible for me"—but I will not be mastered by anything. "Food for the stomach and the stomach for food"—but God will destroy them both. The body is not meant for sexual immorality, but for the Lord, and the Lord for the body. By his power God raised the Lord from the dead, and he will raise us also. Do you not know that your bodies are members of Christ himself? Shall I then take the members of Christ and unite them with a prostitute? Never! Do you not know that he who unites himself with a prostitute is one with her in body? For it is said, "The two will become one flesh."[b] But he who unites himself with the Lord is one with him in spirit.

Flee from sexual immorality. All other sins a man commits are outside his body, but he who sins sexually sins against his own body. Do you not know that your body is a temple of the Holy Spirit, who is in you, whom you have received from God? You are not your own; you were bought at a price. Therefore honor God with your body.

> *"By his power God raised the Lord from the dead,*
> *and he will raise us also."*

FROM OSWALD CHAMBERS

  ⁖ Our Lord rose to an absolutely new life, to a life He did not live before He was incarnate; He rose to a life that had never been before. There had been resurrections before the resurrection of Jesus Christ, but they were all resuscitations to the same kind of life as heretofore. Jesus Christ rose to a totally new life, and to a totally different relationship to men and women. The resurrection of Jesus Christ grants Him the right to give His own destiny to any human being—viz., to make us the sons and daughters of God. His resurrection means that we are raised to His risen life, not to our old life. "Like as Christ was raised up from the dead by the glory of the Father, even so we also should walk in newness of life . . . we shall be also in the likeness of His resurrection" (Rom. 6:4-5).
PR 113

  ⁖ Christ's resurrection deity means that He can take us into union with God, and the way into that relationship of oneness is by the Cross and the Resurrection. The weakest saint can experience the power of the deity of the Son of God if he is willing to "let go." The whole almighty power of God is on our behalf, and when we realize this, life becomes the implicit life of the child. No wonder Jesus said—"Let not your heart be troubled"! (John 14:1) The characteristic of the saintly life is abandon to God, not a settling down on our whiteness. God is not making hothouse plants, but sons and daughters of God, men and women with a strong family likeness to Jesus Christ. PR 115

> Thank God that the almighty power of Jesus Christ is for us. All power is vested in Him in heaven and on earth, and He says, "Lo, I am with you all the days" (Matt. 28:20). All the power of the deity of Christ is ours through His resurrection. PR 117

---

a. Or *matters, do you appoint as judges men of little account in the church?*
b. Gen. 2:24

19

1 CORINTHIANS 7

MATTERS OF MARRIAGE

Now for the matters you wrote about: It is good for a man not to marry. But since there is so much immorality, each man should have his own wife, and each woman her own husband. The husband should fulfill his marital duty to his wife, and likewise the wife to her husband. The wife's body does not belong to her alone but also to her husband. In the same way, the husband's body does not belong to him alone but also to his wife. Do not deprive each other except by mutual consent and for a time, so that you may devote yourselves to prayer. Then come together again so that Satan will not tempt you because of your lack of self-control. I say this as a concession, not as a command. I wish that all men were as I am. But each man has his own gift from God; one has this gift, another has that.

Now to the unmarried and the widows I say: It is good for them to stay unmarried, as I am. But if they cannot control themselves, they should marry, for it is better to marry than to burn with passion.

To the married I give this command (not I, but the Lord): A wife must not separate from her husband. But if she does, she must remain unmarried or else be reconciled to her husband. And a husband must not divorce his wife.

To the rest I say this (I, not the Lord): If any brother has a wife who is not a believer and she is willing to live with him, he must not divorce her. And if a woman has a husband who is not a believer and he is willing to live with her, she must not divorce him. For the unbelieving husband has been sanctified through his wife, and the unbelieving wife has been sanctified through her believing husband. Otherwise your children would be unclean, but as it is, they are holy.

But if the unbeliever leaves, let him do so. A believing man or woman is not bound in such circumstances; God has called us to live in peace. How do you know, wife, whether you will save your husband? Or, how do you know, husband, whether you will save your wife?

Nevertheless, each one should retain the place in life that the Lord assigned to him and to which God has called him. This is the rule I lay down in all the churches. Was a man already circumcised when he was called? He should not become uncircumcised. Was a man uncircumcised when he was called? He should not be circumcised. Circumcision is nothing and uncircumcision is nothing. Keeping God's commands is what counts. Each one should remain in the situation which he was in when God called him. Were you a slave when you were called? Don't let it trouble you — although if you can gain your freedom, do so. For he who was a slave when he was called by the Lord is the Lord's freedman; similarly, he who was a free man when he was called is Christ's slave. You were bought at a price; do not become slaves of men. Brothers, each man, as responsible to God, should remain in the situation God called him to.

Now about virgins: I have no command from the Lord, but I give a judgment as one who by the Lord's mercy is trustworthy. Because of the present crisis, I think that it is good for you to remain as you are. Are you married? Do not seek a divorce. Are you unmarried? Do not look for a wife. But if you do marry, you have not sinned; and if a virgin marries, she has not sinned. But those who marry will face many troubles in this life, and I want to spare you this.

What I mean, brothers, is that the time is short. From now on those who have wives should live as if they had none; those who mourn, as if they did not; those who are happy, as if they were not; those who buy something, as if it were not theirs to keep; those who use the things of the world, as if not engrossed in them. For this world in its present form is passing away.

I would like you to be free from concern. An unmarried man is concerned about the Lord's affairs — how he can please the Lord. But a married man is concerned about the affairs of this world — how he can please his wife — and his interests are divided. An unmarried woman or virgin is concerned about the Lord's affairs: Her aim is to be devoted to the Lord in both body and spirit. But

a married woman is concerned about the affairs of this world—
how she can please her husband. I am saying this for your own
good, not to restrict you, but that you may live in a right way in
undivided devotion to the Lord.

If anyone thinks he is acting improperly toward the virgin he is
engaged to, and if she is getting along in years and he feels he
ought to marry, he should do as he wants. He is not sinning. They
should get married. But the man who has settled the matter in
his own mind, who is under no compulsion but has control over
his own will, and who has made up his mind not to marry the
virgin—this man also does the right thing. So then, he who marries the virgin does right, but he who does not marry her does
even better.[a]

A woman is bound to her husband as long as he lives. But if
her husband dies, she is free to marry anyone she wishes, but he
must belong to the Lord. In my judgment, she is happier if she
stays as she is—and I think that I too have the Spirit of God.

*"The time is short. . . . This world in its present form
is passing away."*

FROM OSWALD CHAMBERS

❧ How many of us spend our time expecting that we will be something we are not. "Oh the time is coming when I am going to be so
and so." It never will come, the time is always *now*. MFL 60

❧ Spend plenty of time with God, let other things go, but don't neglect Him. And beware of practical work. NKW 137

❧ We can choke God's word with a yawn; we can hinder the time that
should be spent with God by remembering we have other things to
do. "I haven't time!" Of course you have not time! *Take* time,
strangle some other interests, and make time to realize that the
center of power in your life is the Lord Jesus Christ and His Atonement. OBH 124

❧ Let us examine ourselves the next time we say, "I have not time,"
or "I give all the time I can to the study of God's Word," "I give all
the time I can to praying." God grant me that we may be put on the

alert on these lines that we may not be found lying to the Holy Ghost. WG 103

ᴫ Remember we have all the time there is. The majority of us waste time and want to encroach on eternity. MFL 65

ᴫ What is the world? The set of people with the ambitions, religious or otherwise, that are not identified with the Lord Jesus Christ. AUG 102

ᴫ To be "of" the world means to belong to the set that organizes its religion, its business, its social life, and pleasures without any concern as to how it affects Jesus Christ, as to whether He lived or died matters nothing at all. BE 34

ᴫ The counsel of the Spirit of God to the saints is that they must allow nothing worldly in themselves while living among the worldly in the world. Those who live otherworldly in this world are the men and women who have been regenerated and who dare to live their life according to the principles of Jesus. BE 35

ᴫ The sign for the world without God is a circle, complete in and for itself; the sign for the Christian is the Cross. The Christian knows by bitter yet blessed conviction of sin that no man is sufficient for himself, and he thereby enters into identification with the Cross of Calvary; and he longs and prays and works to see the sinful, self-centered world broken up and made the occasion for the mighty Cross to have its way, whereby men may come to God and God come down to men. HGM 118

ᴫ The line where the world ends and Christianity begins alters in every generation. What was worldliness in Paul's day is not worldliness in our day; the line is altering all the time. Today the world has taken on so many things out of the church, and the church has taken on so many things out of the world, that it is difficult to know where you are. SHL 17

---

a. Or *If anyone thinks he is not treating his daughter properly, and if she is getting along in years, and he feels she ought to marry, he should do as he wants. He is not sinning. He should let her get married. But the man who has settled the matter in his own mind, who is under no compulsion but has control over his own will, and who has made up his mind to keep the virgin unmarried — this man also does the right thing. So then, he who gives his virgin in marriage does right, but he who does not give her in marriage does even better.*

20

FOOD SACRIFICED TO IDOLS

ow about food sacrificed to idols: We know that we all possess knowledge.[a] Knowledge puffs up, but love builds up. The man who thinks he knows something does not yet know as he ought to know. But the man who loves God is known by God.

So then, about eating food sacrificed to idols: We know that an idol is nothing at all in the world and that there is no God but one. For even if there are so-called gods, whether in heaven or on earth (as indeed there are many "gods" and many "lords"), yet for us there is but one God, the Father, from whom all things came and for whom we live; and there is but one Lord, Jesus Christ, through whom all things came and through whom we live.

But not everyone knows this. Some people are still so accustomed to idols that when they eat such food they think of it as having been sacrificed to an idol, and since their conscience is weak, it is defiled. But food does not bring us near to God; we are no worse if we do not eat, and no better if we do.

Be careful, however, that the exercise of your freedom does not become a stumbling block to the weak. For if anyone with a weak conscience sees you who have this knowledge eating in an idol's temple, won't he be emboldened to eat what has been sacrificed to idols? So this weak brother, for whom Christ died, is destroyed by your knowledge. When you sin against your brothers in this way and wound their weak conscience, you sin against Christ. Therefore, if what I eat causes my brother to fall into sin, I will never eat meat again, so that I will not cause him to fall.

The Rights of an Apostle

Am I not free? Am I not an apostle? Have I not seen Jesus our Lord? Are you not the result of my work in the Lord? Even though I may not be an apostle to others, surely I am to you! For you are the seal of my apostleship in the Lord.

This is my defense to those who sit in judgment on me. Don't we have the right to food and drink? Don't we have the right to take a believing wife along with us, as do the other apostles and the Lord's brothers and Cephas?[b] Or is it only I and Barnabas who must work for a living?

Who serves as a soldier at his own expense? Who plants a vineyard and does not eat of its grapes? Who tends a flock and does not drink of the milk? Do I say this merely from a human point of view? Doesn't the Law say the same thing? For it is written in the Law of Moses: "Do not muzzle an ox while it is treading out the grain."[c] Is it about oxen that God is concerned? Surely he says this for us, doesn't he? Yes, this was written for us, because when the plowman plows and the thresher threshes, they ought to do so in the hope of sharing in the harvest. If we have sown spiritual seed among you, is it too much if we reap a material harvest from you? If others have this right of support from you, shouldn't we have it all the more?

But we did not use this right. On the contrary, we put up with anything rather than hinder the gospel of Christ. Don't you know that those who work in the temple get their food from the temple, and those who serve at the altar share in what is offered on the altar? In the same way, the Lord has commanded that those who preach the gospel should receive their living from the gospel.

But I have not used any of these rights. And I am not writing this in the hope that you will do such things for me. I would rather die than have anyone deprive me of this boast. Yet when I preach the gospel, I cannot boast, for I am compelled to preach. Woe to me if I do not preach the gospel! If I preach voluntarily, I have a reward; if not voluntarily, I am simply discharging the trust committed to me. What then is my reward? Just this: that in preaching the gospel I may offer it free of charge, and so not make use of my rights in preaching it.

Though I am free and belong to no man, I make myself a slave to everyone, to win as many as possible. To the Jews I became like a Jew, to win the Jews. To those under the law I became like one under the law (though I myself am not under the law), so as to win those under the law. To those not having the law I became like one not having the law (though I am not free from God's law but am under Christ's law), so as to win those not having the law. To the weak I became weak, to win the weak. I have become all things to all men so that by all possible means I might save some. I do all this for the sake of the gospel, that I may share in its blessings.

Do you not know that in a race all the runners run, but only one gets the prize? Run in such a way as to get the prize. Everyone who competes in the games goes into strict training. They do it to get a crown that will not last; but we do it to get a crown that will last forever. Therefore I do not run like a man running aimlessly; I do not fight like a man beating the air. No, I beat my body and make it my slave so that after I have preached to others, I myself will not be disqualified for the prize.

"There is but one Lord, Jesus Christ, through whom all things came and through whom we live."

FROM OSWALD CHAMBERS

ᴈᴥ Jesus Christ is not an individual iota of a man; He is the whole of the human race centered before God in one person. He is God and man in one. Man is lifted up to God in Christ, and God is brought down to man in Christ. Jesus Christ nowhere said, "He that hath seen man hath seen the Father"; but He did say that God was manifest in human flesh in His own person that He might become the generation center for the same manifestation in every human being, and the place of His travail pangs is the Incarnation, Calvary, and the Resurrection. AUG 70

ᴈᴥ The character of Jesus Christ is exhibited in the New Testament, and it appeals to us all. He lived His life straight down in the ordinary amalgam of human life, and He claims that the character He manifested is possible for any man if he will come in by the door He provides. AUG 81

ᴈᴥ Jesus Christ is a fact; He is the most honorable and the holiest

Man, and two things necessarily follow—first, He is the least likely to be deceived about Himself; second, He is least likely to deceive anyone else. AUG 82

❧ Jesus Christ claims that He can do in human nature what human nature cannot do for itself, viz., "Destroy the works of the devil" (1 John 3:8), remove the wrong heredity, and put in the right one. He can satisfy the last aching abyss of the human heart; He can put the key into our hands which will give the solution to every problem that ever stretched before our minds. He can soothe by His pierced hands the wildest sorrow with which Satan or sin or death ever racked humanity. There is nothing for which Jesus Christ is not amply sufficient and over which He cannot make us more than conquerors. BE 111

❧ What weakness! Our Lord lived thirty years in Nazareth with His brethren who did not believe on Him; He lived three years of popularity, scandal, and hatred; fascinated a dozen illiterate men who at the end of three years all forsook Him and fled; and finally He was taken by the powers that be and crucified outside the city wall. Judged from every standpoint, save the standpoint of the Spirit of God, His life was a most manifest expression of weakness, and the idea would be strong to those in the pagan world who thought anything about Him that surely now He and His crazy tale were stamped out. CD VOL. 2, 144

❧ The task which confronted Jesus Christ was that He had to bring man, who is a sinner, back to God, forgive him his sin, and make him as holy as He is Himself; and He did it single-handed. The revelation is that Jesus Christ, the last Adam, was "made to be sin," the thing which severed man from God, and that He put away sin by the sacrifice of Himself—"that we might become the righteousness of God in Him" (2 Cor. 5:21). He lifted the human race back, not to where it was in the first Adam, He lifted it back to where it never was, viz., to where He is Himself. CHI 15

❧ Jesus Christ is not only Savior, He is King, and He has the right to exact anything and everything from us at His own discretion. HGM 129

---

a. Or *"We all possess knowledge,"* as you say
b. That is, Peter
c. Deut. 25:4

21

1 CORINTHIANS 10

WARNINGS FROM ISRAEL'S HISTORY

For I do not want you to be ignorant of the fact, brothers, that our forefathers were all under the cloud and that they all passed through the sea. They were all baptized into Moses in the cloud and in the sea. They all ate the same spiritual food and drank the same spiritual drink; for they drank from the spiritual rock that accompanied them, and that rock was Christ. Nevertheless, God was not pleased with most of them; their bodies were scattered over the desert.

Now these things occurred as examples[a] to keep us from setting our hearts on evil things as they did. Do not be idolaters, as some of them were; as it is written: "The people sat down to eat and drink and got up to indulge in pagan revelry."[b] We should not commit sexual immorality, as some of them did — and in one day twenty-three thousand of them died. We should not test the Lord, as some of them did — and were killed by snakes. And do not grumble, as some of them did — and were killed by the destroying angel.

These things happened to them as examples and were written down as warnings for us, on whom the fulfillment of the ages has come. So, if you think you are standing firm, be careful that you don't fall! No temptation has seized you except what is common to man. And God is faithful; he will not let you be tempted beyond what you can bear. But when you are tempted, he will also provide a way out so that you can stand up under it.

IDOL FEASTS AND THE LORD'S SUPPER

Therefore, my dear friends, flee from idolatry. I speak to sensible people; judge for yourselves what I say. Is not the cup of thanks-

105

giving for which we give thanks a participation in the blood of Christ? And is not the bread that we break a participation in the body of Christ? Because there is one loaf, we, who are many, are one body, for we all partake of the one loaf.

Consider the people of Israel: Do not those who eat the sacrifices participate in the altar? Do I mean then that a sacrifice offered to an idol is anything, or that an idol is anything? No, but the sacrifices of pagans are offered to demons, not to God, and I do not want you to be participants with demons. You cannot drink the cup of the Lord and the cup of demons too; you cannot have a part in both the Lord's table and the table of demons. Are we trying to arouse the Lord's jealousy? Are we stronger than he?

THE BELIEVER'S FREEDOM

"Everything is permissible" — but not everything is beneficial. "Everything is permissible" — but not everything is constructive. Nobody should seek his own good, but the good of others.

Eat anything sold in the meat market without raising questions of conscience, for, "The earth is the Lord's, and everything in it."[c]

If some unbeliever invites you to a meal and you want to go, eat whatever is put before you without raising questions of conscience. But if anyone says to you, "This has been offered in sacrifice," then do not eat it, both for the sake of the man who told you and for conscience' sake[d] — the other man's conscience, I mean, not yours. For why should my freedom be judged by another's conscience? If I take part in the meal with thankfulness, why am I denounced because of something I thank God for?

So whether you eat or drink or whatever you do, do it all for the glory of God. Do not cause anyone to stumble, whether Jews, Greeks or the church of God — even as I try to please everybody in every way. For I am not seeking my own good but the good of many, so that they may be saved.

"No temptation has seized you except what is common to man.
And God is faithful; he will not let you be tempted
beyond what you can bear. . . .
He will also provide a way out so that you can stand up under it."

FROM OSWALD CHAMBERS

~ Jesus Christ was tempted, and so shall we be tempted when we are rightly related to God. BP 191

~ To be raised above temptation belongs to God only. DI 75

~ How are we to face the tempter? By prayer? No. With the Word of God? No. Face the tempter with Jesus Christ, and He will apply the Word of God to you, and the temptation will cease. DI 76

~ We are apt to imagine that our Lord was only tempted once and that then His temptations were over. His temptations went on from the first moment of His conscious life to the last, because His holiness was not the holiness of Almighty God, but the holiness of man, which can only progress by means of the things that go against it. LG 152

~ Temptations in the life of faith are not accidents; each temptation is part of a plan, a step in the progress of faith. NKW 117

~ Temptation must come, and we do not know what it is until we meet it. When we do meet it, we must not debate with God, but stand absolutely true to Him no matter what it costs us personally, and we will find that the onslaught will leave us with higher and purer affinities than before. PR 70

~ Temptation is not sin; temptation must always be possible for our sonship to be of worth to God. It would be no credit for God to bring mechanical slaves to glory—"for it became Him . . . in bringing many sons unto glory" (Heb. 2:10)—not slaves, not useless channels, but vigorous, alert, wide-awake men and women, with all their powers and faculties devoted absolutely to God. PS 50

~ There is a limit to temptation. "God is faithful, who will not suffer you to be tempted above that ye are able" (1 Cor. 10:13). God does not save us from temptations, but He succors us in the middle of them. PS 59

~ The word *temptation* has come down in the world; we are apt to use it wrongly. Temptation is not sin; it is the thing we are bound to meet if we are human. Not to be tempted would be to be beneath contempt. Many of us, however, suffer from temptations from which we have no business to suffer, simply because we have refused to let God lift us to a higher plane where we would face temptations of another order.

A man's disposition on the inside, i.e., what he possesses in his personality, determines what he is tempted by on the outside. The temptation fits the nature of the one tempted, and reveals the possibilities of the nature. Every man has the setting of his own temptation, and the temptation will come along the line of the ruling disposition.

Temptation is a suggested shortcut to the realization of the highest at which I aim — not toward what I understand as good. Temptation is something that completely baffles me for a while; I do not know whether the thing is right or wrong. Temptation yielded to is lust deified, and is a proof that it was timidity that prevented the sin before.

Temptation is not something we may escape; it is essential to the full-orbed life of a man. Beware lest you think you are tempted as no one else is tempted, what you go through is the common inheritance of the race, not something no one ever went through before. God does not save us from temptations; He succors us in the midst of them. MUH 261

---

a. Or *types;* also in verse 11
b. Exodus 32:6
c. Psalm 24:1
d. Some manuscripts *conscience' sake, for "the earth is the Lord's and everything in it"*

22

PROPRIETY IN WORSHIP

Follow my example, as I follow the example of Christ. I praise you for remembering me in everything and for holding to the teachings,[a] just as I passed them on to you.

Now I want you to realize that the head of every man is Christ, and the head of the woman is man, and the head of Christ is God. Every man who prays or prophesies with his head covered dishonors his head. And every woman who prays or prophesies with her head uncovered dishonors her head — it is just as though her head were shaved. If a woman does not cover her head, she should have her hair cut off; and if it is a disgrace for a woman to have her hair cut or shaved off, she should cover her head. A man ought not to cover his head,[b] since he is the image and glory of God; but the woman is the glory of man. For man did not come from woman, but woman from man; neither was man created for woman, but woman for man. For this reason, and because of the angels, the woman ought to have a sign of authority on her head.

In the Lord, however, woman is not independent of man, nor is man independent of woman. For as woman came from man, so also man is born of woman. But everything comes from God. Judge for yourselves: Is it proper for a woman to pray to God with her head uncovered? Does not the very nature of things teach you that if a man has long hair, it is a disgrace to him, but that if a woman has long hair, it is her glory? For long hair is given to her as a covering. If anyone wants to be contentious about this, we have no other practice — nor do the churches of God.

THE LORD'S SUPPER

In the following directives I have no praise for you, for your meetings do more harm than good. In the first place, I hear that when you come together as a church, there are divisions among you, and to some extent I believe it. No doubt there have to be differences among you to show which of you have God's approval. When you come together, it is not the Lord's Supper you eat, for as you eat, each of you goes ahead without waiting for anybody else. One remains hungry, another gets drunk. Don't you have homes to eat and drink in? Or do you despise the church of God and humiliate those who have nothing? What shall I say to you? Shall I praise you for this? Certainly not!

For I received from the Lord what I also passed on to you: The Lord Jesus, on the night he was betrayed, took bread, and when he had given thanks, he broke it and said, "This is my body, which is for you; do this in remembrance of me." In the same way, after supper he took the cup, saying, "This cup is the new covenant in my blood; do this, whenever you drink it, in remembrance of me." For whenever you eat this bread and drink this cup, you proclaim the Lord's death until he comes.

Therefore, whoever eats the bread or drinks the cup of the Lord in an unworthy manner will be guilty of sinning against the body and blood of the Lord. A man ought to examine himself before he eats of the bread and drinks of the cup. For anyone who eats and drinks without recognizing the body of the Lord eats and drinks judgment on himself. That is why many among you are weak and sick, and a number of you have fallen asleep. But if we judged ourselves, we would not come under judgment. When we are judged by the Lord, we are being disciplined so that we will not be condemned with the world.

So then, my brothers, when you come together to eat, wait for each other. If anyone is hungry, he should eat at home, so that when you meet together it may not result in judgment.

And when I come I will give further directions.

"If we judged ourselves, we would not come under judgment."

FROM OSWALD CHAMBERS

ᴣᴕ If we judge ourselves by one another, we do not feel condemned ... but immediately Jesus Christ is in the background — His life, His language, His looks, His labors, we feel judged instantly. "It is for judgment that I have come into the world" (John 9:39). HGM 43

ᴣᴕ We cannot get away from the penetration of Jesus Christ. If I see the mote in my brother's eye, it is because I have a beam in my own. . . . If I have let God remove the beam from my own outlook by His mighty grace, I will carry with me the implicit sunlight confidence that what God has done for me He can easily do for you, because you have only a splinter and I had a log of wood! SSM 81

ᴣᴕ We have to learn to see things from Jesus Christ's standpoint. Our judgment is warped in every particular in which we do not allow it to be illuminated by Jesus Christ. MFL 125

ᴣᴕ The standard for the judgment of Christians is our Lord. PS 44

ᴣᴕ The Bible says that a man knows by the way he is made that certain things are wrong, and as he obeys or disobeys the ordinance of God written in his spirit, he will be judged. BP 240

ᴣᴕ Which of us would dare stand before God and say, "My God, judge me as I have judged my fellowmen"? We have judged our fellowmen as sinners; if God had judged us like that, we would be in hell. God judges us through the marvelous Atonement of Jesus Christ. SSM 80

ᴣᴕ God's condemnations as well as His promises are conditional; as long as we remain with the wrong disposition unremoved, every truth of God will harden us and ripen us for judgment. HGM 109

ᴣᴕ Most of us suspend judgment about ourselves. We find reasons for not accusing ourselves entirely; consequently, when we find anything so definite and intense as the Bible revelation we are apt to say it exaggerates, until we are smitten with the knowledge of what we are like in God's sight. OPG 54

---

a. Or *traditions*
b. Or *Every man who prays or prophesies with long hair dishonors his head. And every woman who prays or prophesies with no covering of hair on her head dishonors*

her head — she is just like one of the "shorn women." If a woman has no covering, let her be for now with short hair, but since it is a disgrace for a woman to have her hair shorn or shaved, she should grow it again. A man ought not to have long hair

<p style="text-align: center;">

23

1 CORINTHIANS 12–13

SPIRITUAL GIFTS

N ow about spiritual gifts, brothers, I do not want you to be ignorant. You know that when you were pagans, somehow or other you were influenced and led astray to mute idols. Therefore I tell you that no one who is speaking by the Spirit of God says, "Jesus be cursed," and no one can say, "Jesus is Lord," except by the Holy Spirit.

There are different kinds of gifts, but the same Spirit. There are different kinds of service, but the same Lord. There are different kinds of working, but the same God works all of them in all men.

Now to each one the manifestation of the Spirit is given for the common good. To one there is given through the Spirit the message of wisdom, to another the message of knowledge by means of the same Spirit, to another faith by the same Spirit, to another gifts of healing by that one Spirit, to another miraculous powers, to another prophecy, to another distinguishing between spirits, to another speaking in different kinds of tongues, and to still another the interpretation of tongues.[a] All these are the work of one and the same Spirit, and he gives them to each one, just as he determines.

ONE BODY, MANY PARTS

The body is a unit, though it is made up of many parts; and though all its parts are many, they form one body. So it is with Christ. For we were all baptized by one Spirit into one body — whether Jews or Greeks, slave or free — and we were all given the one Spirit to drink.

Now the body is not made up of one part but of many. If the foot should say, "Because I am not a hand, I do not belong to the body," it would not for that reason cease to be part of the body. And if the ear should say, "Because I am not an eye, I do not belong to the body," it would not for that reason cease to be part of the body. If the whole body were an eye, where would the sense of hearing be? If the whole body were an ear, where would the sense of smell be? But in fact God has arranged the parts in the body, every one of them, just as he wanted them to be. If they were all one part, where would the body be? As it is, there are many parts, but one body.

The eye cannot say to the hand, "I don't need you!" And the head cannot say to the feet, "I don't need you!" On the contrary, those parts of the body that seem to be weaker are indispensable, and the parts that we think are less honorable we treat with special honor. And the parts that are unpresentable are treated with special modesty, while our presentable parts need no special treatment. But God has combined the members of the body and has given greater honor to the parts that lacked it, so that there should be no division in the body, but that its parts should have equal concern for each other. If one part suffers, every part suffers with it; if one part is honored, every part rejoices with it.

Now you are the body of Christ, and each one of you is a part of it. And in the church God has appointed first of all apostles, second prophets, third teachers, then workers of miracles, also those having gifts of healing, those able to help others, those with gifts of administration, and those speaking in different kinds of tongues. Are all apostles? Are all prophets? Are all teachers? Do all work miracles? Do all have gifts of healing? Do all speak in tongues? Do all interpret? But eagerly desire the greater gifts.

LOVE

And now I will show you the most excellent way.

If I speak in the tongues[e] of men and of angels, but have not love, I am only a resounding gong or a clanging cymbal. If I have the gift of prophecy and can fathom all mysteries and all knowledge, and if I have a faith that can move mountains, but have not love, I am nothing. If I give all I possess to the poor and surrender my body to the flames,[f] but have not love, I gain nothing.

Love is patient, love is kind. It does not envy, it does not boast, it is not proud. It is not rude, it is not self-seeking, it is not easily angered, it keeps no record of wrongs. Love does not delight in evil but rejoices with the truth. It always protects, always trusts, always hopes, always perseveres.

Love never fails. But where there are prophecies, they will cease; where there are tongues, they will be stilled; where there is knowledge, it will pass away. For we know in part and we prophesy in part, but when perfection comes, the imperfect disappears. When I was a child, I talked like a child, I thought like a child, I reasoned like a child. When I became a man, I put childish ways behind me. Now we see but a poor reflection as in a mirror; then we shall see face to face. Now I know in part; then I shall know fully, even as I am fully known.

And now these three remain: faith, hope and love. But the greatest of these is love.

"These three remain: faith, hope, and love.
But the greatest of these is love."

FROM OSWALD CHAMBERS

⤷ Love to be anything at all must be personal; to love without hating is an impossibility, and the stronger and more emphatic the love, the more intense is its obverse, hatred. God loves the world so much that He hates with a perfect hatred the thing that switched men wrong; and Calvary is the measure of His hatred. BE 32

⤷ Love in the Bible is *one;* it is unique, and the human element is but one aspect of it. It is a love so mighty, so absorbing, so intense that all the mind is emancipated and entranced by God; all the heart is transfigured by the same devotion; all the soul in its living, working, waking, sleeping moments is indwelt and surrounded and enwheeled in the rest of this love. CD VOL. 2, 154

⤷ There is only one being who loves perfectly, and that is God, yet the New Testament distinctly states that we are to love as God does. So the first step is obvious: If ever we are going to have perfect love in our hearts, we must have the very nature of God in us. CHI 88

⤷ The one characteristic of love is that it thinks of nothing for itself; it is absorbed in God. IWP 21

❧ God is love, not, God is loving. God and love are synonymous. Love is not an attribute of God; it is God; whatever God is, love is. If your conception of love does not agree with justice and judgment and purity and holiness, then your idea of love is wrong. It is not love you conceive of in your mind, but some vague infinite foolishness, all tears and softness and of infinite weakness. LG 9

❧ "Keep yourselves in the love of God" Jude 21), not "keep on loving God," none can do that. When once you have understood the truth about your own heart's sinfulness, think not again of it, but look at the great, vast, illimitable magnificence of the love of God. LG 19

❧ If human love does not carry a man beyond himself, it is not love. If love is always discreet, always wise, always sensible and calculating, never carried beyond itself, it is not love at all. It may be affection, it may be warmth of feeling, but it has not the true nature of love in it. MUH 52

---

a. Or *languages;* also in verse 28
b. Or *with;* or *in*
c. Or *other languages*
d. Or *But you are eagerly desiring*
e. Or *languages*
f. Some early manuscripts *body that I may boast*

24

1 CORINTHIANS 14

GIFTS OF PROPHECY AND TONGUES

Follow the way of love and eagerly desire spiritual gifts, especially the gift of prophecy. For anyone who speaks in a tongue[a] does not speak to men but to God. Indeed, no one understands him; he utters mysteries with his spirit.[b] But everyone who prophesies speaks to men for their strengthening, encouragement and comfort. He who speaks in a tongue edifies himself, but he who prophesies edifies the church. I would like every one of you to speak in tongues,[c] but I would rather have you prophesy. He who prophesies is greater than one who speaks in tongues,[c] unless he interprets, so that the church may be edified.

Now, brothers, if I come to you and speak in tongues, what good will I be to you, unless I bring you some revelation or knowledge or prophecy or word of instruction? Even in the case of lifeless things that make sounds, such as the flute or harp, how will anyone know what tune is being played unless there is a distinction in the notes? Again, if the trumpet does not sound a clear call, who will get ready for battle? So it is with you. Unless you speak intelligible words with your tongue, how will anyone know what you are saying? You will just be speaking into the air. Undoubtedly there are all sorts of languages in the world, yet none of them is without meaning. If then I do not grasp the meaning of what someone is saying, I am a foreigner to the speaker, and he is a foreigner to me. So it is with you. Since you are eager to have spiritual gifts, try to excel in gifts that build up the church.

For this reason anyone who speaks in a tongue should pray that he may interpret what he says. For if I pray in a tongue, my spirit prays, but my mind is unfruitful. So what shall I do? I will

117

pray with my spirit, but I will also pray with my mind; I will sing with my spirit, but I will also sing with my mind. If you are praising God with your spirit, how can one who finds himself among those who do not understand[d] say "Amen" to your thanksgiving, since he does not know what you are saying? You may be giving thanks well enough, but the other man is not edified.

I thank God that I speak in tongues more than all of you. But in the church I would rather speak five intelligible words to instruct others than ten thousand words in a tongue.

Brothers, stop thinking like children. In regard to evil be infants, but in your thinking be adults. In the Law it is written:

"Through men of strange tongues
    and through the lips of foreigners
I will speak to this people,
    but even then they will not listen to me,"[e]

says the Lord.

Tongues, then, are a sign, not for believers but for unbelievers; prophecy, however, is for believers, not for unbelievers. So if the whole church comes together and everyone speaks in tongues, and some who do not understand[f] or some unbelievers come in, will they not say that you are out of your mind? But if an unbeliever or someone who does not understand[g] comes in while everybody is prophesying, he will be convinced by all that he is a sinner and will be judged by all, and the secrets of his heart will be laid bare. So he will fall down and worship God, exclaiming, "God is really among you!"

ORDERLY WORSHIP

What then shall we say, brothers? When you come together, everyone has a hymn, or a word of instruction, a revelation, a tongue or an interpretation. All of these must be done for the strengthening of the church. If anyone speaks in a tongue, two—or at the most three—should speak, one at a time, and someone must interpret. If there is no interpreter, the speaker should keep quiet in the church and speak to himself and God.

Two or three prophets should speak, and the others should

118

weigh carefully what is said. And if a revelation comes to some-one who is sitting down, the first speaker should stop. For you can all prophesy in turn so that everyone may be instructed and encouraged. The spirits of prophets are subject to the control of prophets. For God is not a God of disorder but of peace.

As in all the congregations of the saints, women should remain silent in the churches. They are not allowed to speak, but must be in submission, as the Law says. If they want to inquire about something, they should ask their own husbands at home; for it is disgraceful for a woman to speak in the church.

Did the word of God originate with you? Or are you the only people it has reached? If anybody thinks he is a prophet or spiritually gifted, let him acknowledge that what I am writing to you is the Lord's command. If he ignores this, he himself will be ignored.[h]

Therefore, my brothers, be eager to prophesy, and do not forbid speaking in tongues. But everything should be done in a fitting and orderly way.

"Follow the way of love and eagerly desire spiritual gifts, especially the gift of prophecy."

FROM OSWALD CHAMBERS

ɞ The personal Holy Spirit builds us up into the body of Christ. All that Jesus Christ came to do is made ours experimentally by the Holy Spirit, and all His gifts are for the good of the whole body, not for individual exaltation. Individuality must go in order that the personal life may be brought out into fellowship with God. By the baptism of the Holy Ghost, we are delivered from the husk of independent individuality; our personality is awakened and brought into communion with God. We too often divorce what the New Testament never divorces. The baptism of the Holy Ghost is not an experience apart from Christ: It is the evidence of the ascended Christ. It is not the baptism of the Holy Ghost that changes men, but the power of the ascended Christ coming into men's lives by the Holy Ghost that changes them. "Ye shall be witnesses unto Me" (Acts 1:8). This great Pentecostal phrase puts the truth for us in unforgettable words. Witnesses not so much of what Jesus Christ can do, but "witnesses unto Me," a delight to the heart of Jesus, a satisfaction to Him wherever He places us. MC 131

❧ A saint is made by God—"He made me." Then do not tell God He is a bungling workman. We do that whenever we say "I can't." To say "I can't" literally means we are too strong in ourselves to depend on God. "I can't pray in public; I can't talk in the open air." Substitute "I won't," and it will be nearer the truth. The thing that makes us say "I can't" is that we forget that we must rely entirely on the creative purpose of God and on this characteristic of perfect finish for God.

Much of our difficulty comes because we choose our own work—"Oh well, this is what I am fitted for." Remember that Jesus took a fisherman and turned him into a shepherd. That is symbolical of what He does all the time. The idea that we have to consecrate our gifts to God is a dangerous one. We cannot consecrate what is not ours (1 Cor. 4:7). We have to consecrate ourselves, and leave our gifts alone. God does not ask us to do the thing that is easy to us naturally; He only asks us to do the thing we are perfectly fitted to do by grace. SSY 108

❧ We must not dictate to Jesus as to where we are going to serve Him. There is a theory abroad today that we have to consecrate our gifts to God. We cannot—they are not ours to consecrate; every gift we have has been given to us. Jesus Christ does not take my gifts and use them; He takes me and turns me right about face, and realizes Himself in me for His glory. AUG 99

❧ The gifts of the Spirit are built on God's sovereignty, not on our temperament. AUG 23

❧ The only sign that a particular gift is from the ascended Christ is that it edifies the church. Much of our Christian work today is built on what the apostle pleads it should not be built on, viz., the excellencies of the natural virtues. DI 23

---

a. Or *another language;* also in verses 4, 13-14, 19, 26 and 27
b. Or *by the Spirit*
c. Or *other languages;* also in verses 6, 18, 22-23 and 39
d. Or *among the inquirers*
e. Isaiah 28:11-12; Deut. 28:49
f. Or *some inquirers*
g. Or *or some inquirer*
h. Some manuscripts *If he is ignorant of this, let him be ignorant*

25

1 CORINTHIANS 15

THE RESURRECTION OF CHRIST

 ow, brothers, I want to remind you of the gospel I preached to you, which you received and on which you have taken your stand. By this gospel you are saved, if you hold firmly to the word I preached to you. Otherwise, you have believed in vain.

For what I received I passed on to you as of first importance:[a] that Christ died for our sins according to the Scriptures, that he was buried, that he was raised on the third day according to the Scriptures, and that he appeared to Peter,[b] and then to the Twelve. After that, he appeared to more than five hundred of the brothers at the same time, most of whom are still living, though some have fallen asleep. Then he appeared to James, then to all the apostles, and last of all he appeared to me also, as to one abnormally born.

For I am the least of the apostles and do not even deserve to be called an apostle, because I persecuted the church of God. But by the grace of God I am what I am, and his grace to me was not without effect. No, I worked harder than all of them—yet not I, but the grace of God that was with me. Whether, then, it was I or they, this is what we preach, and this is what you believed.

THE RESURRECTION OF THE DEAD

But if it is preached that Christ has been raised from the dead, how can some of you say that there is no resurrection of the dead? If there is no resurrection of the dead, then not even Christ has been raised. And if Christ has not been raised, our preaching is useless and so is your faith. More than that, we are then found to be false witnesses about God, for we have testified about God that he raised Christ from the dead. But he did not raise him if in fact the dead are not raised. For if the dead are not raised, then Christ has not been raised either. And if Christ has not been raised, your faith is futile; you are still in your sins. Then those also who have fallen asleep in Christ are lost. If only for this life we have hope in Christ, we are to be pitied more than all men.

But Christ has indeed been raised from the dead, the firstfruits of those who have fallen asleep. For since death came through a man, the resurrection of the dead comes also through a man. For as in Adam all die, so in Christ all will be made alive. But each in his own turn: Christ, the firstfruits; then, when he comes, those who belong to him. Then the end will come, when he hands over the kingdom to God the Father after he has destroyed all dominion, authority and power. For he must reign until he has put all his enemies under his feet. The last enemy to be destroyed is death. For he "has put everything under his feet."[c] Now when it says that "everything" has been put under him, it is clear that this does not include God himself, who put everything under Christ. When he has done this, then the Son himself will be made subject to him who put everything under him, so that God may be all in all.

Now if there is no resurrection, what will those do who are baptized for the dead? If the dead are not raised at all, why are people baptized for them? And as for us, why do we endanger ourselves every hour? I die every day—I mean that, brothers—just as surely as I glory over you in Christ Jesus our Lord. If I fought wild beasts in Ephesus for merely human reasons, what have I gained? If the dead are not raised,

"Let us eat and drink,
    for tomorrow we die."[d]

Do not be misled: "Bad company corrupts good character." Come back to your senses as you ought, and stop sinning; for there are some who are ignorant of God—I say this to your shame.

THE RESURRECTION BODY

But someone may ask, "How are the dead raised? With what kind of body will they come?" How foolish! What you sow does not come to life unless it dies. When you sow, you do not plant the body that will be, but just a seed, perhaps of wheat or of something else. But God gives it a body as he has determined, and to each kind of seed he gives its own body. All flesh is not the same: Men have one kind of flesh, animals have another, birds another and fish another. There are also heavenly bodies and there are earthly bodies; but the splendor of the heavenly bodies is one kind, and the splendor of the earthly bodies is another. The sun has one kind of splendor, the moon another and the stars another; and star differs from star in splendor.

So will it be with the resurrection of the dead. The body that is sown is perishable, it is raised imperishable; it is sown in dishonor, it is raised in glory; it is sown in weakness, it is raised in power; it is sown a natural body, it is raised a spiritual body.

If there is a natural body, there is also a spiritual body. So it is written: "The first man Adam became a living being"[e]; the last Adam, a life-giving spirit. The spiritual did not come first, but the natural, and after that the spiritual. The first man was of the dust of the earth, the second man from heaven. As was the earthly man, so are those who are of the earth; and as is the man from heaven, so also are those who are of heaven. And just as we have borne the likeness of the earthly man, so shall we[f] bear the likeness of the man from heaven.

I declare to you, brothers, that flesh and blood cannot inherit the kingdom of God, nor does the perishable inherit the imperishable. Listen, I tell you a mystery: We will not all sleep, but we will all be changed—in a flash, in the twinkling of an eye, at the last trumpet. For the trumpet will sound, the dead will be raised imperishable, and we will be changed. For the perishable must clothe itself with the imperishable, and the mortal with immortality. When the perishable has been clothed with the imperishable, and the mortal with immortality, then the saying that is written will come true: "Death has been swallowed up in victory."[g]

"Where, O death, is your victory?
Where, O death, is your sting?"[h]

The sting of death is sin, and the power of sin is the law. But thanks be to God! He gives us the victory through our Lord Jesus Christ.

Therefore, my dear brothers, stand firm. Let nothing move you. Always give yourselves fully to the work of the Lord, because you know that your labor in the Lord is not in vain.

"If only for this life we have hope in Christ,
we are to be pitied more than all men.
But Christ has indeed been raised from the dead,
the first fruits of those who have fallen asleep."

From Oswald Chambers

❧ The Bible points out that man's spirit is immortal, whether or not he is energized by the Spirit of God; that is, spirit never sleeps. Instead of the spirit sleeping at what we call death, at the breaking away of spirit from the body, the spirit is ten thousand-fold more awake. With the majority of us, our spirits are half-concealed while we are in this body. Remember, spirit and personality are synonymous, but as long as a man is in the body his personality is obscured. Immediately when he dies, his spirit is no more obscured; it is absolutely awake; no limitations now; man is face to face with everything else that is of spirit.

Soul and body depend on each other; spirit does not—spirit is immortal. Soul is simply the spirit expressing itself in the body. Immediately when the body goes, the soul is gone, but the moment the body is brought back, soul is brought back, and spirit, soul, and body will again be together. Spirit has never died, can never die, in the sense in which the body dies; the spirit is immortal, either in immortal life or in immortal death. There is no such thing as annihilation taught in the Bible. The separation of spirit from body and soul is temporary. The resurrection is the resurrection of the body.

Our Lord never speaks of the resurrection of spirit; the spirit does not need resurrecting. He speaks of a resurrection body for glorification and a resurrection body for damnation. "The hour is coming, in which all that are in the graves shall hear His voice, and shall come forth; they that have done good, unto the resurrection of life; and they that have done evil, unto the resurrection of damnation" (John 5:28-29). We know what the resurrection body for glorification will be like: it will be like "His glorious body"; but all we know about the resurrection of the bad is that Jesus Christ . . . says that there will be a resurrection to damnation. The question of eternal punishment is a fearful one, but let no one say that Jesus Christ did not say anything about it; He did. BP 259

❧ We have all known the thrilling yesterday—when we first entered into the realization of love, or of friendship, or of the joy of life. If all that we have is the human, it will end in bitter tears—not sometimes, but every time. The only way in which bitter tears can be evaded is either by a man's shallowness, or by his coming into a totally new relation to the Lord Jesus Christ through His Resurrection. PH 123

---

a. Or *you at the first*
b. Greek *Cephas*
c. Psalm 8:6
d. Isaiah 22:13
e. Gen. 2:7
f. Some early manuscripts *so let us*
g. Isaiah 25:8
h. Hosea 13:14

26

THE COLLECTION FOR GOD'S PEOPLE

ow about the collection for God's people: Do what I told the Galatian churches to do. On the first day of every week, each one of you should set aside a sum of money in keeping with his income, saving it up, so that when I come no collections will have to be made. Then, when I arrive, I will give letters of introduction to the men you approve and send them with your gift to Jerusalem. If it seems advisable for me to go also, they will accompany me.

PERSONAL REQUESTS

After I go through Macedonia, I will come to you—for I will be going through Macedonia. Perhaps I will stay with you awhile, or even spend the winter, so that you can help me on my journey, wherever I go. I do not want to see you now and make only a passing visit; I hope to spend some time with you, if the Lord permits. But I will stay on at Ephesus until Pentecost, because a great door for effective work has opened to me, and there are many who oppose me.

If Timothy comes, see to it that he has nothing to fear while he is with you, for he is carrying on the work of the Lord, just as I am. No one, then, should refuse to accept him. Send him on his way in peace so that he may return to me. I am expecting him along with the brothers.

Now about our brother Apollos: I strongly urged him to go to you with the brothers. He was quite unwilling to go now, but he will go when he has the opportunity.

Be on your guard; stand firm in the faith; be men of courage; be strong. Do everything in love.

You know that the household of Stephanas were the first converts in Achaia, and they have devoted themselves to the service of the saints. I urge you, brothers, to submit to such as these and to everyone who joins in the work, and labors at it. I was glad when Stephanas, Fortunatus and Achaicus arrived, because they have supplied what was lacking from you. For they refreshed my spirit and yours also. Such men deserve recognition.

FINAL GREETINGS

The churches in the province of Asia send you greetings. Aquila and Priscilla[a] greet you warmly in the Lord, and so does the church that meets at their house. All the brothers here send you greetings. Greet one another with a holy kiss.

I, Paul, write this greeting in my own hand.

If anyone does not love the Lord—a curse be on him. Come, O Lord![b]

The grace of the Lord Jesus be with you.

My love to all of you in Christ Jesus. Amen.[c]

"Be on your guard; stand firm in the faith;
be men of courage; be strong. Do everything in love."

FROM OSWALD CHAMBERS

⁊ There is a method of making disciples which is not sanctioned by our Lord. It is an excessive pressing of people to be reconciled to God in a way that is unworthy of the dignity of the Gospel. The pleading is on the line of: Jesus has done so much for us; cannot we do something out of gratitude to Him? This method of getting people into relationship to God out of pity for Jesus is never recognized by our Lord. It does not put sin in its right place, nor does it put the more serious aspect of the Gospel in its right place. Our Lord never pressed anyone to follow Him unconditionally; nor did He wish to be followed merely out of an impulse of enthusiasm. He never pleaded, He never entrapped; He made discipleship intensely narrow and pointed out certain things which could never be in those who followed Him. Today there is a tendency to take the harshness out of our Lord's statements. What Jesus says is hard; it is only easy when it comes to those who are His disciples. AUG 49

❧ The distinction between a saved soul and a disciple is fundamental. The stern conditions laid down by our Lord for discipleship are not the conditions of salvation; discipleship is a much closer and more conscious relationship. BSG 23

❧ To make disciples, then, we must have been made disciples ourselves. There is no royal road to sainthood and discipleship. The way of the Cross is the only way. We see God only from a pure heart, never from an able intellect. CD VOL. 2, 113

❧ Jesus Christ always said, "If any man will be My disciple"—He did not clamor for him, or buttonhole him. He never took a man off his guard, or used a revivalistic meeting to get a man out of his wits and then say, "Believe in Me," but, "Take time and consider what you are doing; if you would be My disciple, you must lose your 'soul,' i.e., your way of reasoning about things." SA 87

❧ We have to do our utmost as disciples to prove that we appreciate God's utmost for us, and to learn never to allow "I can't" to creep in. "Oh, I am not a saint; I can't do that." If that thought comes in, we are a disgrace to Jesus Christ. God's salvation is a glad thing, but it is a holy, difficult thing that tests us for all we are worth. SSM 96

❧ The walk of a disciple is gloriously difficult but gloriously certain. SSM 104

❧ We are called to be unobtrusive disciples, not heroes. When we are right with God, the tiniest thing done out of love to Him is more precious to Him than any eloquent preaching of a sermon. We have introduced into our conception of Christianity heroic notions that come from paganism and not from the teaching of our Lord. SSY 68

❧ We have become so taken up with the idea of being prepared for something in the future that that is the conception we have of discipleship. It is true, but it is also untrue. The attitude of the Christian life is that we must be prepared *now*, this second; this is the time. SSY 72

---

a. Greek *Prisca*, a variant of *Priscilla*
b. In Aramaic the expression *Come, O Lord* is *Marana tha*
c. Some manuscripts do not have *Amen*.

128

27

2 CORINTHIANS 1–2

THE GOD OF ALL COMFORT

Paul, an apostle of Christ Jesus by the will of God, and Timothy our brother,

To the church of God in Corinth, together with all the saints throughout Achaia:

Grace and peace to you from God our Father and the Lord Jesus Christ.

Praise be to the God and Father of our Lord Jesus Christ, the Father of compassion and the God of all comfort, who comforts us in all our troubles, so that we can comfort those in any trouble with the comfort we ourselves have received from God. For just as the sufferings of Christ flow over into our lives, so also through Christ our comfort overflows. If we are distressed, it is for your comfort and salvation; if we are comforted, it is for your comfort, which produces in you patient endurance of the same sufferings we suffer. And our hope for you is firm, because we know that just as you share in our sufferings, so also you share in our comfort.

We do not want you to be uninformed, brothers, about the hardships we suffered in the province of Asia. We were under great pressure, far beyond our ability to endure, so that we despaired even of life. Indeed, in our hearts we felt the sentence of death. But this happened that we might not rely on ourselves but on God, who raises the dead. He has delivered us from such a deadly peril, and he will deliver us. On him we have set our hope that he will continue to deliver us, as you help us by your prayers. Then many will give thanks on our[a] behalf for the gracious favor granted us in answer to the prayers of many.

PAUL'S CHANGE OF PLANS

Now this is our boast: Our conscience testifies that we have conducted ourselves in the world, and especially in our relations with you, in the holiness and sincerity that are from God. We have done so not according to worldly wisdom but according to God's grace. For we do not write you anything you cannot read or understand. And I hope that, as you have understood us in part, you will come to understand fully that you can boast of us just as we will boast of you in the day of the Lord Jesus.

Because I was confident of this, I planned to visit you first so that you might benefit twice. I planned to visit you on my way to Macedonia and to come back to you from Macedonia, and then to have you send me on my way to Judea. When I planned this, did I do it lightly? Or do I make my plans in a worldly manner so that in the same breath I say, "Yes, yes" and "No, no"?

But as surely as God is faithful, our message to you is not "Yes" and "No." For the Son of God, Jesus Christ, who was preached among you by me and Silas[b] and Timothy, was not "Yes" and "No," but in him it has always been "Yes." For no matter how many promises God has made, they are "Yes" in Christ. And so through him the "Amen" is spoken by us to the glory of God. Now it is God who makes both us and you stand firm in Christ. He anointed us, set his seal of ownership on us, and put his Spirit in our hearts as a deposit, guaranteeing what is to come.

I call God as my witness that it was in order to spare you that I did not return to Corinth. Not that we lord it over your faith, but we work with you for your joy, because it is by faith you stand firm. So I made up my mind that I would not make another painful visit to you. For if I grieve you, who is left to make me glad but you whom I have grieved? I wrote as I did so that when I came I should not be distressed by those who ought to make me rejoice. I had confidence in all of you, that you would all share my joy. For I wrote you out of great distress and anguish of heart and with many tears, not to grieve you but to let you know the depth of my love for you.

FORGIVENESS FOR THE SINNER

If anyone has caused grief, he has not so much grieved me as he has grieved all of you, to some extent — not to put it too severely.

The punishment inflicted on him by the majority is sufficient for him. Now instead, you ought to forgive and comfort him, so that he will not be overwhelmed by excessive sorrow. I urge you, therefore, to reaffirm your love for him. The reason I wrote you was to see if you would stand the test and be obedient in everything. If you forgive anyone, I also forgive him. And what I have forgiven — if there was anything to forgive — I have forgiven in the sight of Christ for your sake, in order that Satan might not outwit us. For we are not unaware of his schemes.

MINISTERS OF THE NEW COVENANT

Now when I went to Troas to preach the gospel of Christ and found that the Lord had opened a door for me, I still had no peace of mind, because I did not find my brother Titus there. So I said good-by to them and went on to Macedonia.

But thanks be to God, who always leads us in triumphal procession in Christ and through us spreads everywhere the fragrance of the knowledge of him. For we are to God the aroma of Christ among those who are being saved and those who are perishing. To the one we are the smell of death; to the other, the fragrance of life. And who is equal to such a task? Unlike so many, we do not peddle the word of God for profit. On the contrary, in Christ we speak before God with sincerity, like men sent from God.

"No matter how many promises God has made,
they are 'Yes' in Christ."

FROM OSWALD CHAMBERS

ॐ At times it appears as if God has not only forsaken His Word, but has deliberately deceived us. We asked Him for a particular thing, or related ourselves to Him along a certain line, and expected that it would mean the fulness of blessing, and actually it has meant the opposite — upset, trouble, and difficulty all around, and we are staggered, until we learn that by this very discipline God is bringing us to the place of entire abandonment to Himself.

Never settle down in the middle of the dance of circumstances and say that you have been mistaken in your natural interpretation of God's promise to you because the immediate aftermath is devastation; say that God did give you the promise, and stick to it, and slowly God will bring you into the perfect, detailed fulfillment of that promise. When and where the fulfillment will take place depends upon God and yourself, but never doubt the absolute fulfillment of God's Word, and remember that the beginning of the fulfillment lies in your acquiescence in God's will. Remain true to God, although it means the sword going through the natural, and you will be brought into a supernaturally clear agreement with God. We are not introduced to Christianity by explanations, but we must labor at the exposition of Christianity until we satisfactorily unfold it through God's grace and our own effort. NKW 22

❧ One of the greatest demands of God on the human spirit is to believe that God is good when His providence seems to prohibit the fulfillment of what He has promised. The one character in the Bible who sustains this strain grandly is Abraham. Paul in summing up the life of Abraham points to it as his greatest quality—"Abraham believed God" (Rom. 4:3). NKW 99

❧ The majority of us know nothing about waiting; we don't wait, we endure. Waiting means that we go on in the perfect certainty of God's goodness—no dumps or fear. The attitude of the human heart toward God who promises should be to give Him credit for being as honest as He ought to be, and then to go on in the actual life as if no promise had been made. That is faithful waiting. NKW 98

❧ By the discipline of obedience, I come to the place Abraham reached and see God as He is. The promises of God are of no use to me until by obedience I understand the nature of God. We read some things in the Bible 365 times and they mean nothing to us; then all of a sudden we see what they mean, because in some particular we have obeyed God, and instantly His character is revealed. "For all the promises of God are in Him yea" (2 Cor. 1:20). The "yea" must be born of obedience; when by the obedience of our life, we say "Amen, so let it be," to a promise, then that promise is made ours. NKW 128

---

a. Many manuscripts *your*
b. Greek *Silvanus,* a variant of *Silas*

132

28

MINISTERS OF A NEW AGREEMENT

Are we beginning to commend ourselves again? Or do we need, like some people, letters of recommendation to you or from you? You yourselves are our letter, written on our hearts, known and read by everybody. You show that you are a letter from Christ, the result of our ministry, written not with ink but with the Spirit of the living God, not on tablets of stone but on tablets of human hearts.

Such confidence as this is ours through Christ before God. Not that we are competent in ourselves to claim anything for ourselves, but our competence comes from God. He has made us competent as ministers of a new covenant—not of the letter but of the Spirit; for the letter kills, but the Spirit gives life.

THE GLORY OF THE NEW COVENANT

Now if the ministry that brought death, which was engraved in letters on stone, came with glory, so that the Israelites could not look steadily at the face of Moses because of its glory, fading though it was, will not the ministry of the Spirit be even more glorious? If the ministry that condemns men is glorious, how much more glorious is the ministry that brings righteousness! For what was glorious has no glory now in comparison with the surpassing glory. And if what was fading away came with glory, how much greater is the glory of that which lasts!

Therefore, since we have such a hope, we are very bold. We are not like Moses, who would put a veil over his face to keep the Israelites from gazing at it while the radiance was fading away. But their minds were made dull, for to this day the same veil

133

remains when the old covenant is read. It has not been removed, because only in Christ is it taken away. Even to this day when Moses is read, a veil covers their hearts. But whenever anyone turns to the Lord, the veil is taken away. Now the Lord is the Spirit, and where the Spirit of the Lord is, there is freedom. And we, who with unveiled faces all reflect[a] the Lord's glory, are being transformed into his likeness with ever-increasing glory, which comes from the Lord, who is the Spirit.

Treasures in Jars of Clay

Therefore, since through God's mercy we have this ministry, we do not lose heart. Rather, we have renounced secret and shameful ways; we do not use deception, nor do we distort the word of God. On the contrary, by setting forth the truth plainly we commend ourselves to every man's conscience in the sight of God. And even if our gospel is veiled, it is veiled to those who are perishing. The god of this age has blinded the minds of unbelievers, so that they cannot see the light of the gospel of the glory of Christ, who is the image of God. For we do not preach ourselves, but Jesus Christ as Lord, and ourselves as your servants for Jesus' sake. For God, who said, "Let light shine out of darkness,"[b] made his light shine in our hearts to give us the light of the knowledge of the glory of God in the face of Christ.

But we have this treasure in jars of clay to show that this all-surpassing power is from God and not from us. We are hard pressed on every side, but not crushed; perplexed, but not in despair; persecuted, but not abandoned; struck down, but not destroyed. We always carry around in our body the death of Jesus, so that the life of Jesus may also be revealed in our body. For we who are alive are always being given over to death for Jesus' sake, so that his life may be revealed in our mortal body. So then, death is at work in us, but life is at work in you.

It is written: "I believed; therefore I have spoken."[c] With that same spirit of faith we also believe and therefore speak, because we know that the one who raised the Lord Jesus from the dead will also raise us with Jesus and present us with you in his presence. All this is for your benefit, so that the grace that is reaching more and more people may cause thanksgiving to overflow to the glory of God.

Therefore we do not lose heart. Though outwardly we are wasting away, yet inwardly we are being renewed day by day. For our light and momentary troubles are achieving for us an eternal glory that far outweighs them all. So we fix our eyes not on what is seen, but on what is unseen. For what is seen is temporary, but what is unseen is eternal.

"Now the Lord is the Spirit,
and where the Spirit of the Lord is,
there is freedom."

FROM OSWALD CHAMBERS

❧ We call liberty allowing the other fellow to please himself to the same extent as we please ourselves. True liberty is the ability earned by practice to do the right thing. There is no such thing as a gift of freedom; freedom must be earned. The counterfeit of freedom is independence. When the Spirit of God deals with sin, it is independence that He touches; that is why the preaching of the Gospel awakens resentment as well as craving. Independence must be blasted right out of a Christian; there must be only liberty, which is a very different thing. Spiritually, liberty means the ability to fulfill the Law of God, and it establishes the rights of other people. BE 25

❧ The reason man is not free is that within his personality there is a disposition which has been allowed to enslave his will, the disposition of sin. Man's destiny is determined by his disposition; he cannot alter his disposition, but he can choose to let God alter it. Jesus said, "Whosoever committeth sin is the servant of sin" (John 8:34); but He also said, "If the Son therefore shall make you free, ye shall be free indeed" (John 8:36), i.e., free in essence. We are free only when the Son sets us free, but we are free to choose whether or not we will be made free. In the experience of regeneration, a man takes the step of choosing to let God alter his disposition. When the Holy Spirit comes into a man, He brings His own generating will power and makes a man free in will. Will simply means the whole nature active, and when the Holy Spirit comes in and energizes a man's will, he is able to do what he never could do before, viz., he is able to do God's will. (Phil. 2:13) MFL 28

❧ The only liberty a saint has is the liberty not to use his liberty. BE 25

135

᷾ What is the difference between liberty and license? Liberty is the ability to perform the Law, perfect freedom to fulfill all the demands of the Law. To be free from the Law means that I am the living Law of God; there is no independence of God in my makeup. License is rebellion against all law. If my heart does not become the center of divine love, it may become the center of diabolical license. BE 136

᷾ License simply means—"I will not be bound by any laws but my own." This spirit resents God's Law and will not have anything to do with it—"I shall rule my body as I choose, I shall rule my social relationships and my religious life as I like, and I will not allow God or any creed or doctrine to rule me." That is the way license begins to work. BP 136

᷾ Our destiny is not determined for us, but it is determined by us. Man's free will is part of God's sovereign will. We have freedom to take which course we choose, but not freedom to determine the end of that choice. God makes clear what He desires; we must choose, and the result of the choice is not the inevitableness of law, but the inevitableness of God. CHI 66

a. Or *contemplate*
b. Gen. 1:3
c. Psalm 116:10

OUR HEAVENLY DWELLING

Now we know that if the earthly tent we live in is destroyed, we have a building from God, an eternal house in heaven, not built by human hands. Meanwhile we groan, longing to be clothed with our heavenly dwelling, because when we are clothed, we will not be found naked. For while we are in this tent, we groan and are burdened, because we do not wish to be unclothed but to be clothed with our heavenly dwelling, so that what is mortal may be swallowed up by life. Now it is God who has made us for this very purpose and has given us the Spirit as a deposit, guaranteeing what is to come.

Therefore we are always confident and know that as long as we are at home in the body we are away from the Lord. We live by faith, not by sight. We are confident, I say, and would prefer to be away from the body and at home with the Lord. So we make it our goal to please him, whether we are at home in the body or away from it. For we must all appear before the judgment seat of Christ, that each one may receive what is due him for the things done while in the body, whether good or bad.

THE MINISTRY OF RECONCILIATION

Since, then, we know what it is to fear the Lord, we try to persuade men. What we are is plain to God, and I hope it is also plain to your conscience. We are not trying to commend ourselves to you again, but are giving you an opportunity to take pride in us, so that you can answer those who take pride in what is seen rather than in what is in the heart. If we are out of our mind, it is for the sake of God; if we are in our right mind, it is for you. For Christ's love compels us, because we are convinced that one died for all, and therefore all died. And he died for all, that those who live should no longer live for themselves but for him who died for them and was raised again.

So from now on we regard no one from a worldly point of view. Though we once regarded Christ in this way, we do so no longer. Therefore, if anyone is in Christ, he is a new creation; the old has gone, the new has come! All this is from God, who reconciled us to himself through Christ and gave us the ministry of reconciliation: that God was reconciling the world to himself in Christ, not counting men's sins against them. And he has committed to us the message of reconciliation. We are therefore Christ's ambassadors, as though God were making his appeal through us. We implore you on Christ's behalf: Be reconciled to God. God made him who had no sin to be sin[a] for us, so that in him we might become the righteousness of God.

> *"If anyone is in Christ, he is a new creation;*
> *the old has gone, the new has come!"*

FROM OSWALD CHAMBERS

➣ The Bible reveals that the natural virtues are remnants of what the human race was as God designed it, i.e., the natural virtues belong to an order that is no longer appearing. The "man of old" has to pass and the "new man" has to dominate, but in the meantime there is chaos. The great thing to realize is that our physical nature is the same after we are born again as we were before; the difference is in the ruling disposition. SH 176

➣ When we are born again, the Holy Spirit begins to work His new creation in us, and there will come a time when there is nothing remaining of the old life. Our old gloomy outlook disappears, as does our old attitude toward things, and "all things are of God" (5:18). How are we going to get a life that has no lust, no self-interest, and is not sensitive to the ridicule of others? How will we have the type of love that "is kind . . . is not provoked, [and] thinks no evil"? (1 Cor. 13:4-5) The only way is by allowing nothing of the old life to remain, and by having only simple, perfect trust in God — such a trust that we no longer want God's blessings, but only want

God Himself. Have we come to the point where God can withdraw His blessings from us without our trust in Him being affected? Once we truly see God at work, we will never be concerned again about the things that happen, because we are actually trusting in our Father in heaven, whom the world cannot see. MUH-UE 10/23

⚘ Jesus Christ claims that He can do in human nature what human nature cannot do for itself, viz., "Destroy the works of the devil" (1 John 3;8), remove the wrong heredity, and put in the right one. He can satisfy the last aching abyss of the human heart; He can put the key into our hands which will give the solution to every problem that ever stretched before our minds. He can soothe by His pierced hands the wildest sorrow with which Satan or sin or death ever racked humanity. There is nothing for which Jesus Christ is not amply sufficient and over which He cannot make us more than conquerors. BE 111

⚘ The task which confronted Jesus Christ was that He had to bring man, who is a sinner, back to God, forgive him his sin, and make him as holy as He is Himself; and He did it single-handed. The revelation is that Jesus Christ, the last Adam, was "made to be sin," the thing which severed man from God, and that He put away sin by the sacrifice of Himself—"that we might become the righteousness of God in Him" (2 Cor. 5:21). He lifted the human race back, not to where it was in the first Adam; He lifted it back to where it never was, viz.: to where He is Himself. CHI 15

⚘ Jesus Christ came to do what no human being can do: He came to redeem men, to alter their disposition, to plant in them the Holy Spirit, to make them new creatures. Christianity is not the obliteration of the old, but the transfiguration of the old. Jesus Christ did not come to teach men to be holy: He came to make men holy. His teaching has no meaning for us unless we enter into His life by the means of His death. The Cross is the great central point. SSY 154

---

a. Or *be a sin offering*

139

30

2 CORINTHIANS 6

NOW IS THE DAY OF SALVATION

s God's fellow workers we urge you not to receive God's grace in vain. For he says,

"In the time of my favor I heard you,
and in the day of salvation I helped you."[a]

I tell you, now is the time of God's favor, now is the day of salvation.

PAUL'S HARDSHIPS

We put no stumbling block in anyone's path, so that our ministry will not be discredited. Rather, as servants of God we commend ourselves in every way: in great endurance; in troubles, hardships and distresses; in beatings, imprisonments and riots; in hard work, sleepless nights and hunger; in purity, understanding, patience and kindness; in the Holy Spirit and in sincere love; in truthful speech and in the power of God; with weapons of righteousness in the right hand and in the left; through glory and dishonor, bad report and good report; genuine, yet regarded as impostors; known, yet regarded as unknown; dying, and yet we live on; beaten, and yet not killed; sorrowful, yet always rejoicing; poor, yet making many rich; having nothing, and yet possessing everything.

We have spoken freely to you, Corinthians, and opened wide our hearts to you. We are not withholding our affection from you, but you are withholding yours from us. As a fair exchange — I speak as to my children — open wide your hearts also.

DO NOT BE YOKED WITH UNBELIEVERS

Do not be yoked together with unbelievers. For what do right-eousness and wickedness have in common? Or what fellowship can light have with darkness? What harmony is there between Christ and Belial[b]? What does a believer have in common with an unbeliever? What agreement is there between the temple of God and idols? For we are the temple of the living God. As God has said: "I will live with them and walk among them, and I will be their God, and they will be my people."[c]

"Therefore come out from them
and be separate,

says the Lord.

Touch no unclean thing,
and I will receive you."[d]
"I will be a Father to you,
and you will be my sons and daughters,

says the Lord Almighty."[e]

"As God's fellow workers
we urge you not to receive God's grace in vain. . . .
I tell you, now is the time of God's favor,
now is the day of salvation."

FROM OSWALD CHAMBERS

❧ The essence of the Gospel of God working through conscience and conduct is that it shows itself at once in action. God can make simple, guileless people out of cunning, crafty people; that is the marvel of the grace of God. It can take the strands of evil and twistedness out of a man's mind and imagination and make him simple toward God, so that his life becomes radiantly beautiful by the miracle of God's grace. BP 206

❧ The phrase "a sinner saved by grace" means that a man is no longer a sinner; if he is, he is not saved. PS 25

❧ The miracle of the grace of God is that He can make the past as though it had never been. RTR 33 ᴥ Salvation is based on the *revelation* fact that God has redeemed the world from the possibility of condemnation on account of sin. The experience of salvation means that a man can be regenerated, can have the disposition of the Son of God put into him, viz., the Holy Spirit. DI 56

ᴥ Salvation is sudden, but the working of it out in our lives is never sudden. It is moment by moment, here a little and there a little. God educates us down to the scruple. MFL 120

ᴥ We cannot do anything for our salvation, but we must do something to manifest it; we must work it out. OBH 81

ᴥ When I am saved by God's almighty grace, I realize that I am delivered completely from what He has condemned—and *that* is salvation; I don't palliate it any longer, but agree with God's verdict on it on the Cross. At the back of all the condemnation of God put "Calvary." OPG 16

ᴥ Salvation to be experimental in me is always a judgment inasmuch as it is concerned with some kind of separation. The Cross condemns men to salvation. OPG 20

ᴥ Unless our salvation works out through our fingertips and everywhere else, there is nothing to it; it is religious humbug. PH 101

ᴥ If you have been making a great profession in your religious life but begin to find that the Holy Spirit is scrutinizing you, let His searchlight go straight down, and He will not only search you, He will put everything right that is wrong; He will make the past as though it had never been; He will "restore the years the locust hath eaten" (Joel 2:25); He will "blot out the handwriting of ordinances that is against you" (Col. 2:14); He will put His Spirit within you and cause you to walk in His ways; He will make you pure in the deepest recesses of your personality. Thank God, Jesus Christ's salvation is a flesh-and-blood reality! SHL 51

---

a. Isaiah 49:8
b. Greek *Beliar,* a variant of *Belial*
c. Lev. 26:12; Jer. 32:38; Ezek. 37:27
d. Isaiah 52:11; Ezek. 20:34, 41
e. 2 Sam. 7:14; 7:8

31

2 CORINTHIANS 7

PAUL'S JOY

Since we have these promises, dear friends, let us purify ourselves from everything that contaminates body and spirit, perfecting holiness out of reverence for God.

Make room for us in your hearts. We have wronged no one, we have corrupted no one, we have exploited no one. I do not say this to condemn you; I have said before that you have such a place in our hearts that we would live or die with you. I have great confidence in you; I take great pride in you. I am greatly encouraged; in all our troubles my joy knows no bounds.

For when we came into Macedonia, this body of ours had no rest, but we were harassed at every turn—conflicts on the outside, fears within. But God, who comforts the downcast, comforted us by the coming of Titus, and not only by his coming but also by the comfort you had given him. He told us about your longing for me, your deep sorrow, your ardent concern for me, so that my joy was greater than ever.

Even if I caused you sorrow by my letter, I do not regret it. Though I did regret it—I see that my letter hurt you, but only for a little while—yet now I am happy, not because you were made sorry, but because your sorrow led you to repentance. For you became sorrowful as God intended and so were not harmed in any way by us. Godly sorrow brings repentance that leads to salvation and leaves no regret, but worldly sorrow brings death. See what this godly sorrow has produced in you: what earnestness, what eagerness to clear yourselves, what indignation, what alarm, what longing, what concern, what readiness to see justice done. At every point you have proved yourselves to be innocent in this matter. So even though I wrote to you, it was not on account of the one who did the wrong or of the injured party, but rather that before God you could see for yourselves how devoted to us you are. By all this we are encouraged.

In addition to our own encouragement, we were especially delighted to see how happy Titus was, because his spirit has been refreshed by all of you. I had boasted to him about you, and you have not embarrassed me. But just as everything we said to you was true, so our boasting about you to Titus has proved to be true as well. And his affection for you is all the greater when he remembers that you were all obedient, receiving him with fear and trembling. I am glad I can have complete confidence in you.

"Since we have these promises . . . let us purify ourselves
from everything that contaminates body and spirit,
perfecting holiness out of reverence for God.

FROM OSWALD CHAMBERS

⚥ God's perspective is that through His promises I will come to recognize His claim of ownership on me. For example, do I realize that my "body is the temple of the Holy Spirit," or am I condoning some habit in my body which clearly could not withstand the light of God on it? (1 Cor. 6:19) God formed His Son in me through sanctification, setting me apart from sin and making me holy in His sight (see Gal. 4:19). But I must begin to transform my natural life into spiritual life by obedience to Him. God instructs us even in the smallest details of life. And when He brings you conviction of sin, do not "confer with flesh and blood," but cleanse yourself from it at once (Gal. 1:16). Keep yourself cleansed in your daily walk.

I must cleanse myself from all filthiness in my flesh and my spirit until both are in harmony with the nature of God. Is the mind of my spirit in perfect agreement with the life of the Son of God in me, or am I mentally rebellious and defiant? Am I allowing the mind of Christ to be formed in me? (See Phil. 2:5.) MUH 3/17

⚥ Holiness is the characteristic of the man after God's own heart. BE 16

⚥ What Jesus Christ does in new birth is to put in a disposition that transforms morality into holiness. He came to put into the man who knows he needs it His own heredity of holiness, to bring him into a oneness with God which he never had through natural birth. CHI 22

❧ Holiness is the only sign that a man is repentant in the New Testament sense, and a holy man is not one who has his eyes set on his own whiteness, but one who is personally and passionately devoted to the Lord who saved him. CHI 123

❧ Personal holiness is never the ground of my acceptance with God; the only ground of acceptance is the death of the Lord Jesus Christ. NKW 123

❧ The Spirit of God who wrought out that marvelous life in the Incarnation will baptize us into the very same life, not into a life like it, but into His life until the very holiness of Jesus is gifted to us. It is not something we work out in Him; it is in Him, and He manifests it through us while we abide in Him. OBH 17

❧ The one marvelous secret of a holy life is not in imitating Jesus, but in letting the perfections of Jesus manifest themselves in our mortal flesh. OBH 19

145

32

2 CORINTHIANS 8–9

GENEROSITY ENCOURAGED

And now, brothers, we want you to know about the grace that God has given the Macedonian churches. Out of the most severe trial, their overflowing joy and their extreme poverty welled up in rich generosity. For I testify that they gave as much as they were able, and even beyond their ability. Entirely on their own, they urgently pleaded with us for the privilege of sharing in this service to the saints. And they did not do as we expected, but they gave themselves first to the Lord and then to us in keeping with God's will. So we urged Titus, since he had earlier made a beginning, to bring also to completion this act of grace on your part. But just as you excel in everything—in faith, in speech, in knowledge, in complete earnestness and in your love for us—[a]see that you also excel in this grace of giving.

I am not commanding you, but I want to test the sincerity of your love by comparing it with the earnestness of others. For you know the grace of our Lord Jesus Christ, that though he was rich, yet for your sakes he became poor, so that you through his poverty might become rich.

And here is my advice about what is best for you in this matter: Last year you were the first not only to give but also to have the desire to do so. Now finish the work, so that your eager willingness to do it may be matched by your completion of it, according to your means. For if the willingness is there, the gift is acceptable according to what one has, not according to what he does not have.

Our desire is not that others might be relieved while you are hard pressed, but that there might be equality. At the present time your plenty will supply what they need, so that in turn their plenty will supply what you need. Then there will be equality, as it is written: "He who gathered much did not have too much, and he who gathered little did not have too little."[b]

TITUS SENT TO CORINTH

I thank God, who put into the heart of Titus the same concern I have for you. For Titus not only welcomed our appeal, but he is coming to you with much enthusiasm and on his own initiative. And we are sending along with him the brother who is praised by all the churches for his service to the gospel. What is more, he was chosen by the churches to accompany us as we carry the offering, which we administer in order to honor the Lord himself and to show our eagerness to help. We want to avoid any criticism of the way we administer this liberal gift. For we are taking pains to do what is right, not only in the eyes of the Lord but also in the eyes of men.

In addition, we are sending with them our brother who has often proved to us in many ways that he is zealous, and now even more so because of his great confidence in you. As for Titus, he is my partner and fellow worker among you; as for our brothers, they are representatives of the churches and an honor to Christ. Therefore show these men the proof of your love and the reason for our pride in you, so that the churches can see it.

There is no need for me to write to you about this service to the saints. For I know your eagerness to help, and I have been boasting about it to the Macedonians, telling them that since last year you in Achaia were ready to give; and your enthusiasm has stirred most of them to action. But I am sending the brothers in order that our boasting about you in this matter should not prove hollow, but that you may be ready, as I said you would be. For if any Macedonians come with me and find you unprepared, we—not to say anything about you—would be ashamed of having been so confident. So I thought it necessary to urge the brothers to visit you in advance and finish the arrangements for the generous gift you had promised. Then it will be ready as a generous gift, not as one grudgingly given.

SOWING GENEROUSLY

Remember this: Whoever sows sparingly will also reap sparingly, and whoever sows generously will also reap generously. Each

148

man should give what he has decided in his heart to give, not reluctantly or under compulsion, for God loves a cheerful giver. And God is able to make all grace abound to you, so that in all things at all times, having all that you need, you will abound in every good work. As it is written:

"He has scattered abroad his gifts to the poor;
his righteousness endures forever."[c]

Now he who supplies seed to the sower and bread for food will also supply and increase your store of seed and will enlarge the harvest of your righteousness. You will be made rich in every way so that you can be generous on every occasion, and through us your generosity will result in thanksgiving to God.

This service that you perform is not only supplying the needs of God's people but is also overflowing in many expressions of thanks to God. Because of the service by which you have proved yourselves, men will praise God for the obedience that accompanies your confession of the gospel of Christ, and for your generosity in sharing with them and with everyone else. And in their prayers for you their hearts will go out to you, because of the surpassing grace God has given you. Thanks be to God for his indescribable gift!

"Just as you excel in everything,
in faith, in speech, in knowledge,
in complete earnestness and in your love for us —
see that you also excel in this grace of giving."

FROM OSWALD CHAMBERS

   ❦ If you feel remarkably generous, then be generous at once; act it out. If you don't, it will react and make you mean. BE 73

   ❦ We never get credit spiritually for impulsive giving. If suddenly we feel we should give a shilling to a poor man, we get no credit from God for giving it; there is no virtue in it whatever. As a rule, that sort of giving is a relief to our feelings; it is not an indication of a generous character but rather an indication of a lack of generosity.

149

God never estimates what we give from impulse. We are given credit for what we determine in our hearts to give—for the giving that is governed by a fixed determination. The Spirit of God revolutionizes our philanthropic instincts. Much of our philanthropy is simply the impulse to save ourselves an uncomfortable feeling. The Spirit of God alters all that. Our attitude toward giving is that we give for Jesus Christ's sake, and from no other motive. God holds us responsible for the way we use this power of voluntary choice. BP 108

❧ Our giving is to be proportionate to all we have received of the infinite giving of God. "Freely ye have received, freely give" (Matt. 10:8). Not how much we give, but what we do not give is the test of our Christianity. When we speak of giving, we nearly always think only of money. Money is the life-blood of most of us. We have a remarkable trick—when we give money, we don't give sympathy; and when we give sympathy, we don't give money. CHI 77

❧ Watch your motive for giving presents; it is a good way of discerning what a mean sneak you are capable of being. The giving of presents is one of the touchstones of character. If your relationship with God is not right in your present-giving, you will find there is an abomination of self-interest in it somewhere; even though you do it out of a warm-hearted impulse, there is a serpent-insinuation in it. It creeps into all our charity unless the life is right with God. OPG 59

❧ Don't be careful whether men receive what you give in the right way or the wrong way; see to it that you don't withhold your hand. As long as you have something to give, give; let the consequences be what they may. SHH 144

❧ Have no other motive in giving than to please God. In modern philanthropy, we are "egged on" with other motives: It will do them good; they need the help; they deserve it. Jesus Christ never brings out that aspect in His teaching; He allows no other motive in giving than to please God. SSM 57

a. Some manuscripts *in our love for you*
b. Exodus 16:18
c. Psalm 112:9

33

2 CORINTHIANS 10

PAUL'S DEFENSE OF HIS MINISTRY

B y the meekness and gentleness of Christ, I appeal to you—I, Paul, who am "timid" when face to face with you, but "bold" when away! I beg you that when I come I may not have to be as bold as I expect to be toward some people who think that we live by the standards of this world. For though we live in the world, we do not wage war as the world does. The weapons we fight with are not the weapons of the world. On the contrary, they have divine power to demolish strongholds. We demolish arguments and every pretension that sets itself up against the knowledge of God, and we take captive every thought to make it obedient to Christ. And we will be ready to punish every act of disobedience, once your obedience is complete.

You are looking only on the surface of things.[a] If anyone is confident that he belongs to Christ, he should consider again that we belong to Christ just as much as he. For even if I boast somewhat freely about the authority the Lord gave us for building you up rather than pulling you down, I will not be ashamed of it. I do not want to seem to be trying to frighten you with my letters. For some say, "His letters are weighty and forceful, but in person he is unimpressive and his speaking amounts to nothing." Such people should realize that what we are in our letters when we are absent, we will be in our actions when we are present.

We do not dare to classify or compare ourselves with some who commend themselves. When they measure themselves by themselves and compare themselves with themselves, they are not wise. We, however, will not boast beyond proper limits, but will confine our boasting to the field God has assigned to us, a field that reaches even to you. We are not going too far in our

151

boasting, as would be the case if we had not come to you, for we did get as far as you with the gospel of Christ. Neither do we go beyond our limits by boasting of work done by others.[b] Our hope is that, as your faith continues to grow, our area of activity among you will greatly expand, so that we can preach the gospel in the regions beyond you. For we do not want to boast about work already done in another man's territory. But, "Let him who boasts boast in the Lord."[c] For it is not the one who commends himself who is approved, but the one whom the Lord commends.

> *"We demolish arguments and every pretension*
> *that sets itself up against the knowledge of God,*
> *and we take captive every thought*
> *to make it obedient to Christ."*

FROM OSWALD CHAMBERS

❧ Determinedly demolish some things. Deliverance from sin is not the same as deliverance from human nature. There are things in human nature, such as prejudices, that the saint can destroy only through sheer neglect. But there are other things that have to be destroyed through violence, that is, through God's divine strength imparted by His Spirit. There are some things over which we are not to fight, but only to "stand still, and see the salvation of the Lord" (Ex. 14:13). But every theory or thought that raises itself up as a fortified barrier "against the knowledge of God" is to be determinedly demolished by drawing on God's power, not through human effort or by compromise (see 2 Cor. 10:4).
MUH 9/8

❧ To bring every thought into captivity is the last thing we do, and it is not done easily. In the beginning we have to do violence to our old ways of thinking just as at sanctification we had to do violence to our old ways of living. Intellect in a saint is the last thing to become identified with Jesus Christ. BSG 67

❧ It is because we have failed to realize that God requires intellectual vigor on the part of a saint that the devil gets his hold on the stagnant mental life of so many. To be transformed by the renewing of our mind means the courageous lifting of all our problems, individual, family, social, and civic, into the spiritual domain, and habitually working out a life of practical holiness there. It is not an easy task, but a gloriously difficult one, requiring the mightiest effort of our human nature, a task which lifts us into thinking God's thoughts after Him. CHI 83

ᔆ Obedience is the basis of Christian thinking. Never be surprised if there are whole areas of thinking that are not clear; they never will be until you obey. DI 80

ᔆ People won't go through the labor of thinking; consequently, snares get hold of them, and remember, thinking is a tremendous labor. We have to labor to "bring every thought into captivity to the obedience of Christ." GW 104

ᔆ The old idea that we cannot help evil thoughts has become so ingrained in our minds that most of us accept it as a fact. But if it is true, then Paul is talking nonsense when he tells us to choose our thinking, to think only on those things that are true, and honorable, and just, and pure. MFL 35

ᔆ God will not make me think like Jesus; I have to do it myself. I have to bring every thought into captivity to the obedience of Christ. "Abide in Me"—in intellectual matters, in money matters, in every one of the matters that make human life what it is. It is not a handbox life. MUH 166

ᔆ We do not think on the basis of Christianity at all. We are taught to think like pagans for six days a week and to reverse the order for one day; consequently, in critical moments we think as pagans and our religion is left in the limbo of the inarticulate. Our thinking is based not on Hebrew wisdom and confidence in God, but on the wisdom of the Greeks which is removed from practical life, and on that basis we persuade ourselves that if a man knows a thing is wrong he will not do it. That is not true. The plague with me, apart from the grace of God, is that I know what is right, but I'm hanged if I'll do it! What I want to know is, can anyone tell me of a power that will alter my "want to"? SHH 106

---

a. Or *Look at the obvious facts*
b. Or *"We, however, will not boast about things that cannot be measured, but we will boast according to the standard of measurement that the God of measure has assigned us—a measurement that relates even to you. . . . Neither do we boast about things that cannot be measured in regard to the work done by others.*
c. Jer. 9:24

34

PAUL AND THE FALSE APOSTLES

I hope you will put up with a little of my foolishness; but you are already doing that. I am jealous for you with a godly jealousy. I promised you to one husband, to Christ, so that I might present you as a pure virgin to him. But I am afraid that just as Eve was deceived by the serpent's cunning, your minds may somehow be led astray from your sincere and pure devotion to Christ. For if someone comes to you and preaches a Jesus other than the Jesus we preached, or if you receive a different spirit from the one you received, or a different gospel from the one you accepted, you put up with it easily enough. But I do not think I am in the least inferior to those "super-apostles." I may not be a trained speaker, but I do have knowledge. We have made this perfectly clear to you in every way.

Was it a sin for me to lower myself in order to elevate you by preaching the gospel of God to you free of charge? I robbed other churches by receiving support from them so as to serve you. And when I was with you and needed something, I was not a burden to anyone, for the brothers who came from Macedonia supplied what I needed. I have kept myself from being a burden to you in any way, and will continue to do so. As surely as the truth of Christ is in me, nobody in the regions of Achaia will stop this boasting of mine. Why? Because I do not love you? God knows I do! And I will keep on doing what I am doing in order to cut the ground from under those who want an opportunity to be considered equal with us in the things they boast about.

For such men are false apostles, deceitful workmen, masquerading as apostles of Christ. And no wonder, for Satan himself masquerades as an angel of light. It is not surprising, then, if his servants masquerade as servants of righteousness. Their end will be what their actions deserve.

PAUL BOASTS ABOUT HIS SUFFERINGS

I repeat: Let no one take me for a fool. But if you do, then receive me just as you would a fool, so that I may do a little boasting. In this self-confident boasting I am not talking as the Lord would, but as a fool. Since many are boasting in the way the world does, I too will boast. You gladly put up with fools since you are so wise! In fact, you even put up with anyone who enslaves you or exploits you or takes advantage of you or pushes himself forward or slaps you in the face. To my shame I admit that we were too weak for that!

What anyone else dares to boast about—I am speaking as a fool—I also dare to boast about. Are they Hebrews? So am I. Are they Israelites? So am I. Are they Abraham's descendants? So am I. Are they servants of Christ? (I am out of my mind to talk like this.) I am more. I have worked much harder, been in prison more frequently, been flogged more severely, and been exposed to death again and again. Five times I received from the Jews the forty lashes minus one. Three times I was beaten with rods, once I was stoned, three times I was shipwrecked, I spent a night and a day in the open sea, I have been constantly on the move. I have been in danger from rivers, in danger from bandits, in danger from my own countrymen, in danger from Gentiles; in danger in the city, in danger in the country, in danger at sea; and in danger from false brothers. I have labored and toiled and have often gone without sleep; I have known hunger and thirst and have often gone without food; I have been cold and naked. Besides everything else, I face daily the pressure of my concern for all the churches. Who is weak, and I do not feel weak? Who is led into sin, and I do not inwardly burn?

If I must boast, I will boast of the things that show my weakness. The God and Father of the Lord Jesus, who is to be praised forever, knows that I am not lying. In Damascus the governor under King Aretas had the city of the Damascenes guarded in order to arrest me. But I was lowered in a basket from a window in the wall and slipped through his hands.

*"Satan . . . masquerades as an angel of light.
It is not surprising, then, if his servants masquerade
as servants of righteousness."*

FROM OSWALD CHAMBERS

✞ Satan counterfeits the Holy Spirit. BFB 8

✞ The pretensions of Satan are clear. He is the god of this world, and he will not allow relationship to the true God. Satan's attitude is that of a pretender to the throne; he claims it as his right. Wherever and whenever the rule of God is recognized by man, Satan proceeds to instill the tendency of mutiny and rebellion and lawlessness. BP 20

✞ Men are responsible for doing wrong things, and they do wrong things because of the wrong disposition in them. The moral cunning of our nature makes us blame Satan when we know perfectly well we should blame ourselves; the true blame for sins lies in the wrong disposition in us. In all probability Satan is as much upset as the Holy Ghost is when men fall into external sin, but for a different reason. When men go into external sin and upset their lives, Satan knows perfectly well that they will want another ruler, a Savior and Deliverer; as long as Satan can keep men in peace and unity and harmony apart from God, he will do so. BP 24

✞ Satan . . . is as subtle as God is good, and he tries to counterfeit everything God does, and if he cannot counterfeit it, he will limit it. Do not be ignorant of his devices! BP 101

✞ "Resist the devil" (James 4:7), not attack him. BSG 29

✞ Health and happiness is what is wanted today and Jesus Christ is simply exploited. We who name the name of Christ, are we beginning to discern what Satan is after? He is trying to fatigue out of us what God has put in, viz., the possibility of being of value to God. Our only safety is to watch our Lord and Savior. BSG 31

✞ Satan is not removed now from the presence of the saints, but the saint is still kept in the world where the evil one rules; consequently, the saint is continually being badgered by the evil one. Jesus

157

prayed not that we should be taken out of the world, but that we should be kept from the evil one (John 17:15). IWP 28

❧ God does not deal with Satan directly; man must deal with Satan because man is responsible for his introduction. That is why God became incarnate. Put it in any other way—God could banish Satan in two seconds; but it is man who, through the redemption, is to overcome Satan, and much more than overcome him, he is to do that which will exhibit the perfect fulfillment of this prophecy. Jesus Christ, the last Adam, took on Him our human form, and it is through His seed in that human form that Satan is to be overcome. OPG 9

35

2 CORINTHIANS 12

PAUL'S VISION AND HIS THORN

I must go on boasting. Although there is nothing to be gained, I will go on to visions and revelations from the Lord. I know a man in Christ who fourteen years ago was caught up to the third heaven. Whether it was in the body or out of the body I do not know—God knows. And I know that this man—whether in the body or apart from the body I do not know, but God knows—was caught up to paradise. He heard inexpressible things, things that man is not permitted to tell. I will boast about a man like that, but I will not boast about myself, except about my weaknesses. Even if I should choose to boast, I would not be a fool, because I would be speaking the truth. But I refrain, so no one will think more of me than is warranted by what I do or say.

To keep me from becoming conceited because of these surpassingly great revelations, there was given me a thorn in my flesh, a messenger of Satan, to torment me. Three times I pleaded with the Lord to take it away from me. But he said to me, "My grace is sufficient for you, for my power is made perfect in weakness." Therefore I will boast all the more gladly about my weaknesses, so that Christ's power may rest on me. That is why, for Christ's sake, I delight in weaknesses, in insults, in hardships, in persecutions, in difficulties. For when I am weak, then I am strong.

PAUL'S CONCERN FOR THE CORINTHIANS

I have made a fool of myself, but you drove me to it. I ought to have been commended by you, for I am not in the least inferior to the "super-apostles," even though I am nothing. The things that mark an apostle—signs, wonders and miracles—were done among you with great perseverance. How were you inferior to the other churches, except that I was never a burden to you? Forgive me this wrong!

Now I am ready to visit you for the third time, and I will not be a burden to you, because what I want is not your possessions but you. After all, children should not have to save up for their parents, but parents for their children. So I will very gladly spend for you everything I have and expend myself as well. If I love you more, will you love me less? Be that as it may, I have not been a burden to you. Yet, crafty fellow that I am, I caught you by trickery! Did I exploit you through any of the men I sent you? I urged Titus to go to you and I sent our brother with him. Titus did not exploit you, did he? Did we not act in the same spirit and follow the same course?

Have you been thinking all along that we have been defending ourselves to you? We have been speaking in the sight of God as those in Christ; and everything we do, dear friends, is for your strengthening. For I am afraid that when I come I may not find you as I want you to be, and you may not find me as you want me to be. I fear that there may be quarreling, jealousy, outbursts of anger, factions, slander, gossip, arrogance and disorder. I am afraid that when I come again my God will humble me before you, and I will be grieved over many who have sinned earlier and have not repented of the impurity, sexual sin and debauchery in which they have indulged.

"[God] said to me, 'My grace is sufficient for you,
for my power is made perfect in weakness.' "

FROM OSWALD CHAMBERS

≈ The realization that my Lord has enabled me to be a worker keeps me strong enough never to be weak. Conscious obtrusive weakness is natural unthankful strength; it means I refuse to be made strong by Him. When I say I am too weak, it means I am too strong; and whenever I say "I can't," it means "I won't." When Jesus Christ enables me, I am omnipotently strong all the time. Paul talks in paradoxes, "For when I am weak, then am I strong." AUG 11

❧ The "strong man" idea is the one that appeals to men—the strong man physically, morally, strong in every way; the kingdoms of men are to be founded on strong men and the weakest are to go to the wall. History proves, however, that it is the strongest that go to the wall, not the weakest. GW 100

❧ No one can remain under and endure what God puts a servant of His through unless he has the power of God. We read that our Lord was "crucified through weakness" (2 Cor. 13:4), yet it took omnipotent might to make Him weak like that. LG 95

❧ "He was crucified through weakness" (2 Cor. 13:4). Jesus Christ represents God limiting His own power for one purpose: He died for the weak, for the ungodly, for sinners, and for no one else. "I came not to call the righteous, but sinners to repentance (Matt. 9:13). No chain is stronger than its weakest link. MFL 106

❧ Until we are rightly related to God, we deify pluck and heroism. We will do anything that is heroic, anything that puts the inspiration of strain on us; but when it comes to submitting to being a weak thing for God, it takes Almighty God to do it. "We are weak in Him" (2 Cor. 13:4). PH 56

❧ "Be strong in the Lord" (Eph. 6:10)—we much prefer to be strong *for* the Lord. The only way to be strong *in* the Lord is to be "weak in Him." RTR 62

❧ No power on earth or in hell can conquer the Spirit of God in human spirit; it is an inner unconquerableness. If you have the whine in you, kick it out ruthlessly. It is a positive crime to be weak in God's strength. RTR 65

❧ The source of physical strength in spiritual life is different from what it is in natural life. In natural life we draw our strength direct from without, in spiritual life we draw our physical strength, consciously or unconsciously, from communion with God. SHL 108

36

2 CORINTHIANS 13

FINAL WARNINGS

T his will be my third visit to you. "Every matter must be established by the testimony of two or three witnesses."[a] I already gave you a warning when I was with you the second time. I now repeat it while absent: On my return I will not spare those who sinned earlier or any of the others, since you are demanding proof that Christ is speaking through me. He is not weak in dealing with you, but is powerful among you. For to be sure, he was crucified in weakness, yet he lives by God's power. Likewise, we are weak in him, yet by God's power we will live with him to serve you.

Examine yourselves to see whether you are in the faith; test yourselves. Do you not realize that Christ Jesus is in you—unless, of course, you fail the test? And I trust that you will discover that we have not failed the test. Now we pray to God that you will not do anything wrong. Not that people will see that we have stood the test but that you will do what is right even though we may seem to have failed. For we cannot do anything against the truth, but only for the truth. We are glad whenever we are weak but you are strong; and our prayer is for your perfection. This is why I write these things when I am absent, that when I come I may not have to be harsh in my use of authority—the authority the Lord gave me for building you up, not for tearing you down.

FINAL GREETINGS

Finally, brothers, good-by. Aim for perfection, listen to my appeal, be of one mind, live in peace. And the God of love and peace will be with you.

Greet one another with a holy kiss. All the saints send their greetings.
May the grace of the Lord Jesus Christ, and the love of God, and the fellowship of the Holy Spirit be with you all.

> *"Aim for perfection . . . be of one mind,
> live in peace."*

FROM OSWALD CHAMBERS

> ❧ Perfect life does not mean perfection. Perfection means perfect attainment in everything. Perfect life means the perfect adjustment of all our relationships to God, nothing out of joint, everything rightly related; then we can begin to live the perfect life, that is, we can begin to attain. BP 141

> ❧ Size yourself up with a good sense of humor—"me, perfect!" That is what Jesus Christ has undertaken to do. DI 72

> ❧ The Bible reveals that "that which is perfect" is a Being. God is the only perfect being; no human being is perfect apart from God. IWP 9

> ❧ We are to be perfect as our Father in heaven is perfect, not by struggle and effort, but by the impartation of that which is perfect. IWP 9

> ❧ Do we really want to be perfect? Beware of mental quibbling over the word perfect. Perfection does not mean the full maturity and consummation of a man's powers, but perfect fitness for doing the will of God. IWP 17

> ❧ Supposing Jesus Christ can perfectly adjust me to God, put me so perfectly right that I shall be on the footing where I can do the will of God, do I really want Him to do it? Do I want God at all costs to make me perfect? A great deal depends on what is the real deep desire of our hearts. IWP 117

> ❧ God always ignores the present perfection for the ultimate perfection. He is not concerned about making you blessed and happy just now; He is working out His ultimate perfection all the time—"that they may be one even as We are" (John 17:11) MUH 118

---

a. Deut. 19:15

37

GALATIANS 1

NO OTHER GOSPEL

 aul, an apostle — sent not from men nor by man, but by Jesus Christ and God the Father, who raised him from the dead — and all the brothers with me,

To the churches in Galatia:

Grace and peace to you from God our Father and the Lord Jesus Christ, who gave himself for our sins to rescue us from the present evil age, according to the will of our God and Father, to whom be glory for ever and ever. Amen.

I am astonished that you are so quickly deserting the one who called you by the grace of Christ and are turning to a different gospel — which is really no gospel at all. Evidently some people are throwing you into confusion and are trying to pervert the gospel of Christ. But even if we or an angel from heaven should preach a gospel other than the one we preached to you, let him be eternally condemned! As we have already said, so now I say again: If anybody is preaching to you a gospel other than what you accepted, let him be eternally condemned!

Am I now trying to win the approval of men, or of God? Or am I trying to please men? If I were still trying to please men, I would not be a servant of Christ.

PAUL CALLED BY GOD

I want you to know, brothers, that the gospel I preached is not something that man made up. I did not receive it from any man, nor was I taught it; rather, I received it by revelation from Jesus Christ.

For you have heard of my previous way of life in Judaism, how intensely I persecuted the church of God and tried to destroy it. I was advancing in Judaism beyond many Jews of my own age and was extremely zealous for the traditions of my fathers. But when God, who set me apart from birth[a] and called me by his grace, was pleased to reveal his Son in me so that I might preach him among the Gentiles, I did not consult any man, nor did I go up to Jerusalem to see those who were apostles before I was, but I went immediately into Arabia and later returned to Damascus.

Then after three years, I went up to Jerusalem to get acquainted with Peter[b] and stayed with him fifteen days. I saw none of the other apostles—only James, the Lord's brother. I assure you before God that what I am writing you is no lie. Later I went to Syria and Cilicia. I was personally unknown to the churches of Judea that are in Christ. They only heard the report: "The man who formerly persecuted us is now preaching the faith he once tried to destroy." And they praised God because of me.

"[Christ] gave himself for our sins
to rescue us from the present evil age."

From Oswald Chambers

Ș "Seek ye first the kingdom of God" (Matt. 6:33)—and apply it to modern life and you will find its statements are either those of a madman or of God incarnate. AUG 63

Ș If we try to live the life Jesus Christ lived, modern civilization will fling us out like waste material; we are no good, we do not add anything to the hard cash of the times we live in, and the sooner we are flung out the better. HG 28

Ș Jesus knew He was here for His Father's purpose, and He never allowed the cares of civilization to bother Him. He did nothing to add to the wealth of the civilization in which He lived. He earned nothing; modern civilization would not have tolerated Him for two minutes. HG 28

Ș God engineers us out of our sequestered places and brings us into elemental conditions, and we get a taste of what the world is like

166

because of the disobedience of man. We realize then that our hold on God has been a civilized hold, we have not really believed in Him at all. HGM 92

  ❧ There is a rivalry between men, and we have made it a good thing; we have made ambition and competition the very essence of civilized life. No wonder there is no room for Jesus Christ, and no room for the Bible. We are all so scientifically orthodox nowadays, so materialistic and certain that rationalism is the basis of things, that we make the Bible out to be the most revolutionary, unorthodox, and heretical of books. SHH 45

  ❧ The birds of civilization come and lodge in the branches of the spiritual tree, and men say, "Now this is what is to be!" and they have not seen God's purpose at all. If we do not see God's purpose, we shall continually be misled by externals. SSY 80

  ❧ What is needed today is Christian sociology, not sociology Christianized. One way in which God will reintroduce the emphasis on the Gospel is by bringing into His service men and women who not only understand the problems, but who have learned that the secret of the whole thing is supernatural regeneration, that is, personal holiness wrought by the grace of God. SSY 154

---

a. Or *from my mother's womb*
b. Greek *Cephas*

167

38

GALATIANS 2

PAUL ACCEPTED BY THE APOSTLES

Fourteen years later I went up again to Jerusalem, this time with Barnabas. I took Titus along also. I went in response to a revelation and set before them the gospel that I preach among the Gentiles. But I did this privately to those who seemed to be leaders, for fear that I was running or had run my race in vain. Yet not even Titus, who was with me, was compelled to be circumcised, even though he was a Greek. [This matter arose] because some false brothers had infiltrated our ranks to spy on the freedom we have in Christ Jesus and to make us slaves. We did not give in to them for a moment, so that the truth of the gospel might remain with you.

As for those who seemed to be important—whatever they were makes no difference to me; God does not judge by external appearance—those men added nothing to my message. On the contrary, they saw that I had been entrusted with the task of preaching the gospel to the Gentiles,[a] just as Peter had been to the Jews.[b] For God, who was at work in the ministry of Peter as an apostle to the Jews, was also at work in my ministry as an apostle to the Gentiles. James, Peter[c] and John, those reputed to be pillars, gave me and Barnabas the right hand of fellowship when they recognized the grace given to me. They agreed that we should go to the Gentiles, and they to the Jews. All they asked was that we should continue to remember the poor, the very thing I was eager to do.

PAUL OPPOSES PETER

When Peter came to Antioch, I opposed him to his face, because he was clearly in the wrong. Before certain men came from

James, he used to eat with the Gentiles. But when they arrived, he began to draw back and separate himself from the Gentiles because he was afraid of those who belonged to the circumcision group. The other Jews joined him in his hypocrisy, so that by their hypocrisy even Barnabas was led astray.

When I saw that they were not acting in line with the truth of the gospel, I said to Peter in front of them all, "You are a Jew, yet you live like a Gentile and not like a Jew. How is it, then, that you force Gentiles to follow Jewish customs?

"We who are Jews by birth and not 'Gentile sinners' know that a man is not justified by observing the law, but by faith in Jesus Christ. So we, too, have put our faith in Christ Jesus that we may be justified by faith in Christ and not by observing the law, because by observing the law no one will be justified.

"If, while we seek to be justified in Christ, it becomes evident that we ourselves are sinners, does that mean that Christ promotes sin? Absolutely not! If I rebuild what I destroyed, I prove that I am a lawbreaker. For through the law I died to the law so that I might live for God. I have been crucified with Christ and I no longer live, but Christ lives in me. The life I live in the body, I live by faith in the Son of God, who loved me and gave himself for me. I do not set aside the grace of God, for if righteousness could be gained through the law, Christ died for nothing!"[d]

> *"I have been crucified with Christ and I no longer live,*
> *but Christ lives in me . . . by faith in the Son of God."*

FROM OSWALD CHAMBERS

≈ The teaching of self-realization is the great opponent of the doctrine of sanctification — "I have to realize myself as a separate individual, must educate and develop myself so that I fulfill the purpose of my being." Self-realization and self-consciousness are ways in which the principle of sin works out, and in Galatians 2:20 Paul is referring to the time and the place where he got rid of his "soul" in this respect. There is nothing in the nature of self-realization or of self-consciousness in our Lord.

People will say glibly, "Oh yes, I have been crucified with Christ," while their whole life is stamped with self-realization. Once identification with the death of Jesus has really taken place, self-realization does not appear again. To be "crucified with Christ" means that in obedience to the Spirit granted to me at regeneration, I eagerly and willingly go to the Cross and crucify self-realization forever. The crucifixion of the flesh is the willing action of an obedient regenerate man or woman. "And they that are Christ's have crucified the flesh with the affections and lusts" (Gal. 5:24). Obey the Spirit of God and the Word of God, and it will be as clear as a sunbeam what you have to do; it is an attitude of will toward God, an absolute abandon, a glad sacrifice of the soul in unconditional surrender. Then comes the marvelous revelation—"I have been crucified with Christ"—not, "I am being crucified," or, "I hope to be crucified by and by"; not, "I am getting nearer to the place where I shall be crucified with Christ," but, "I have been crucified with Christ—I realize it and know it." BE 89

꣓ To be "crucified with Christ" means that in obedience to the Spirit granted to me at regeneration, I eagerly and willingly go to the Cross and crucify self-realization forever. BE 88

꣓ Crucifixion means death. BP 261

꣓ "I am crucified with Christ"—it is a real definite personal experience. CV VOL. 1, 132.

꣓ If once a man has heard the appeal of Jesus from the cross, he begins to find there is something there that answers the cry of the human heart and the problem of the whole world. What we have to do as God's servants is to lift up Christ crucified. IWP 61

꣓ When we tell God that we want at all costs to be identified with the death of Jesus Christ, at that instant a supernatural identification with His death takes place, and we know with a knowledge that our "old man" is crucified with Christ, and we prove it forever after by the amazing ease with which the supernatural life of God in us enables us to do His will. That is why the bedrock of Christianity is personal, passionate devotion to the Lord Jesus. PH 164

---

a. Greek *uncircumcised*
b. Greek *circumcised;* also in verses 8 and 9
c. Greek *Cephas;* also in verses 11 and 14
d. Some interpreters end the quotation after verse 14.

39

GALATIANS 3

FAITH OR OBSERVANCE OF THE LAW

You foolish Galatians! Who has bewitched you? Before your very eyes Jesus Christ was clearly portrayed as crucified. I would like to learn just one thing from you: Did you receive the Spirit by observing the law, or by believing what you heard? Are you so foolish? After beginning with the Spirit, are you now trying to attain your goal by human effort? Have you suffered so much for nothing — if it really was for nothing? Does God give you his Spirit and work miracles among you because you observe the law, or because you believe what you heard?

Consider Abraham: "He believed God, and it was credited to him as righteousness."[a] Understand, then, that those who believe are children of Abraham. The Scripture foresaw that God would justify the Gentiles by faith, and announced the gospel in advance to Abraham: "All nations will be blessed through you." So those who have faith are blessed along with Abraham, the man of faith.[b]

All who rely on observing the law are under a curse, for it is written: "Cursed is everyone who does not continue to do everything written in the Book of the Law."[c] Clearly no one is justified before God by the law, because, "The righteous will live by faith."[d] The law is not based on faith; on the contrary, "The man who does these things will live by them."[e] Christ redeemed us from the curse of the law by becoming a curse for us, for it is written: "Cursed is everyone who is hung on a tree."[f] He redeemed us in order that the blessing given to Abraham might come to the Gentiles through Christ Jesus, so that by faith we might receive the promise of the Spirit.

The Law and the Promise

Brothers, let me take an example from everyday life. Just as no one can set aside or add to a human covenant that has been duly established, so it is in this case. The promises were spoken to Abraham and to his seed. The Scripture does not say "and to seeds," meaning many people, but "and to your seed,"[g] meaning one person, who is Christ. What I mean is this: The law, introduced 430 years later, does not set aside the covenant previously established by God and thus do away with the promise. For if the inheritance depends on the law, then it no longer depends on a promise; but God in his grace gave it to Abraham through a promise.

What, then, was the purpose of the law? It was added because of transgressions until the Seed to whom the promise referred had come. The law was put into effect through angels by a mediator. A mediator, however, does not represent just one party; but God is one.

Is the law, therefore, opposed to the promises of God? Absolutely not! For if a law had been given that could impart life, then righteousness would certainly have come by the law. But the Scripture declares that the whole world is a prisoner of sin, so that what was promised, being given through faith in Jesus Christ, might be given to those who believe.

Before this faith came, we were held prisoners by the law, locked up until faith should be revealed. So the law was put in charge to lead us to Christ[h] that we might be justified by faith. Now that faith has come, we are no longer under the supervision of the law.

Sons of God

You are all sons of God through faith in Christ Jesus, for all of you who were baptized into Christ have clothed yourselves with Christ. There is neither Jew nor Greek, slave nor free, male nor female, for you are all one in Christ Jesus. If you belong to Christ, then you are Abraham's seed, and heirs according to the promise.

"Clearly no one is justified before God by the law,
because 'The righteous will live by faith.' "

172

FROM OSWALD CHAMBERS

꙳ It is absurd to tell a man he must believe this and that; in the mean-time he can't! Skepticism is produced by telling men what to believe. We are in danger of putting the cart before the horse and saying a man must believe certain things before he can be a Christian; his beliefs are the effect of his being a Christian, not the cause of it. Our Lord's word *believe* does not refer to an intellectual act, but to a moral act. With Him "to believe" means "to commit." AUG 78

꙳ The one thing that tells is the great fundamental rock: "Believe also in Me" (John 14:1). Many know a good deal about salvation, but not much about this intense patience of "hanging in" in perfect certainty to the fact that what Jesus Christ says is true. AUG 117

꙳ The reason people disbelieve God is not because they do not un-derstand with their heads—we understand very few things with our heads—but because they have turned their hearts in another direc-tion. BP 144

꙳ Faith means that I commit myself to Jesus, project myself absolute-ly on to Him, sink or swim—and you do both; you sink out of yourself and swim into Him. CHI 60

꙳ Believe what you do believe and stick to it, but don't profess to believe more than you intend to stick to. If you say you believe God is love, stick to it, though all Providence becomes a pandemonium shouting that God is cruel to allow what He does. DI 12

꙳ Beware of worshiping Jesus as the Son of God and professing your faith in Him as the Savior of the world while you blaspheme Him by the complete evidence in your daily life that He is powerless to do anything in and through you. DI 5

꙳ We all have faith in good principles, in good management, in good common sense, but who among us has faith in Jesus Christ? Physi-cal courage is grand, moral courage is grander, but the man who trusts Jesus Christ in the face of the terrific problems of life is worth a whole crowd of heroes. HG 61

꙳ Nowadays the tendency is to switch away from "the righteousness which is of God by faith" (Phil. 3:9), and to put the emphasis on doing things. You cannot do anything at all that does not become, in the rugged language of Isaiah, "as filthy rags," if it is divorced from living faith in Jesus Christ. If we have the tiniest hankering after believing we can be justified by what we have done, we are on the wrong side of the Cross. HG 108

ॐ Believe steadfastly on Him, and all you come up against will develop your faith. MUH 242

ॐ Faith is unutterable trust in God, trust which never dreams that He will not stand by us. MUH 242

ॐ There is only one way to live the life of faith and that is to *live* it. NKW 70

ॐ It is never our merit God looks at but our faith. If there is only one strand of faith among all the corruption within us, God will take hold of that one strand. NKW 80

---

a. Gen. 15:6
b. Gen. 12:3; 18:18; 22:18
c. Deut. 27:26
d. Hab. 2:4
e. Lev. 18:5
f. Deut. 21:23
g. Gen. 12:7; 13:15; 24:7
h. Or *charge until Christ came*

40

GALATIANS 4

PAUL'S CONCERN FOR THE GALATIANS

What I am saying is that as long as the heir is a child, he is no different from a slave, although he owns the whole estate. He is subject to guardians and trustees until the time set by his father. So also, when we were children, we were in slavery under the basic principles of the world. But when the time had fully come, God sent his Son, born of a woman, born under law, to redeem those under law, that we might receive the full rights of sons. Because you are sons, God sent the Spirit of his Son into our hearts, the Spirit who calls out, "Abba,ª Father." So you are no longer a slave, but a son; and since you are a son, God has made you also an heir.

Formerly, when you did not know God, you were slaves to those who by nature are not gods. But now that you know God — or rather are known by God — how is it that you are turning back to those weak and miserable principles? Do you wish to be enslaved by them all over again? You are observing special days and months and seasons and years! I fear for you, that somehow I have wasted my efforts on you.

I plead with you, brothers, become like me, for I became like you. You have done me no wrong. As you know, it was because of an illness that I first preached the gospel to you. Even though my illness was a trial to you, you did not treat me with contempt or scorn. Instead, you welcomed me as if I were an angel of God, as if I were Christ Jesus himself. What has happened to all your joy? I can testify that, if you could have done so, you would have torn out your eyes and given them to me. Have I now become your enemy by telling you the truth?

Those people are zealous to win you over, but for no good.

What they want is to alienate you [from us], so that you may be zealous for them. It is fine to be zealous, provided the purpose is good, and to be so always and not just when I am with you. My dear children, for whom I am again in the pains of childbirth until Christ is formed in you, how I wish I could be with you now and change my tone, because I am perplexed about you!

HAGAR AND SARAH

Tell me, you who want to be under the law, are you not aware of what the law says? For it is written that Abraham had two sons, one by the slave woman and the other by the free woman. His son by the slave woman was born in the ordinary way; but his son by the free woman was born as the result of a promise.

These things may be taken figuratively, for the women represent two covenants. One covenant is from Mount Sinai and bears children who are to be slaves: This is Hagar. Now Hagar stands for Mount Sinai in Arabia and corresponds to the present city of Jerusalem, because she is in slavery with her children. But the Jerusalem that is above is free, and she is our mother. For it is written:

"Be glad, O barren woman,
　who bears no children;
break forth and cry aloud,
　you who have no labor pains;
because more are the children of the desolate woman
　than of her who has a husband."[b]

Now you, brothers, like Isaac, are children of promise. At that time the son born in the ordinary way persecuted the son born by the power of the Spirit. It is the same now. But what does the Scripture say? "Get rid of the slave woman and her son, for the slave woman's son will never share in the inheritance with the free woman's son."[c] Therefore, brothers, we are not children of the slave woman, but of the free woman.

"You are no longer a slave, but a son; and since you are a son,
God has made you also an heir."

FROM OSWALD CHAMBERS

➣ Adam is called the son of God. There is only one other "Son of God" in the Bible, and He is Jesus Christ. Yet we are called "sons of God," but how? By being reinstated through the Atonement of Jesus Christ. This is an important point. We are not the sons of God by natural generation. Adam did not come into the world as we do; neither did Adam come into the world as Jesus Christ came. Adam was not "begotten"; Jesus Christ was. Adam was "created." God created Adam; He did not beget him. We are all generated; we are not created beings. Adam was the "son of God," and God created him as well as everything else that was created. BP 6

➣ Why does God take such a long time? Because of what He is after, viz., "bringing many sons unto glory" (Heb. 2:10). It takes time to make a son. We are not made sons of God by magic; we are saved in the great supernatural sense by the sovereign work of God's grace, but sonship is a different matter. I have to become a son of God by deliberate discernment and understanding and chastisement, not by spiritual necromancy, imagining I can ascend to heaven in leaps and bounds. The "shortcut" would make men mechanisms, not sons, with no discernment of God. If God did not shield His only begotten Son from any of the requirements of sonship (see Heb. 5:8), He will not shield us from all the requirements of being His sons and daughters by adoption. PH 100

➣ On the basis of the redemption God expects us to erect characters worthy of the sons of God. He does not expect us to carry on "evangelical capers," but to manifest the life of the Son of God in our mortal flesh. LG 122

➣ He has undertaken to take the vilest piece of stuff that humanity and the devil have put together, and to transform this into a son of God. SA 41

➣ Jesus Christ is bringing many sons to glory, and He will not shield us from any of the requirements of sonship. He will say at certain times to the world, the flesh, and the devil, "Do your worst; I know that 'greater is He that is in you than he that is in the world' " (1 John 4:4). God's grace does not turn out milksops, but men and women with a strong family likeness to Jesus Christ. Thank God He does give us difficult things to do! A man's heart would burst if

177

there were no way to show his gratitude. "I beseech you therefore, brethren," says Paul, "by the mercies of God, that ye present your bodies a *living sacrifice*" (Rom. 12:1). SSM 96

---

a. Aramaic for *Father*
b. Isaiah 54:1
c. Gen. 21:10

41

GALATIANS 5

FREEDOM IN CHRIST

t is for freedom that Christ has set us free. Stand firm, then, and do not let yourselves be burdened again by a yoke of slavery.

Mark my words! I, Paul, tell you that if you let yourselves be circumcised, Christ will be of no value to you at all. Again I declare to every man who lets himself be circumcised that he is obligated to obey the whole law. You who are trying to be justified by law have been alienated from Christ; you have fallen away from grace. But by faith we eagerly await through the Spirit the righteousness for which we hope. For in Christ Jesus neither circumcision nor uncircumcision has any value. The only thing that counts is faith expressing itself through love.

You were running a good race. Who cut in on you and kept you from obeying the truth? That kind of persuasion does not come from the one who calls you. "A little yeast works through the whole batch of dough." I am confident in the Lord that you will take no other view. The one who is throwing you into confusion will pay the penalty, whoever he may be. Brothers, if I am still preaching circumcision, why am I still being persecuted? In that case the offense of the cross has been abolished. As for those agitators, I wish they would go the whole way and emasculate themselves!

LIFE BY THE SPIRIT

You, my brothers, were called to be free. But do not use your freedom to indulge the sinful nature[a]; rather, serve one another in love. The entire law is summed up in a single command: "Love your neighbor as yourself."[b] If you keep on biting and devouring each other, watch out or you will be destroyed by each other. So I say, live by the Spirit, and you will not gratify the desires of the sinful nature. For the sinful nature desires what is contrary to the Spirit, and the Spirit what is contrary to the sinful nature. They are in conflict with each other, so that you do not do what you want. But if you are led by the Spirit, you are not under law.

The acts of the sinful nature are obvious: sexual immorality, impurity and debauchery; idolatry and witchcraft; hatred, discord, jealousy, fits of rage, selfish ambition, dissensions, factions and envy; drunkenness, orgies, and the like. I warn you, as I did before, that those who live like this will not inherit the kingdom of God.

But the fruit of the Spirit is love, joy, peace, patience, kindness, goodness, faithfulness, gentleness and self-control. Against such things there is no law. Those who belong to Christ Jesus have crucified the sinful nature with its passions and desires. Since we live by the Spirit, let us keep in step with the Spirit. Let us not become conceited, provoking and envying each other.

"Live by the Spirit, and you will not gratify
the desires of the sinful nature."

FROM OSWALD CHAMBERS

❧ The Holy Ghost is seeking to awaken men out of lethargy. He is pleading, yearning, blessing, pouring benedictions on men, convicting and drawing them nearer, for one purpose only, that they may receive Him so that He may make them holy men and women exhibiting the life of Jesus Christ. BE 99

❧ The Holy Spirit alone makes Jesus real; the Holy Spirit alone expounds His Cross, the Holy Spirit alone convicts of sin; the Holy Spirit alone does in us what Jesus *did* for us. BE 99

❧ Immediately the Holy Spirit comes in as life and as light, He will chase through every avenue of our minds. His light will penetrate every recess of our hearts; He will chase His light through every affection of our souls, and make us know what sin is. The Holy Spirit convicts of sin; man does not. BP 37

❧ Mind the Holy Spirit, mind His light, mind His convictions, mind His guidance, and slowly and surely the sensual personality will be turned into a spiritual personality. BP 50

❧ The thought is unspeakably full of glory that God the Holy Ghost can come into my heart and fill it so full that the life of God will manifest itself all through this body which used to manifest exactly the opposite. If I am willing and determined to keep in the light and obey the Spirit, then the characteristics of the indwelling Christ will manifest themselves. BP 146

❧ When the Holy Spirit comes in, unbelief is turned out and the energy of God is put into us; we are then enabled to will and to do of His good pleasure. When the Holy Spirit comes in, He sheds abroad the love of God in our hearts, so that we are able to show our fellows the same love that God has shown to us. When the Holy Spirit comes in, He makes us as "light," and our righteousness will exceed the righteousness of the most moral upright natural man because the supernatural has been made natural in us. BP 222

❧ It is extraordinary how things fall off from a man like autumn leaves once he comes to the place where there is no rule but that of the personal domination of the Holy Spirit. DI 20

❧ There is nothing so still and gentle as the checks of the Holy Spirit; if they are yielded to, emancipation is the result; but let them be trifled with, and there will come a hardening of the life away from God. Don't "quench the Spirit" (1 Thes. 5:19). DI 22

❧ The Holy Ghost destroys my personal private life and turns it into a thoroughfare for God. RTR 42

---

a. Or *the flesh;* also in verses 16-17, 19 and 24
b. Lev. 19:18

42

GALATIANS 6

DOING GOOD TO ALL

Brothers, if someone is caught in a sin, you who are spiritual should restore him gently. But watch yourself, or you also may be tempted. Carry each other's burdens, and in this way you will fulfill the law of Christ. If anyone thinks he is something when he is nothing, he deceives himself. Each one should test his own actions. Then he can take pride in himself, without comparing himself to somebody else, for each one should carry his own load.

Anyone who receives instruction in the word must share all good things with his instructor.

Do not be deceived: God cannot be mocked. A man reaps what he sows. The one who sows to please his sinful nature, from that nature[a] will reap destruction; the one who sows to please the Spirit, from the Spirit will reap eternal life. Let us not become weary in doing good, for at the proper time we will reap a harvest if we do not give up. Therefore, as we have opportunity, let us do good to all people, especially to those who belong to the family of believers.

NOT CIRCUMCISION BUT A NEW CREATION

See what large letters I use as I write to you with my own hand!

Those who want to make a good impression outwardly are trying to compel you to be circumcised. The only reason they do this is to avoid being persecuted for the cross of Christ. Not even those who are circumcised obey the law, yet they want you to be circumcised that they may boast about your flesh. May I never boast except in the cross of our Lord Jesus Christ, through which the world has been crucified to me, and I to the world. Neither circumcision nor uncircumcision means anything; what counts is a new creation. Peace and mercy to all who follow this rule, even to the Israel of God.

Finally, let no one cause me trouble, for I bear on my body the marks of Jesus.

The grace of our Lord Jesus Christ be with your spirit, brothers. Amen.

> *"The one who sows to please his sinful nature,*
> *from that nature will reap destruction;*
> *the one who sows to please the Spirit,*
> *from the Spirit will reap eternal life."*

From Oswald Chambers

> ✍ Carnality and its suspicions only ever arise from its own nature, and it can see in other people what it is most likely to see in itself if placed under similar conditions. Every judgment carnality brings against another is a revelation of carnality. "Set a thief to watch a thief." Moral lepers are the first to detect moral leprosy in others, and most often, it is not in the other person at all, but merely a revelation of carnality. Read how strong God's Word is on "busybodies" (see 1 Peter 4:15; 1 Tim. 5:13).
>
> "Study to shut up and mind your own business." This is a full and free translation of 1 Thessalonians 4:11 that should be engraved on carnality's tombstone.
>
> Carnality disguised is suspicious. It will not suffer long, it cannot be kind, it does envy, it is always rash and puffed up, will behave itself unseemly, always seeks its own, is easily provoked, always takes account of the evil, rejoices in iniquity when it is discovered, and cannot rejoice with the truth, cannot bear anything, will believe scarcely anything, and endures nothing. Carnality always fails.
>
> Carnality undisguised is hell. It is adulterous, fornicating, unclean, lascivious, idolatrous, spiritualistic, hateful, at variance, emulating, wrathful, a strife maker, seditious, a heretic, envious, murderous, a drunkard, a reveller, etc. (Gal. 5:19-20). Carnality shall have its part in the lake which burns with fire and brimstone (Rev. 21:8).
>
> Sanctification discerns whatsoever things are true, whatsoever things are just, whatsoever things are pure, whatsoever thing are lovely, whatsoever things are of good report. Sanctification discerns

183

any virtue and anything praiseworthy and delights in these. Sanctification and spiritual discernment are easily entreated, full of mercy and good fruits, and never seem what they are not (see James 3:17). GR, 1/31/07

---

a. Or *his flesh, from the flesh*

43

EPHESIANS 1

SPIRITUAL BLESSINGS IN CHRIST

aul, an apostle of Christ Jesus by the will of God,
To the saints in Ephesus,[a] the faithful[b] in Christ
Jesus:
Grace and peace to you from God our Father and
the Lord Jesus Christ.

Praise be to the God and Father of our Lord Jesus Christ, who
has blessed us in the heavenly realms with every spiritual blessing
in Christ. For he chose us in him before the creation of the world
to be holy and blameless in his sight. In love he[c] predestined us
to be adopted as his sons through Jesus Christ, in accordance
with his pleasure and will—to the praise of his glorious grace,
which he has freely given us in the One he loves. In him we have
redemption through his blood, the forgiveness of sins, in accordance with the riches of God's grace that he lavished on us with
all wisdom and understanding. And he[d] made known to us the
mystery of his will according to his good pleasure, which he
purposed in Christ, to be put into effect when the times will have
reached their fulfillment—to bring all things in heaven and on
earth together under one head, even Christ.

In him we were also chosen,[e] having been predestined according to the plan of him who works out everything in confor-
mity with the purpose of his will, in order that we, who were the
first to hope in Christ, might be for the praise of his glory.
And you also were included in Christ when you heard the word
of truth, the gospel of your salvation. Having believed, you
were marked in him with a seal, the promised Holy Spirit, who
is a deposit guaranteeing our inheritance until the redemption of those who are God's possession—to the praise of his
glory.

Thanksgiving and Prayer

For this reason, ever since I heard about your faith in the Lord Jesus and your love for all the saints, I have not stopped giving thanks for you, remembering you in my prayers. I keep asking that the God of our Lord Jesus Christ, the glorious Father, may give you the Spirit^f of wisdom and revelation, so that you may know him better. I pray also that the eyes of your heart may be enlightened in order that you may know the hope to which he has called you, the riches of his glorious inheritance in the saints, and his incomparably great power for us who believe. That power is like the working of his mighty strength, which he exerted in Christ when he raised him from the dead and seated him at his right hand in the heavenly realms, far above all rule and authority, power and dominion, and every title that can be given, not only in the present age but also in the one to come. And God placed all things under his feet and appointed him to be head over everything for the church, which is his body, the fullness of him who fills everything in every way.

"God . . . has blessed us in the heavenly realms
with every spiritual blessing in Christ."

From Oswald Chambers

‽ Any man, every man, we ourselves, may partake of this marvelous raising up whereby God puts us into the wonderful life of His Son, and the very qualities of Jesus Christ are imparted to us. There is plenty of room to grow in the heavenly places; room for the head to grow, for the heart to grow, for the bodily relationships to grow, for the spirit to grow—plenty of room for every phase of us to grow into the realization of what a marvelous being our Lord Jesus Christ is. OBH 32

‽ *"Heavenly places in Christ Jesus."* That is where God raises us. We do not get there by climbing, by aspiring, by struggling, by consecration, or by vows; God lifts us right straight up out of sin, inability and weakness, lust and disobedience, wrath and self-seeking—lifts us right up out of all this, "up, up to the whiter than snow shine," to the heavenly places where Jesus Christ lived when He was on earth, and where He lives to this hour in the fullness of the pleni-tude of His power. May God never relieve us from the wonder of it. We are lifted up into that inviolable place that cannot be defiled, and Paul states that God can raise us up there *now*, and that the wonder of sitting in the heavenly places in Christ Jesus is to be manifested in our lives while we are here on earth. OBH 32

❧ "And made us sit together." Sit? But I have to earn my living! Sit? But I am in the midst of the wild turmoil of city life! Sit? But I have my calling in life and my ambitions to fulfill! Paul says that God has raised us up and made us *sit* together in heavenly places in Christ Jesus. We must have in our minds that by "heavenly places" is meant all that Jesus Christ was when He was down here, and all that He is revealed to be now by the Word; and God raises us up to sit together with Him there. There is ample time and ample room to grow in the heavenly places. OBH 33

❧ We are lifted up into that inviolable place that cannot be defiled, and Paul states that God can raise us up there *now*, and that the wonder of sitting in the heavenly places in Christ Jesus is to be manifested in our lives while we are here on earth. OBH 32

❧ The marvelous characteristic of the Spirit of God in you and me when we are raised up to the heavenly places in Christ Jesus is that we look to the Creator, and see that the marvelous being who made the world and upholds all things by the word of His power is the one who keeps us in every particular. OBH 33

❧ Jesus Christ tells us to take the lessons of our lives from the things men never look at — "Consider the lilies"; "Behold the fowls of the air" (see Matt. 6:26, 28). How often do we look at clouds, or grass, at sparrows, or flowers? Why, we have no time to look at them, we are in the rush of things — it is absurd to sit dreaming about spar-rows and trees and clouds! Thank God, when He raises us to the heavenly places, He manifests in us the very mind that was in Christ Jesus, unhasting and unresting, calm, steady, and strong. OBH 33

---

a. Some early manuscripts do not have *in Ephesus*.
b. Or *believers who are*
c. Or *sight in love. He*
d. Or *us. With all wisdom and understanding, he*
e. Or *were made heirs*
f. Or *a spirit*

44

MADE ALIVE IN CHRIST

As for you, you were dead in your transgressions and sins, in which you used to live when you followed the ways of this world and of the ruler of the kingdom of the air, the spirit who is now at work in those who are disobedient. All of us also lived among them at one time, gratifying the cravings of our sinful nature[a] and following its desires and thoughts. Like the rest, we were by nature objects of wrath. But because of his great love for us, God, who is rich in mercy, made us alive with Christ even when we were dead in transgressions—it is by grace you have been saved. And God raised us up with Christ and seated us with him in the heavenly realms in Christ Jesus, in order that in the coming ages he might show the incomparable riches of his grace, expressed in his kindness to us in Christ Jesus. For it is by grace you have been saved, through faith—and this not from yourselves, it is the gift of God—not by works, so that no one can boast. For we are God's workmanship, created in Christ Jesus to do good works, which God prepared in advance for us to do.

ONE IN CHRIST

Therefore, remember that formerly you who are Gentiles by birth and called "uncircumcised" by those who call themselves "the circumcision" (that done in the body by the hands of men)—remember that at that time you were separate from Christ, excluded from citizenship in Israel and foreigners to the covenants of the promise, without hope and without God in the world. But now in Christ Jesus you who once were far away have been brought near through the blood of Christ.

For he himself is our peace, who has made the two one and has destroyed the barrier, the dividing wall of hostility, by abolishing in his flesh the law with its commandments and regulations. His purpose was to create in himself one new man out of the two, thus making peace, and in this one body to reconcile both of them to God through the cross, by which he put to death their hostility. He came and preached peace to you who were far away and peace to those who were near. For through him we both have access to the Father by one Spirit.

Consequently, you are no longer foreigners and aliens, but fellow citizens with God's people and members of God's household, built on the foundation of the apostles and prophets, with Christ Jesus himself as the chief cornerstone. In him the whole building is joined together and rises to become a holy temple in the Lord. And in him you too are being built together to become a dwelling in which God lives by his Spirit.

> *"We are God's workmanship,*
> *created in Christ Jesus to do good works,*
> *which God prepared in advance for us to do."*

From Oswald Chambers

≈ The stamp of the worker gripped by God is that, slowly and surely, one here and another there is being won for God. AUG 9

≈ To recognize that my Lord counts us faithful removes the last snare of idealizing natural pluck. If we have the idea that we must face the difficulties with pluck, we have never recognized the truth that He has counted us faithful; it is His work in me He is counting worthy, not my work for Him. The truth is we have nothing to fear and nothing to overcome because He is all in all, and we are more than conquerors through Him. The recognition of this truth is not flattering to the worker's sense of heroics, but it is amazingly glorifying to the work of Christ. He counts us worthy because He has done everything for us. It is a shameful thing for Christians to talk about "getting the victory"; by this time the Victor ought to have got us so completely that it is His victory all the time, not ours. AUG 11

- Don't insult God by despising His ordinary ways in your life by saying, "Those things are beneath me." God has no special line; anything that is ordinary and human is His line. DI 87

- When a worker jealously guards his secret life with God, the public life will take care of itself. DI 88

- Remember, in estimating other lives there is always one fact more you don't know. You don't know why some men turn to God and others don't; it is hidden in the inscrutable part of a man's nature. DI 88

- Never talk for the sake of making the other person see you are in the right. Talk only that he may see the right, and when he does see it, you will be so obliterated that he will forget to say, "Thank you." DI 88

- The difference between a Christian worker and one who does not know Jesus Christ is just this—that a Christian worker can never meet anyone of whom he can despair. If we do despair of anyone, it is because we have never met Jesus Christ ourselves. HG 44

- We are not here to do work *for* God; we are here to be workers *with* Him, those through whom He can do His work. NKW 137

- So many of us put prayer and consecration in place of God's work; we make ourselves the workers. God is the Worker, and He is after spirituality. God does nothing other than the profound; we have to do the practical. OBH 132

- The saint must become like His Master, utterly unobtrusive. For "we preach not ourselves, but Christ Jesus as Lord, and ourselves as your servants for Jesus' sake" (2 Cor. 4:5). If you are serving men for their sakes, you will soon have the heart knocked out of you; but if you are personally and passionately devoted to the Lord Jesus Christ, then you can spend yourselves to the last ebb because your motive is love to the Lord. PH 134

---

a. Or *our flesh*

190

45

EPHESIANS 3

PAUL THE PREACHER TO THE GENTILES

For this reason I, Paul, the prisoner of Christ Jesus for the sake of you Gentiles—

Surely you have heard about the administration of God's grace that was given to me for you, that is, the mystery made known to me by revelation, as I have already written briefly. In reading this, then, you will be able to understand my insight into the mystery of Christ, which was not made known to men in other generations as it has now been revealed by the Spirit to God's holy apostles and prophets. This mystery is that through the gospel the Gentiles are heirs together with Israel, members together of one body, and sharers together in the promise in Christ Jesus.

I became a servant of this gospel by the gift of God's grace given me through the working of his power. Although I am less than the least of all God's people, this grace was given me: to preach to the Gentiles the unsearchable riches of Christ, and to make plain to everyone the administration of this mystery, which for ages past was kept hidden in God, who created all things. His intent was that now, through the church, the manifold wisdom of God should be made known to the rulers and authorities in the heavenly realms, according to his eternal purpose which he accomplished in Christ Jesus our Lord. In him and through faith in him we may approach God with freedom and confidence. I ask you, therefore, not to be discouraged because of my sufferings for you, which are your glory.

A PRAYER FOR THE EPHESIANS

For this reason I kneel before the Father, from whom his whole family[a] in heaven and on earth derives its name. I pray that out of his glorious riches he may strengthen you with power through his Spirit in your inner being, so that Christ may dwell in your hearts through faith. And I pray that you, being rooted and established in love, may have power, together with all the saints, to grasp how wide and long and high and deep is the love of Christ, and to know this love that surpasses knowledge—that you may be filled to the measure of all the fullness of God.

Now to him who is able to do immeasurably more than all we ask or imagine, according to his power that is at work within us, to him be glory in the church and in Christ Jesus throughout all generations, for ever and ever! Amen.

"In [Christ] and through faith in him we may
approach God with freedom and confidence."

FROM OSWALD CHAMBERS

⁊⁀ When once a saint puts his confidence in the election of God, no tribulation or affliction can ever touch that confidence. When we realize that there is no hope of deliverance in human wisdom, or in human rectitude, or in anything that we can do . . . accept the justification of God and . . . stand true to the election of God in Christ Jesus. This is the finest cure for spiritual degeneration or for spiritual sulks. CD VOL. 1, 156

⁊⁀ The one thing Satan tries to shake is our confidence in God. HG 28

⁊⁀ Confidence in the natural world is self-reliance, in the spiritual world it is God-reliance. IYA 32

⁊⁀ We won't walk before God because we are not confident in Him, and the proof that we are not confident in God is that occasionally we get into the sulks. If you are walking with God, it is impossible to be in the sulks. Never have the idea that you have disobeyed when you know you have not; the reason you say so is because you are not walking in the permanent light of faith. NKW 60

⁊⁀ It is nonsense to imagine that God expects me to discern all that is clear to His own mind; all He asks of me is to maintain perfect confidence in Himself. Faith springs from the indwelling of the life of God in me. OPG 37

192

✙ The great object of the enemy of our souls is to make us fling away our confidence in God; to do this is nothing less than spiritual suicide. OPG 57

✙ God expects His children to be so confident in Him that in a crisis they are the ones upon whom He can rely. PH 39

✙ There is no more glorious opportunity than the day in which we live for proving in personal life and in every way that we are confident in God. PH 41

✙ A great point is reached spiritually when we stop worrying God over personal matters or over any matter. God expects of us the one thing that glorifies Him—and that is to remain absolutely confident in Him, remembering what He has said beforehand, and sure that His purpose will be fulfilled. RTR 67

✙ We can get to God as Creator apart from Jesus Christ, but never to God as our Father save through Him. Let us receive this inspired idea of our Lord's right into our inmost willing heart, believe it, and pray in the confidence of it. CD VOL. 2, 24

✙ "There am I in the midst of them." A wonderful picture—a group of our Lord's children around the knees of the Heavenly Father, making their requests known in familiarity, in awe and reverence, in simplicity and confidence in Him, and in humble certainty that He is there. CD VOL. 2, 45

✙ The only way to get into the relationship of "asking" is to get into the relationship of absolute reliance on the Lord Jesus. *"And this is the confidence that we have in Him."* DI 39

✙ So many of us limit our praying because we are not reckless in our confidence in God. In the eyes of those who do not know God, it is madness to trust Him, but when we pray in the Holy Ghost we begin to realize the resources of God, that He is our perfect Heavenly Father, and we are His children. IYA 62

✙ The only one who prays in the Holy Ghost is the child, the child-spirit in us, the glad spirit of utter confidence in God. IYA 64

---

a. Or *whom all fatherhood*

193

46

EPHESIANS 4

UNITY IN THE BODY OF CHRIST

A s a prisoner for the Lord, then, I urge you to live a life worthy of the calling you have received. Be completely humble and gentle; be patient, bearing with one another in love. Make every effort to keep the unity of the Spirit through the bond of peace. There is one body and one Spirit— just as you were called to one hope when you were called—one Lord, one faith, one baptism; one God and Father of all, who is over all and through all and in all.

But to each one of us grace has been given as Christ apportioned it. This is why it[a] says:

"When he ascended on high,
he led captives in his train
and gave gifts to men."[b]

(What does "he ascended" mean except that he also descended to the lower, earthly regions[c]? He who descended is the very one who ascended higher than all the heavens, in order to fill the whole universe.) It was he who gave some to be apostles, some to be prophets, some to be evangelists, and some to be pastors and teachers, to prepare God's people for works of service, so that the body of Christ may be built up until we all reach unity in the faith and in the knowledge of the Son of God and become mature, attaining to the whole measure of the fullness of Christ.

Then we will no longer be infants, tossed back and forth by the waves, and blown here and there by every wind of teaching and by the cunning and craftiness of men in their deceitful scheming. Instead, speaking the truth in love, we will in all things grow up into him who is the Head, that is, Christ. From him the whole body, joined and held together by every supporting ligament, grows and builds itself up in love, as each part does its work.

LIVING AS CHILDREN OF LIGHT

So I tell you this, and insist on it in the Lord, that you must no longer live as the Gentiles do, in the futility of their thinking. They are darkened in their understanding and separated from the life of God because of the ignorance that is in them due to the hardening of their hearts. Having lost all sensitivity, they have given themselves over to sensuality so as to indulge in every kind of impurity, with a continual lust for more.

You, however, did not come to know Christ that way. Surely you heard of him and were taught in him in accordance with the truth that is in Jesus. You were taught, with regard to your former way of life, to put off your old self, which is being corrupted by its deceitful desires; to be made new in the attitude of your minds; and to put on the new self, created to be like God in true righteousness and holiness.

Therefore each of you must put off falsehood and speak truthfully to his neighbor, for we are all members of one body. "In your anger do not sin"[d]: Do not let the sun go down while you are still angry, and do not give the devil a foothold. He who has been stealing must steal no longer, but must work, doing something useful with his own hands, that he may have something to share with those in need.

Do not let any unwholesome talk come out of your mouths, but only what is helpful for building others up according to their needs, that it may benefit those who listen. And do not grieve the Holy Spirit of God, with whom you were sealed for the day of redemption. Get rid of all bitterness, rage and anger, brawling and slander, along with every form of malice. Be kind and compassionate to one another, forgiving each other, just as in Christ God forgave you.

"[Christ] gave [gifts] . . . to prepare God's people
for works of service,
so that the body of Christ may be built up
until we all reach unity in the faith."

From Oswald Chambers

❧ Christian service is not our work; loyalty to Jesus is our work. DI 85

❧ The value of our work depends on whether we can direct men to Jesus Christ. DI 85

❧ It is much easier to do Christian work than to be concentrated on God's point of view. DI 89

❧ If we are paying attention to the source, rivers of living water will pour out of us, but if immediately we stop paying attention to the source, the outflow begins to dry up. We have nothing to do with our "useability," but only with our relationship to Jesus Christ; nothing must be allowed to come in between. IWP 45

❧ So many of us put prayer and work and consecration in place of the working of God; we make ourselves the workers. God is the Worker, we work out what He works in. IWP 63

❧ We have a way of saying—"What a wonderful power that man or woman would be in God's service." Reasoning on man's broken virtues makes us fix on the wrong thing. The only way any man or woman can ever be of service to God is when he or she is willing to renounce all their natural excellencies and determine to be weak in Him—"I am here for one thing only, for Jesus Christ to manifest Himself in me." That is to be the steadfast habit of a Christian's life. MFL 106

❧ Beware of anything that competes with loyalty to Jesus Christ. The greatest competitor of devotion to Jesus is service for Him. It is easier to serve than to be drunk to the dregs. The one aim of the call of God is the satisfaction of God, not a call to do something for Him. We are not sent to battle for God, but to be used by God in His battlings. MUH 18

❧ Jesus Christ calls service what we are to Him, not what we do for Him. MUH 171

❧ With us, Christian service is something we do; with Jesus Christ it is not what we do *for* Him, but what we *are* to Him that He calls service. Our Lord always puts the matter of discipleship on the basis of

197

devotion not to a belief or a creed, but to Himself. There is no argument about it, and no compulsion, simply—"If you would be My disciple, you must be devoted to Me" (see Luke 14:33). PH 144

ɞ "To serve the living God" (see 1 Thes. 1:9). This means a life laid down for Jesus, a life of narrowed interests, a life that deliberately allows itself to be swamped by a crowd of paltry things. It is not fanaticism, it is the steadfast, flint-like attitude of heart and mind and body for one purpose—spoilt for everything saving as we can be used to win souls for Jesus. PS 22

ɞ Looking for opportunities to serve God is an impertinence; every time and all the time is our opportunity of serving God. RTR 52

ɞ God never uses in His service those who are sentimentally devoted to Him; He uses only those who are holy within in heart and holy without in practice. SHL 120

ɞ My contact with the nature of God has made me realize what I can do for God. Service is the outcome of what is fitted to my nature; God's call is fitted to His nature, and I never hear His call until I have received His nature. When I have received his nature, then His nature and mine work together; the Son of God reveals Himself in me, and I, the natural man, serve the Son of God in ordinary ways, out of sheer downright devotion to Him. SSY 12

ɞ Our Lord pays not the remotest attention to natural abilities or natural virtues; He heeds only one thing—Does that man discern who I am? Does he know the meaning of My Cross? The men and women Jesus Christ is going to use in His enterprises are those in whom He has done everything. SSY 49

ɞ Whether our work is a success or a failure has nothing to do with us. Our call is not to successful service, but to faithfulness. SSY 123

---

a. Or *God*
b. Psalm 68:18
c. Or *the depths of the earth*
d. Psalm 4:4

47

LIVE A LIFE OF LOVE

Be imitators of God, therefore, as dearly loved children and live a life of love, just as Christ loved us and gave himself up for us as a fragrant offering and sacrifice to God.

But among you there must not be even a hint of sexual immorality, or of any kind of impurity, or of greed, because these are improper for God's holy people. Nor should there be obscenity, foolish talk or coarse joking, which are out of place, but rather thanksgiving. For of this you can be sure: No immoral, impure or greedy person—such a man is an idolater—has any inheritance in the kingdom of Christ and of God.[a] Let no one deceive you with empty words, for because of such things God's wrath comes on those who are disobedient. Therefore do not be partners with them.

For you were once darkness, but now you are light in the Lord. Live as children of light (for the fruit of the light consists in all goodness, righteousness and truth) and find out what pleases the Lord. Have nothing to do with the fruitless deeds of darkness, but rather expose them. For it is shameful even to mention what the disobedient do in secret. But everything exposed by the light becomes visible, for it is light that makes everything visible. This is why it is said:

> "Wake up, O sleeper,
> rise from the dead,
> and Christ will shine on you."

Be very careful, then, how you live—not as unwise but as wise, making the most of every opportunity, because the days are evil. Therefore do not be foolish, but understand what the Lord's will is. Do not get drunk on wine, which leads to debauchery. Instead, be filled with the Spirit. Speak to one another with psalms, hymns and spiritual songs. Sing and make music in your heart to the Lord, always giving thanks to God the Father for everything, in the name of our Lord Jesus Christ.

Submit to one another out of reverence for Christ.

WIVES AND HUSBANDS

Wives, submit to your husbands as to the Lord. For the husband is the head of the wife as Christ is the head of the church, his body, of which he is the Savior. Now as the church submits to Christ, so also wives should submit to their husbands in everything.

Husbands, love your wives, just as Christ loved the church and gave himself up for her to make her holy, cleansing her[b] by the washing with water through the word, and to present her to himself as a radiant church, without stain or wrinkle or any other blemish, but holy and blameless. In this same way, husbands ought to love their wives as their own bodies. He who loves his wife loves himself. After all, no one ever hated his own body, but he feeds and cares for it, just as Christ does the church—for we are members of his body. "For this reason a man will leave his father and mother and be united to his wife, and the two will become one flesh."[c] This is a profound mystery—but I am talking about Christ and the church. However, each one of you also must love his wife as he loves himself, and the wife must respect her husband.

"Live as children of light . . .
and find out what pleases the Lord.
Have nothing to do with the fruitless deeds of darkness,
but rather expose them."

FROM OSWALD CHAMBERS

⚭ Nothing is cleaner or grander or sweeter than light. Light cannot be soiled; a sunbeam may shine into the dirtiest puddle, but it is never soiled. A sheet of white paper can be soiled, as can almost any white substance, but you cannot soil light. BP 173

⚭ God is a light so bright that the first vision of Himself is dark with excess of light. CD VOL. 1, 52

❧ As long as you are in the dark you do not know what God is doing; immediately when you get into the light, you discover it. HGM 53

❧ "Ye are the light of the world" (Matt. 5:14). We have the idea that we are going to shine in heaven, but we are to shine down here, "in the midst of a crooked and perverse nation" (Phil. 2:15). We are to shine as lights in the world in the squalid places, and it cannot be done by putting on a brazen smile, the light must be there all the time. LG 45

❧ In actual life we must be always in the light, and we cease to be in the light when we want to explain why we did a thing. The significant thing about our Lord is that He never explained anything; He let mistakes correct themselves because He always lived in the light. There is so much in us that is folded and twisted, but the sign that we are following God is that we keep in the light. LG 66

❧ There is another thing about the possession of light in Jesus Christ: my possession of light is quite different from yours. Each of us has a particular possession of light that no one else can have, and if we refuse to take our possession, everyone else will suffer. OBH 42

❧ One step in the right direction in obedience to the light, and the manifestation of the Son of God in your mortal flesh is as certain as that God is on His throne. When once God's light has come to us through Jesus Christ, we must never hang back, but obey; and we shall not walk in darkness, but will have the light of life. OBH 43

❧ "Let your light so shine before men." (Matt. 5:16). Our light is to shine in the darkness; it is not needed in the light. OBH 75

❧ We all like the twilight in spiritual and moral matters, not the intensity of black and white, not the clear lines of demarcation — saved and unsaved. We prefer things to be hazy, winsome, and indefinite, without the clear light. When the light does come difficulty is experienced, for when a man awakens he sees a great many things. We may feel complacent with a background of drab, but to be brought up against the white background of Jesus Christ is an immensely uncomfortable thing. PH 198

---

a. Or *kingdom of the Christ and God*
b. Or *having cleansed*
c. Gen. 2:24

48

CHILDREN AND PARENTS

hildren, obey your parents in the Lord, for this is right. "Honor your father and mother"—which is the first commandment with a promise—"that it may go well with you and that you may enjoy long life on the earth."[a]

Fathers, do not exasperate your children; instead, bring them up in the training and instruction of the Lord.

SLAVES AND MASTERS

Slaves, obey your earthly masters with respect and fear, and with sincerity of heart, just as you would obey Christ. Obey them not only to win their favor when their eye is on you, but like slaves of Christ, doing the will of God from your heart. Serve wholeheartedly, as if you were serving the Lord, not men, because you know that the Lord will reward everyone for whatever good he does, whether he is slave or free.

And masters, treat your slaves in the same way. Do not threaten them, since you know that he who is both their Master and yours is in heaven, and there is no favoritism with him.

THE ARMOR OF GOD

Finally, be strong in the Lord and in his mighty power. Put on the full armor of God so that you can take your stand against the devil's schemes. For our struggle is not against flesh and blood, but against the rulers, against the authorities, against the powers of this dark world and against the spiritual forces of evil in the heavenly realms. Therefore put on the full armor of God, so that when the day of evil comes, you may be able to stand your ground, and after you have done everything, to stand. Stand firm then, with the belt of truth buckled around your waist, with the breastplate of righteousness in place, and with your feet fitted with the readiness that comes from the gospel of peace. In addition to all this, take up the shield of faith, with which you can extinguish all the flaming arrows of the evil one. Take the helmet of salvation and the sword of the Spirit, which is the word of God. And pray in the Spirit on all occasions with all kinds of prayers and requests. With this in mind, be alert and always keep on praying for all the saints.

Pray also for me, that whenever I open my mouth, words may be given me so that I will fearlessly make known the mystery of the gospel, for which I am an ambassador in chains. Pray that I may declare it fearlessly, as I should.

FINAL GREETINGS

Tychicus, the dear brother and faithful servant in the Lord, will tell you everything, so that you also may know how I am and what I am doing. I am sending him to you for this very purpose, that you may know how we are, and that he may encourage you.

Peace to the brothers, and love with faith from God the Father and the Lord Jesus Christ. Grace to all who love our Lord Jesus Christ with an undying love.

"Put on the full armor of God
so that you can take your stand
against the devil's schemes."

FROM OSWALD CHAMBERS

   ✍ "Wherefore take unto you the whole armor of God." It is not given; we have to take it. It is there for us to put on, understanding what we are doing. We have the idea that prayer is for special times, but we have to put on the armor of God for the continual practice of prayer, so that any struggling onslaught of the powers of darkness cannot touch the position of prayer. When we pray easily, it is because Satan is completely defeated in his onslaughts; when we pray difficultly, it is because Satan is gaining a victory. We have not been continuously practicing; we have not been facing things courageously; we have not been taking our orders from our Lord. Our Lord did not say, "Go" or, "Do"; He said, "Watch and pray."

If we struggle in prayer, it is because the enemy is gaining ground. If prayer is simple to us, it is because we have the victory. There is no such thing as a holiday for the beating of your heart. If there is, the grave comes next. And there is no such thing as a moral or spiritual holiday. If we attempt to take a holiday, the next time we want to pray it is a struggle because the enemy has gained a victory all round, darkness has come down, and spiritual wickedness in high places has enfolded us. If we have to fight, it is because we have disobeyed; we ought to be more than conquerors.

"And having done all, to stand"—a mental state in regard to confidence—no panic. What is it that puts us into a panic? The devil is a bully, but he cannot stand for a second before God. When we stand in the armor of God, he pays no attention to us, but if we tackle the devil in our own strength we are done for. If we stand in God's armor with the strength and courage of God, the devil cannot gain one inch of way, and the position of prayer is held, as far as we are concerned, untouched by his wiles.

Confidence in the natural world is self-reliance; in the spiritual world it is God-reliance. We run away when we have not been practicing, when we have not been doing anything in private; then when there is a new onslaught of the wiles of the devil, we lose heart instantly. Instead of standing, we scuttle, and others have to fill the gap until we are sufficiently ashamed to come back. We cannot stand against the wiles of the devil by our wits. The devil only comes along the lines that God understands, not along the lines we understand, and the only way we can be prepared for him is to do what God tells us—stand complete in His armor, indwelt by His Spirit, in complete obedience to Him. We have not to wait for some great onslaught of the enemy; he is here all the time and he is wily. The secret of the sacred struggle for prayer lies in the fact that we must stand in the armor of God, practicing what God would have us do, then we can hold the position of prayer against all the attacks of the devil. IYA 33

---

a. Deut. 5:16

49

THANKSGIVING AND PRAYER

aul and Timothy, servants of Christ Jesus,
To all the saints in Christ Jesus at Philippi, together with the overseers[a] and deacons:
Grace and peace to you from God our Father and the Lord Jesus Christ.

I thank my God every time I remember you. In all my prayers for all of you, I always pray with joy because of your partnership in the gospel from the first day until now, being confident of this, that he who began a good work in you will carry it on to completion until the day of Christ Jesus.

It is right for me to feel this way about all of you, since I have you in my heart; for whether I am in chains or defending and confirming the gospel, all of you share in God's grace with me. God can testify how I long for all of you with the affection of Christ Jesus.

And this is my prayer: that your love may abound more and more in knowledge and depth of insight, so that you may be able to discern what is best and may be pure and blameless until the day of Christ, filled with the fruit of righteousness that comes through Jesus Christ—to the glory and praise of God.

PAUL'S CHAINS ADVANCE THE GOSPEL

Now I want you to know, brothers, that what has happened to me has really served to advance the gospel. As a result, it has become clear throughout the whole palace guard[b] and to everyone else that I am in chains for Christ. Because of my chains, most of the brothers in the Lord have been encouraged to speak the word of God more courageously and fearlessly.

It is true that some preach Christ out of envy and rivalry, but others out of goodwill. The latter do so in love, knowing that I am put here for the defense of the gospel. The former preach Christ out of selfish ambition, not sincerely, supposing that they can stir up trouble for me while I am in chains.[c] But what does it matter? The important thing is that in every way, whether from false motives or true, Christ is preached. And because of this I rejoice.

Yes, and I will continue to rejoice, for I know that through your prayers and the help given by the Spirit of Jesus Christ, what has happened to me will turn out for my deliverance.[d] I eagerly expect and hope that I will in no way be ashamed, but will have sufficient courage so that now as always Christ will be exalted in my body, whether by life or by death. For to me, to live is Christ and to die is gain. If I am to go on living in the body, this will mean fruitful labor for me. Yet what shall I choose? I do not know! I am torn between the two: I desire to depart and be with Christ, which is better by far; but it is more necessary for you that I remain in the body. Convinced of this, I know that I will remain, and I will continue with all of you for your progress and joy in the faith, so that through my being with you again your joy in Christ Jesus will overflow on account of me.

Whatever happens, conduct yourselves in a manner worthy of the gospel of Christ. Then, whether I come and see you or only hear about you in my absence, I will know that you stand firm in one spirit, contending as one man for the faith of the gospel without being frightened in any way by those who oppose you. This is a sign to them that they will be destroyed, but that you will be saved—and that by God. For it has been granted to you on behalf of Christ not only to believe on him, but also to suffer for him, since you are going through the same struggle you saw I had, and now hear that I still have.

> *"Conduct yourselves in a manner worthy*
> *of the gospel of Christ."*

From Oswald Chambers

> ⁂ When the veil is lifted, we shall find that the seemly conduct of prayer wrought the things of God in men. Let us keep awake and

206

readjust ourselves to our Lord's counsel. He counsels His children to keep alert, to be pure, to yield to no temptation to panic, to false emotion, to illegitimate gain, or to a cowardly sense of futility. We can never be where we are not; we are just where we are; let us keep alert and pray just there for His sake. Then our Lord says we shall be accounted worthy to escape all these things that shall come to pass, and to stand before the Son of man—stand, not lie, nor grovel, nor cry, but stand upright, in the full integrity of Christian manhood and womanhood before the Son of man.

The seemliness of Christian conduct is not consistent adherence to a mere principle of peace, but standing true to Jesus Christ. CD VOL. 1, 117

❧ Righteousness means living and acting in accordance with right and justice, that is, it must express itself in a man's bodily life. "Little children, let no man deceive you: he that doeth righteousness is righteous" (1 John 3:7). Imputed righteousness must never be made to mean that God puts the robe of His righteousness over our moral wrong, like a snowdrift over a rubbish heap; that He pretends we are all right when we are not. The revelation is that "Christ Jesus . . . is made unto us . . . righteousness" (1 Cor. 1:30); it is the distinct impartation of the very life of Jesus on the ground of the Atonement, enabling me to walk in the light as God is in the light, and as long as I remain in the light God sees only the perfections of His Son. We are "accepted in the Beloved" (Eph. 1:6). CHI 81

❧ The only holiness there is is the holiness derived through faith, and faith is the instrument the Holy Spirit uses to organize us into Christ. But do not let us be vague here. Holiness, like sin, is a disposition, not a series of acts. A man can *act* holily, but he has not a holy *disposition.* A saint has had imparted to him the disposition of holiness; therefore holiness must be the characteristic of the life here and now. Entire sanctification is the end of the disposition of sin, but only the beginning of the life of a saint; then comes growth in holiness. The process of sanctification begins at the moment of birth from above and is consummated on the unconditional surrender of my right to myself to Jesus Christ. CHI 81

❧ It is righteous behavior that brings blessing on others, and the heart of faith sees that God is working things out well. HG 45

---

a. Traditionally *bishops*
b. Or *whole palace*
c. Some late manuscripts have verses 16 and 17 in reverse order
d. Or *salvation*

50

PHILIPPIANS 2

IMITATING CHRIST'S HUMILITY

I f you have any encouragement from being united with Christ, if any comfort from his love, if any fellowship with the Spirit, if any tenderness and compassion, then make my joy complete by being like-minded, having the same love, being one in spirit and purpose. Do nothing out of selfish ambition or vain conceit, but in humility consider others better than yourselves. Each of you should look not only to your own interests, but also to the interests of others.

Your attitude should be the same as that of Christ Jesus:

Who, being in very nature[a] God,
did not consider equality with God something
to be grasped,
but made himself nothing,
taking the very nature[b] of a servant,
being made in human likeness.
And being found in appearance as a man,
he humbled himself
and became obedient to death —
even death on a cross!
Therefore God exalted him to the highest place
and gave him the name that is above every name,
that at the name of Jesus every knee should bow,
in heaven and on earth and under the earth,
and every tongue confess that Jesus Christ is Lord,
to the glory of God the Father.

SHINING AS STARS

Therefore, my dear friends, as you have always obeyed—not only in my presence, but now much more in my absence—continue to work out your salvation with fear and trembling, for it is God who works in you to will and to act according to his good purpose.

Do everything without complaining or arguing, so that you may become blameless and pure, children of God without fault in a crooked and depraved generation, in which you shine like stars in the universe as you hold out[c] the word of life—in order that I may boast on the day of Christ that I did not run or labor for nothing. But even if I am being poured out like a drink offering on the sacrifice and service coming from your faith, I am glad and rejoice with all of you. So you too should be glad and rejoice with me.

TIMOTHY AND EPAPHRODITUS

I hope in the Lord Jesus to send Timothy to you soon, that I also may be cheered when I receive news about you. I have no one else like him, who takes a genuine interest in your welfare. For everyone looks out for his own interests, not those of Jesus Christ. But you know that Timothy has proved himself, because as a son with his father he has served with me in the work of the gospel. I hope, therefore, to send him as soon as I see how things go with me. And I am confident in the Lord that I myself will come soon.

But I think it is necessary to send back to you Epaphroditus, my brother, fellow worker and fellow soldier, who is also your messenger, whom you sent to take care of my needs. For he longs for all of you and is distressed because you heard he was ill. Indeed he was ill, and almost died. But God had mercy on him, and not on him only but also on me, to spare me sorrow upon sorrow. Therefore I am all the more eager to send him, so that when you see him again you may be glad and I may have less anxiety. Welcome him in the Lord with great joy, and honor men like him, because he almost died for the work of Christ, risking his life to make up for the help you could not give me.

"Do nothing out of selfish ambition or vain conceit,
but in humility consider others better than yourselves."

FROM OSWALD CHAMBERS

❧ If my love is first of all for God, I shall take no account of the base ingratitude of others, because the mainspring of my service to my fellowmen is love to God. BP 181

❧ We make the mistake of imagining that service for others springs from love of others; the fundamental fact is that supreme love for our Lord alone gives us the motive power of service to any extent for others—"ourselves your servants for Jesus' sake" (2 Cor. 4:5). That means I have to identify myself with God's interests in other people, and God is interested in some extraordinary people, viz., in you and in me, and He is just as interested in the person you dislike as He is in you. CHI 90

❧ We must keep in unbroken touch with God by faith, and see that we give other souls the same freedom and liberty that God gives us. MFL 123

❧ We see the humor of our Heavenly Father in the way He brings around us the type of people who are to us what we have been to Him; now He will watch how we behave toward them. PH 66

❧ God is interested in some strange people; He is interested in the man whom I am inclined to despise. PH 133

❧ The evidence that we are in love with God is that we identify ourselves with His interests in others, and other people are the exact expression of what we ourselves are; that is the humiliating thing! PR 107

❧ A self indwelt by Jesus becomes like Him. "Walk by love, even as Christ also loved you" (Eph. 5:2). Jesus has loved me to the end of all my meanness and selfishness and sin; now, He says, show that same love to others. RTR 40

❧ The apostolic office is not based on faith, but on love. The two working lines for carrying out Jesus Christ's command are, first, the sovereign preference of our person for the person of Jesus Christ; and second, the willing and deliberate identification of our interests with Jesus Christ's interests in other people. SSY 160

211

☙ Not only is the life of the missionary sacred to God, but the lives of others are sacred also, and when one tries to pry into another's concerns, he will receive the rebuke of our Lord — "What is that to thee? Follow thou Me" (John 21:22). SSY 165

---

a. Or *in the form of*
b. Or *the form*
c. Or *hold on to*

51

PHILIPPIANS 3-4

NO CONFIDENCE IN THE FLESH

Finally, my brothers, rejoice in the Lord! It is no trouble for me to write the same things to you again, and it is a safeguard for you.

Watch out for those dogs, those men who do evil, those mutilators of the flesh. For it is we who are the circumcision, we who worship by the Spirit of God, who glory in Christ Jesus, and who put no confidence in the flesh—though I myself have reasons for such confidence.

If anyone else thinks he has reasons to put confidence in the flesh, I have more: circumcised on the eighth day, of the people of Israel, of the tribe of Benjamin, a Hebrew of Hebrews; in regard to the law, a Pharisee; as for zeal, persecuting the church; as for legalistic righteousness, faultless.

But whatever was to my profit I now consider loss for the sake of Christ. What is more, I consider everything a loss compared to the surpassing greatness of knowing Christ Jesus my Lord, for whose sake I have lost all things. I consider them rubbish, that I may gain Christ and be found in him, not having a righteousness of my own that comes from the law, but that which is through faith in Christ—the righteousness that comes from God and is by faith. I want to know Christ and the power of his resurrection and the fellowship of sharing in his sufferings, becoming like him in his death, and so, somehow, to attain to the resurrection from the dead.

PRESSING ON TOWARD THE GOAL

Not that I have already obtained all this, or have already been made perfect, but I press on to take hold of that for which Christ Jesus took hold of me. Brothers, I do not consider myself yet to have taken hold of it. But one thing I do: Forgetting what is behind and straining toward what is ahead, I press on toward the goal to win the prize for which God has called me heavenward in Christ Jesus.

All of us who are mature should take such a view of things. And if on some point you think differently, that too God will make clear to you. Only let us live up to what we have already attained.

Join with others in following my example, brothers, and take note of those who live according to the pattern we gave you. For, as I have often told you before and now say again even with tears, many live as enemies of the cross of Christ. Their destiny is destruction, their god is their stomach, and their glory is in their shame. Their mind is on earthly things. But our citizenship is in heaven. And we eagerly await a Savior from there, the Lord Jesus Christ, who, by the power that enables him to bring everything under his control, will transform our lowly bodies so that they will be like his glorious body.

Therefore, my brothers, you whom I love and long for, my joy and crown, that is how you should stand firm in the Lord, dear friends!

EXHORTATIONS

I plead with Euodia and I plead with Syntyche to agree with each other in the Lord. Yes, and I ask you, loyal yokefellow,[a] help these women who have contended at my side in the cause of the gospel, along with Clement and the rest of my fellow workers, whose names are in the book of life.

Rejoice in the Lord always. I will say it again: Rejoice! Let your gentleness be evident to all. The Lord is near. Do not be anxious about anything, but in everything, by prayer and petition, with thanksgiving, present your requests to God. And the peace of God, which transcends all understanding, will guard your hearts and your minds in Christ Jesus.

Finally, brothers, whatever is true, whatever is noble, whatever is right, whatever is pure, whatever is lovely, whatever is admirable — if anything is excellent or praiseworthy — think about such things. Whatever you have learned or received or heard from me, or seen in me — put it into practice. And the God of peace will be with you.

Thanks for Their Gifts

I rejoice greatly in the Lord that at last you have renewed your concern for me. Indeed, you have been concerned, but you had no opportunity to show it. I am not saying this because I am in need, for I have learned to be content whatever the circumstances. I know what it is to be in need, and I know what it is to have plenty. I have learned the secret of being content in any and every situation, whether well fed or hungry, whether living in plenty or in want. I can do everything through him who gives me strength.

Yet it was good of you to share in my troubles. Moreover, as you Philippians know, in the early days of your acquaintance with the gospel, when I set out from Macedonia, not one church shared with me in the matter of giving and receiving, except you only; for even when I was in Thessalonica, you sent me aid again and again when I was in need. Not that I am looking for a gift, but I am looking for what may be credited to your account. I have received full payment and even more; I am amply supplied, now that I have received from Epaphroditus the gifts you sent. They are a fragrant offering, an acceptable sacrifice, pleasing to God. And my God will meet all your needs according to his glorious riches in Christ Jesus.

To our God and Father be glory for ever and ever. Amen.

Final Greetings

Greet all the saints in Christ Jesus. The brothers who are with me send greetings. All the saints send you greetings, especially those who belong to Caesar's household.

The grace of the Lord Jesus Christ be with your spirit. Amen.

"Do not be anxious about anything, but in everything, by prayer and petition, with thanksgiving, present your requests to God."

From Oswald Chambers

➤ "Take no thought for your life" (Matt. 6:25). These words of our Lord are the most revolutionary of statements. We argue in exactly the opposite way, even the most spiritual of us—"I *must* live, I *must* make so much money, I *must* be clothed and fed." That is how it begins; the great concern of the life is not God, but how we are going to fit ourselves to live. Jesus Christ says, "Reverse the order, get rightly related to Me first, see that you maintain that as the great care of your life, and never put the concentration of your care on the other things." SSM 68

꘎ It is useless to mistake careful consideration of circumstances for that which produces character. We cannot produce an inner life by watching the outer all the time. The lily obeys the law of its life in the surroundings in which it is placed, and Jesus says, as a disciple, consider your hidden life with God; pay attention to the source and God will look after the outflow. Imagine a lily hauling itself out of its pot and saying, "I don't think I look exactly right here." The lily's duty is to obey the law of its life where it is placed by the gardener. "Watch your life with God," says Jesus, "see that that is right and you will grow as the lily." We are all inclined to say, "I should be all right if only I were somewhere else." There is only one way to develop spiritually, and that is by concentrating on God. Don't bother about whether you are growing in grace or whether you are being of use to others, but believe on Jesus and out of you will flow rivers of living water. SSM 69

꘎ "Consider the lilies of the field, how they grow" (Matt. 6:28)—they simply *are*. Take the sea and the air, the sun, the stars, and the moon—they all *are,* and what a ministration they exert! So often we mar God's designed influence through us by our self-conscious effort to be consistent and useful. It seems unreasonable to expect a man to consider the lilies, yet that is the only way he can grow in grace. Jesus Christ's argument is that the men and women who are concentrated on their Father in heaven are those who are the fittest to do the work of the world. They have no ulterior motive in arranging their circumstances in order to produce a fine character. They know it cannot be done in that way. How are you to grow in the knowledge of God? By remaining where you are, and by remembering that your Father knows where you are and the circumstances you are in. Keep concentrated on Him and you will grow spiritually as the lily. SSM 69

---

a. Or *loyal Syzygus*

52

THANKSGIVING AND PRAYER

Paul, an apostle of Christ Jesus by the will of God, and Timothy our brother,

To the holy and faithful[a] brothers in Christ at Colosse:

Grace and peace to you from God our Father.[b]

We always thank God, the Father of our Lord Jesus Christ, when we pray for you, because we have heard of your faith in Christ Jesus and of the love you have for all the saints—the faith and love that spring from the hope that is stored up for you in heaven and that you have already heard about in the word of truth, the gospel that has come to you. All over the world this gospel is bearing fruit and growing, just as it has been doing among you since the day you heard it and understood God's grace in all its truth. You learned it from Epaphras, our dear fellow servant, who is a faithful minister of Christ on our[c] behalf, and who also told us of your love in the Spirit.

For this reason, since the day we heard about you, we have not stopped praying for you and asking God to fill you with the knowledge of his will through all spiritual wisdom and understanding. And we pray this in order that you may live a life worthy of the Lord and may please him in every way: bearing fruit in every good work, growing in the knowledge of God, being strengthened with all power according to his glorious might so that you may have great endurance and patience, and joyfully giving thanks to the Father, who has qualified you[d] to share in the inheritance of the saints in the kingdom of light. For he has rescued us from the dominion of darkness and brought us into the kingdom of the Son he loves, in whom we have redemption,[e] the forgiveness of sins.

The Supremacy of Christ

He is the image of the invisible God, the firstborn over all creation. For by him all things were created: things in heaven and on earth, visible and invisible, whether thrones or powers or rulers or authorities; all things were created by him and for him. He is before all things, and in him all things hold together. And he is the head of the body, the church; he is the beginning and the firstborn from among the dead, so that in everything he might have the supremacy. For God was pleased to have all his fullness dwell in him, and through him to reconcile to himself all things, whether things on earth or things in heaven, by making peace through his blood, shed on the cross.

Once you were alienated from God and were enemies in your minds because of your evil behavior. But now he has reconciled you by Christ's physical body through death to present you holy in his sight, without blemish and free from accusation—if you continue in your faith, established and firm, not moved from the hope held out in the gospel. This is the gospel that you heard and that has been proclaimed to every creature under heaven, and of which I, Paul, have become a servant.

Paul's Labor for the Church

Now I rejoice in what was suffered for you, and I fill up in my flesh what is still lacking in regard to Christ's afflictions, for the sake of his body, which is the church. I have become its servant by the commission God gave me to present to you the word of God in its fullness—the mystery that has been kept hidden for ages and generations, but is now disclosed to the saints. To them God has chosen to make known among the Gentiles the glorious riches of this mystery, which is Christ in you, the hope of glory.

We proclaim him, admonishing and teaching everyone with all wisdom, so that we may present everyone perfect in Christ. To this end I labor, struggling with all his energy, which so powerfully works in me.

"He is the image of the invisible God, the firstborn over all creation. For by him all things were created: things in heaven and on earth, visible and invisible,

whether thrones or powers or rulers or authorities; all things were created by him and for him."

FROM OSWALD CHAMBERS

❧ In presenting Jesus Christ, never present Him as a miraculous being who came down from heaven and worked miracles and who was not related to life as we are; that is not the Gospel of Christ. The Gospel Christ is the Being who came down to earth and lived our life and was possessed of a frame like ours. He became man in order to show the relationship man was to hold to God, and by His death and resurrection He can put any man into that relationship. Jesus Christ is the last word in human nature. AUG 44

❧ Jesus Christ is not an individual iota of a man. He is the whole of the human race centered before God in one Person; He is God and man in one. Man is lifted up to God in Christ, and God is brought down to man in Christ. Jesus Christ nowhere said, "He that hath seen *man* hath seen the Father"; but He did say that God was manifest in human flesh in His own person that He might become the generation center for the same manifestation in every human being, and the place of His travail pangs in the Incarnation, Calvary, and the Resurrection. AUG 70

❧ The character of Jesus Christ is exhibited in the New Testament and it appeals to us all. He lived His life straight down in the ordinary amalgam of human life, and He claims that the character He manifested is possible for any man if he will come in by the door He provides. AUG 81

❧ Jesus Christ never asks anyone to define his position or to understand a creed, but — "Who am I to you?" . . . Jesus Christ makes the whole of human destiny depend on a man's relationship to Himself. AUG 82

❧ Jesus Christ claims that He can do in human nature what human nature cannot do for itself, viz., "Destroy the works of the devil" (1 John 3:8), remove the wrong heredity, and put in the right one. He can satisfy the last aching abyss of the human heart. He can put the key into our hands which will give the solution to every problem that ever stretched before our minds. He can soothe by His pierced hands the wildest sorrow with which Satan or sin or death ever racked humanity. There is nothing for which Jesus Christ is not amply sufficient and over which He cannot make us more than conquerors. BE 111

❧ When the flatteries, the eulogies, the enthusiasms, and the extravagances regarding Jesus Christ have become enshrined sentiments in poetry and music and eloquence, they pass, like fleeting things of mist, colored but for a moment by reflected splendors from the Son of God, and our Lord's own words come with the sublime staying of the simple gentleness of God: "I am the way, and the truth, and the life" (John 14:6). CD VOL. 1, 11

❧ There have been great military geniuses, intellectual giants, geniuses of statesmen, but these only exercise influence over a limited number of men; Jesus Christ exercises unlimited sway over all men because He is the altogether worthy one. CHI 120

---

a. Or *believing*
b. Some manuscripts *Father and the Lord Jesus Christ*
c. Some manuscripts *your*
d. Some manuscripts *us*
e. A few late manuscripts *redemption through his blood*
f. Or *minds, as shown by*

53

ENCOURAGED IN HEART

I want you to know how much I am struggling for you and for those at Laodicea, and for all who have not met me personally. My purpose is that they may be encouraged in heart and united in love, so that they may have the full riches of complete understanding, in order that they may know the mystery of God, namely, Christ,[a] in whom are hidden all the treasures of wisdom and knowledge. I tell you this so that no one may deceive you by fine-sounding arguments. For though I am absent from you in body, I am present with you in spirit and delight to see how orderly you are and how firm your faith in Christ is.

FREEDOM FROM HUMAN REGULATIONS THROUGH LIFE WITH CHRIST

So then, just as you received Christ Jesus as Lord, continue to live in him, rooted and built up in him, strengthened in the faith as you were taught, and overflowing with thankfulness.

See to it that no one takes you captive through hollow and deceptive philosophy, which depends on human tradition and the basic principles of this world rather than on Christ.

For in Christ all the fullness of the Deity lives in bodily form, and you have been given fullness in Christ, who is the head over every power and authority. In him you were also circumcised, in the putting off of the sinful nature,[b] not with a circumcision done by the hands of men but with the circumcision done by Christ, having been buried with him in baptism and raised with him through your faith in the power of God, who raised him from the dead.

When you were dead in your sins and in the uncircumcision of your sinful nature,[c] God made you[d] alive with Christ. He forgave us all our sins, having canceled the written code, with its regulations, that was against us and that stood opposed to us; he took it away, nailing it to the cross. And having disarmed the powers and authorities, he made a public spectacle of them, triumphing over them by the cross.[e]

Therefore do not let anyone judge you by what you eat or drink, or with regard to a religious festival, a New Moon celebration or a Sabbath day. These are a shadow of the things that were to come; the reality, however, is found in Christ. Do not let anyone who delights in false humility and the worship of angels disqualify you for the prize. Such a person goes into great detail about what he has seen, and his unspiritual mind puffs him up with idle notions. He has lost connection with the Head, from whom the whole body, supported and held together by its ligaments and sinews, grows as God causes it to grow.

Since you died with Christ to the basic principles of this world, why, as though you still belonged to it, do you submit to its rules: "Do not handle! Do not taste! Do not touch!"? These are all destined to perish with use, because they are based on human commands and teachings. Such regulations indeed have an appearance of wisdom, with their self-imposed worship, their false humility and their harsh treatment of the body, but they lack any value in restraining sensual indulgence.

"God made you alive with Christ.
He forgave us all our sins,
having canceled the written code, with its regulations,
that was against us and that stood opposed to us;
he took it away, nailing it to the cross."

FROM OSWALD CHAMBERS

⟩⟩ The aspect of the cross in discipleship is lost altogether in the present-day view of following Jesus. The cross is looked upon as something beautiful and simple instead of a stern heroism. Our Lord never said it was easy to be a Christan; He warned men that they would have to face a variety of hardships, which He termed "bearing the cross." AUG 49

222

❧ Most of our emphasis today is on what our Lord's death means to us: the thing that is of importance is that we understand what God means in the Cross. AUG 56

❧ The Cross of Christ is the self-revelation of God, the way God has given Himself. AUG 59

❧ Either the Cross is the only way there is of explaining God, the only way of explaining Jesus Christ, and of explaining the human race, or there is nothing in it at all. BE 61

❧ If the human race apart from the Cross is all right, then the Redemption was a useless waste. BE 61

❧ The Cross did not happen to Jesus: He came on purpose for it. BSG 40

❧ The true portrayal is that the Cross is not the cross of a man, but the Cross of God. The tragedy of the Cross is the hurt to God. In the Cross, God and sinful man merge; consequently the Cross is of more importance than all the world's civilizations. CHI 45

❧ The Cross of Christ alone makes me holy, and it does so the second I am willing to let it. GW 54

❧ Very few of us have any understanding of the reason why Jesus Christ died. If sympathy is all that human beings need, then the Cross of Christ is a farce; there was no need for it. What the world needs is not "a little bit of love," but a surgical operation. MUH 355

❧ The Cross of Christ reveals that the blazing center of the love of God is the holiness of God, not His kindness and compassion. If the divine love pretends I am all right when I am all wrong, then I have a keener sense of justice than the Almighty. PH 65

❧ The cross we have to carry is that we have deliberately given up our right to ourselves to Jesus Christ. PR 92

❧ The cross is the deliberate recognition of what my personal life is for, viz., to be given to Jesus Christ; I have to take up that cross daily and prove that I am no longer my own. Individual independence has gone, and all that is left is personal passionate devotion to Jesus Christ through identification with His Cross. SHL 79

a. Some manuscripts *God, even the Father, and of Christ*
b. Or *the flesh*
c. Or *your flesh*
d. Some manuscripts *us*
e. Or *them in him*

54

RULES FOR HOLY LIVING

ince, then, you have been raised with Christ, set your hearts on things above, where Christ is seated at the right hand of God. Set your minds on things above, not on earthly things. For you died, and your life is now hidden with Christ in God. When Christ, who is your[a] life, appears, then you also will appear with him in glory.

Put to death, therefore, whatever belongs to your earthly nature: sexual immorality, impurity, lust, evil desires and greed, which is idolatry. Because of these, the wrath of God is coming.[b] You used to walk in these ways, in the life you once lived. But now you must rid yourselves of all such things as these: anger, rage, malice, slander, and filthy language from your lips. Do not lie to each other, since you have taken off your old self with its practices and have put on the new self, which is being renewed in knowledge in the image of its Creator. Here there is no Greek or Jew, circumcised or uncircumcised, barbarian, Scythian, slave or free, but Christ is all, and is in all.

Therefore, as God's chosen people, holy and dearly loved, clothe yourselves with compassion, kindness, humility, gentleness and patience. Bear with each other and forgive whatever grievances you may have against one another. Forgive as the Lord forgave you. And over all these virtues put on love, which binds them all together in perfect unity.

Let the peace of Christ rule in your hearts, since as members of one body you were called to peace. And be thankful. Let the word of Christ dwell in you richly as you teach and admonish one another with all wisdom, and as you sing psalms, hymns and spiritual songs with gratitude in your hearts to God. And whatever you do, whether in word or deed, do it all in the name of the Lord Jesus, giving thanks to God the Father through him.

RULES FOR CHRISTIAN HOUSEHOLDS

Wives, submit to your husbands, as is fitting in the Lord.

Husbands, love your wives and do not be harsh with them.

Children, obey your parents in everything, for this pleases the Lord.

Fathers, do not embitter your children, or they will become discouraged.

Slaves, obey your earthly masters in everything; and do it, not only when their eye is on you and to win their favor, but with sincerity of heart and reverence for the Lord. Whatever you do, work at it with all your heart, as working for the Lord, not for men, since you know that you will receive an inheritance from the Lord as a reward. It is the Lord Christ you are serving. Anyone who does wrong will be repaid for his wrong, and there is no favoritism.

"Since then you have been raised with Christ,
set your hearts on things above,
where Christ is seated
at the right hand of God."

FROM OSWALD CHAMBERS

❧ The supreme lesson of the perfectly actual life of faith is to learn how to worship. Faith brings me into personal contact with God before whom I must ever bow. I have to maintain a worshipful relationship to God in everything, and in the beginning this is difficult. NKW 41

❧ Worship is the tryst of sacramental identification with God; we deliberately give back to God the best He has given us that we may be identified with Him in it. SSY 171

❧ Worship of God is the sacramental element in a saint's life. We have to give back to God in worship every blessing He has given to us. SSY 171

225

♞ If we try, as has been tried by psychologists, to take out of the Bible something that agrees with modern science, we shall have to omit many things the Bible says about the heart. According to the Bible the heart is the center: the center of physical life, the center of memory, the center of damnation and of salvation, the center of God's working, and the center of the devil's working, the center from which everything works which molds the human mechanism. BP 100

♞ The heart is the exchange and mart; our words and expressions are simply the coins we use, but the "shop" resides in the heart, the emporium where all the goods are, and that is what God sees but no man can see. BP 102

♞ The heart physically is the center of the body; the heart sentimentally is the center of the soul; and the heart spiritually is the center of the spirit. BP 107

♞ The heart is the altar of which the physical body is the outer court, and whatever is offered on the altar of the heart will tell ultimately through the extremities of the body. "Keep thy heart with all diligence, for out of it are the issues of life" (Prov. 4:23). MFL 113

♞ The Bible term *heart* is best understood if we simply say "me"; it is the central citadel of a man's personality. MFL 113

♞ The human heart must have satisfaction, but there is only one being who can satisfy the last aching abyss of the human heart, and that is our Lord Jesus Christ. PH 52

---

a. Some manuscripts *our*
b. Some early manuscripts *coming on those who are disobedient*

55

COLOSSIANS 4

FURTHER INSTRUCTIONS

Masters, provide your slaves with what is right and fair, because you know that you also have a Master in heaven.

Devote yourselves to prayer, being watchful and thankful. And pray for us, too, that God may open a door for our message, so that we may proclaim the mystery of Christ, for which I am in chains. Pray that I may proclaim it clearly, as I should. Be wise in the way you act toward outsiders; make the most of every opportunity. Let your conversation be always full of grace, seasoned with salt, so that you may know how to answer everyone.

FINAL GREETINGS

Tychicus will tell you all the news about me. He is a dear brother, a faithful minister and fellow servant in the Lord. I am sending him to you for the express purpose that you may know about our[a] circumstances and that he may encourage your hearts. He is coming with Onesimus, our faithful and dear brother, who is one of you. They will tell you everything that is happening here.

My fellow prisoner Aristarchus sends you his greetings, as does Mark, the cousin of Barnabas. (You have received instructions about him; if he comes to you, welcome him.) Jesus, who is called Justus, also sends greetings. These are the only Jews among my fellow workers for the kingdom of God, and they have proved a comfort to me. Epaphras, who is one of you and a servant of Christ Jesus, sends greetings. He is always wrestling in prayer for you, that you may stand firm in all the will of God, mature and fully assured. I vouch for him that he is working hard for you and for those at Laodicea and Hierapolis. Our dear friend Luke, the doctor, and Demas send greetings. Give my greetings to the brothers at Laodicea, and to Nympha and the church in her house.

After this letter has been read to you, see that it is also read in the church of the Laodiceans and that you in turn read the letter from Laodicea.

Tell Archippus: "See to it that you complete the work you have received in the Lord."

I, Paul, write this greeting in my own hand. Remember my chains. Grace be with you.

> *"Devote yourselves to prayer,*
> *being watchful and thankful. And pray for us, too,*
> *that God may open a door for our message,*
> *so that we may proclaim the mystery of Christ."*

FROM OSWALD CHAMBERS

❧ If we look only for results in the earthlies when we pray, we are ill-taught. A praying saint performs far more havoc among the unseen forces of darkness than we have the slightest notion of. "The effectual fervent prayer of a righteous man availeth much" (James 5:16). BP 159

❧ Pray for your friends, and God will turn your captivity also. The emancipation comes as you intercede for them; it is not a mere reaction—it is the way God works. BFB 109

❧ Intercessory prayer is part of the sovereign purpose of God. If there were no saints praying for us, our lives would be infinitely balder than they are; consequently, the responsibility of those who never intercede and who are withholding blessing from other lives is truly appalling. CD VOL. 2, 57

❧ Jesus Christ carries on intercession for us in heaven; the Holy Ghost carries on intercession in us on earth; and we the saints have to carry on intercession for all men. CD VOL. 2, 60

❧ Intercession does not develop the one who intercedes; it blesses the lives of those for whom he interecedes. The reason so few of us intercede is because we don't understand this. DI 41

❧ By intercessory prayer we can hold off Satan from other lives and give the Holy Ghost a chance with them. No wonder Jesus put such tremendous emphasis on prayer! DI 41

❧ Intercessory prayer is the test of our loyalty. GW 61

❧ When we pray for others, the Spirit of God works in the unconscious domain of their being that we know nothing about, and the one we are praying for knows nothing about; but after the passing of time, the conscious life of the one prayed for begins to show signs of unrest and disquiet. We may have spoken until we are worn out, but have never come anywhere near, and we have given up in despair. But if we have been praying, we find on meeting them one day that there is the beginning of a softening in an enquiry and a desire to know something. It is that kind of intercession that does most damage to Satan's kingdom. It is so slight, so feeble in its initial stages that if reason is not wedded to the light of the Holy Spirit, we will never obey it, and yet it is that kind of intercession that the New Testament places most emphasis on, though it has so little to show for it. It seems stupid to think that we can pray and all that will happen, but remember to whom we pray; we pray to a God who understands the unconscious depths of a personality about which we know nothing, and He has told us to pray. The great Master of the human heart said, "Greater works than these shall ye do. . . . And whatsoever ye shall ask in My name, that will I do" (John 14:12; Matt. 21:22) IYA 94

❧ There is only one field of service that has no snares, and that is the field of intercession. All other fields have the glorious but risky snare of publicity; prayer has not. IYA 96

---

a. Some manuscripts *that he may know about your*

56

THANKSGIVING FOR
THE THESSALONIANS' FAITH

Paul, Silas[a] and Timothy,
To the church of the Thessalonians in God the Father and the Lord Jesus Christ:
Grace and peace to you.[b]
We always thank God for all of you, mentioning you in our prayers. We continually remember before our God and Father your work produced by faith, your labor prompted by love, and your endurance inspired by hope in our Lord Jesus Christ.

For we know, brothers loved by God, that he has chosen you, because our gospel came to you not simply with words, but also with power, with the Holy Spirit and with deep conviction. You know how we lived among you for your sake. You became imitators of us and of the Lord; in spite of severe suffering, you welcomed the message with the joy given by the Holy Spirit. And so you became a model to all the believers in Macedonia and Achaia. The Lord's message rang out from you not only in Macedonia and Achaia—your faith in God has become known everywhere. Therefore we do not need to say anything about it, for they themselves report what kind of reception you gave us. They tell how you turned to God from idols to serve the living and true God, and to wait for his Son from heaven, whom he raised from the dead—Jesus, who rescues us from the coming wrath.

PAUL'S MINISTRY IN THESSALONICA

You know, brothers, that our visit to you was not a failure. We had previously suffered and been insulted in Philippi, as you

231

know, but with the help of our God we dared to tell you his gospel in spite of strong opposition. For the appeal we make does not spring from error or impure motives, nor are we trying to trick you. On the contrary, we speak as men approved by God to be entrusted with the gospel. We are not trying to please men but God, who tests our hearts. You know we never used flattery, nor did we put on a mask to cover up greed—God is our witness. We were not looking for praise from men, not from you or anyone else.

As apostles of Christ we could have been a burden to you, but we were gentle among you, like a mother caring for her little children. We loved you so much that we were delighted to share with you not only the gospel of God but our lives as well, because you had become so dear to us. Surely you remember, brothers, our toil and hardship; we worked night and day in order not to be a burden to anyone while we preached the gospel of God to you.

You are witnesses, and so is God, of how holy, righteous and blameless we were among you who believed. For you know that we dealt with each of you as a father deals with his own children, encouraging, comforting and urging you to live lives worthy of God, who calls you into his kingdom and glory.

And we also thank God continually because, when you received the word of God, which you heard from us, you accepted it not as the word of men, but as it actually is, the word of God, which is at work in you who believe. For you, brothers, became imitators of God's churches in Judea, which are in Christ Jesus: You suffered from your own countrymen the same things those churches suffered from the Jews, who killed the Lord Jesus and the prophets and also drove us out. They displease God and are hostile to all men in their effort to keep us from speaking to the Gentiles so that they may be saved. In this way they always heap up their sins to the limit. The wrath of God has come upon them at last.[c]

PAUL'S LONGING TO SEE THE THESSALONIANS

But, brothers, when we were torn away from you for a short time (in person, not in thought), out of our intense longing we made every effort to see you. For we wanted to come to you—certainly

I, Paul, did, again and again—but Satan stopped us. For what is our hope, our joy, or the crown in which we will glory in the presence of our Lord Jesus when he comes? Is it not you? Indeed, you are our glory and joy.

"When you received the word of God . . .
you accepted it not as the word of men, but as it actually is,
the word of God, which is at work in you who believe."

FROM OSWALD CHAMBERS

- When immediately a man becomes spiritual by being born from above, the Bible becomes his authority, because he discerns a law in his conscience that has no objective resting place save in the Bible; and when the Bible is quoted, instantly his intuition says, "Yes, that must be the truth"; not because the Bible says so, but because he discerns what the Bible says to be the Word of God for him. AUG 16

- The Bible is a world of revelation facts, and when you explain the Bible, take into account all the record of it. The Bible nowhere says we have to believe it is the Word of God before we can be Christians. The Bible is not the Word of God to me unless I come at it through what Jesus Christ says; it is of no use to me unless I know Him. AUG 79

- When a man's heart is right with God the mysterious utterances of the Bible are "spirit and life" to him. BSG 42

- The only way to understand the Scriptures is not to accept them blindly, but to read them in the light of a personal relationship to Jesus Christ. BFB 91

- If the Bible agreed with modern science, it would soon be out of date, because, in the very nature of things, modern science is bound to change. BP 5

- The epistles are not the cogitations of men of extraordinary spiritual genius, but the posthumous work of the ascended Christ, and they have therefore a peculiar significance in the program of redemption. The Holy Ghost used these men, with all their personal idiosyncrasies, to convey God's message of salvation to the world. Our Lord, so to speak, incarnated Himself in them—the message of God must always be incarnated, but it remains the message *of God*. CHI 34

❧ Beware of reasoning about God's Word, obey it. DI 9

❧ To use the New Testament as a book of proof is nonsense. If you do not believe that Jesus Christ is the Son of God, the New Testament will not convince you that He is; if you do not believe in the Resurrection, the New Testament will not convince you of it. The New Testament is written for those who do not need convincing. HGM 35

❧ The Bible is not the word of God to us unless we come to it through what Jesus Christ says. The Scriptures, from Genesis to Revelation, are all revelations of Jesus Christ. The context of the Bible is our Lord Himself, and until we are rightly related to Him, the Bible is no more to us than an ordinary book. OBH 127

❧ A remarkable thing about this Book of God is that for every type of human being we come across there is a distinct, clear line laid down here as to the way to apply God's truth to it. The stupid soul, the stubborn soul, the soul that is mentally diseased, the soul that is convicted of sin, the soul with the twisted mind, the sensual soul—every one of the facts that you meet in your daily walk and business has its counterpart here, and God has a word and a revelation fact with regard to every life you come across. WG 13

---

a. Greek *Silvanus,* a variant of *Silas*
b. Some early manuscripts *you from God our Father and the Lord Jesus Christ*
c. Or *them fully*

57

1 THESSALONIANS 3

TIMOTHY'S ENCOURAGING REPORT

So when we could stand it no longer, we thought it best to be left by ourselves in Athens. We sent Timothy, who is our brother and God's fellow worker[a] in spreading the gospel of Christ, to strengthen and encourage you in your faith, so that no one would be unsettled by these trials. You know quite well that we were destined for them. In fact, when we were with you, we kept telling you that we would be persecuted. And it turned out that way, as you well know. For this reason, when I could stand it no longer, I sent to find out about your faith. I was afraid that in some way the tempter might have tempted you and our efforts might have been useless.

But Timothy has just now come to us from you and has brought good news about your faith and love. He has told us that you always have pleasant memories of us and that you long to see us, just as we also long to see you. Therefore, brothers, in all our distress and persecution we were encouraged about you because of your faith. For now we really live, since you are standing firm in the Lord. How can we thank God enough for you in return for all the joy we have in the presence of our God because of you? Night and day we pray most earnestly that we may see you again and supply what is lacking in your faith.

Now may our God and Father himself and our Lord Jesus clear the way for us to come to you. May the Lord make your love increase and overflow for each other and for everyone else, just as ours does for you. May he strengthen your hearts so that you will be blameless and holy in the presence of our God and Father when our Lord Jesus comes with all his holy ones.

"May [the Lord] strengthen your hearts
so that you will be blameless and holy
in the presence of our God and Father
when our Lord Jesus comes with all his holy ones."

From Oswald Chambers

❧ We never can be faultless in this life, but God's Book brings out that we must be blameless, that is, undeserving of censure from God's standpoint, and remember what His standpoint is. He can see into every crook and cranny of my spirit and soul and body, and He demands that I be blameless in all my relationships so that He Himself can see nothing worthy of censure. The revelation is one which shows the supernaturalness of the work of sanctification. It cannot be done by praying, by devoting myself, by believing; it can only be done by the supernatural power of a supernatural God. LG 137

❧ We never can be faultless in this life, for we are in impaired human bodies; but by sanctification we can be blameless. Our disposition can be supernaturally altered until in the simplicity of life before God the whole limit is holy, and if that is to be done, it must be by the great grace of God. LG 138

❧ If we are sanctified by the power of the God of peace, our self life is blameless before Him. There is nothing to hide, and the more we bring our soul under the searchlight of God, the more we realize the ineffable comfort of the supernatural work He has done. LG 139

❧ Can God keep me from stumbling this second? Yes. Can He keep me from sin this second? Yes. Well, that is the whole of life; you cannot live more than a second at a time. If God can keep you blameless this second, He can do it the next. No wonder Jesus Christ said, "Let not your heart be troubled" (John 14:1). We do get troubled when we do not remember the amazing power of God. LG 144

---

a. Some manuscripts *brother and fellow worker;* other manuscripts *brother and God's servant*

58

1 THESSALONIANS 4

LIVING TO PLEASE GOD

Finally, brothers, we instructed you how to live in order to please God, as in fact you are living. Now we ask you and urge you in the Lord Jesus to do this more and more. For you know what instructions we gave you by the authority of the Lord Jesus.

It is God's will that you should be sanctified: that you should avoid sexual immorality; that each of you should learn to control his own body[a] in a way that is holy and honorable, not in passionate lust like the heathen, who do not know God; and that in this matter no one should wrong his brother or take advantage of him. The Lord will punish men for all such sins, as we have already told you and warned you. For God did not call us to be impure, but to live a holy life. Therefore, he who rejects this instruction does not reject man but God, who gives you his Holy Spirit.

Now about brotherly love we do not need to write to you, for you yourselves have been taught by God to love each other. And in fact, you do love all the brothers throughout Macedonia. Yet we urge you, brothers, to do so more and more.

Make it your ambition to lead a quiet life, to mind your own business and to work with your hands, just as we told you, so that your daily life may win the respect of outsiders and so that you will not be dependent on anybody.

THE COMING OF THE LORD

Brothers, we do not want you to be ignorant about those who fall asleep, or to grieve like the rest of men, who have no hope. We believe that Jesus died and rose again and so we believe that

God will bring with Jesus those who have fallen asleep in him. According to the Lord's own word, we tell you that we who are still alive, who are left till the coming of the Lord, will certainly not precede those who have fallen asleep. For the Lord himself will come down from heaven, with a loud command, with the voice of the archangel and with the trumpet call of God, and the dead in Christ will rise first. After that, we who are still alive and are left will be caught up together with them in the clouds to meet the Lord in the air. And so we will be with the Lord forever. Therefore encourage each other with these words.

"God did not call us to be impure,
but to live a holy life.
Therefore, he who rejects this instruction does not reject
man but God, who gives you his Holy Spirit."

FROM OSWALD CHAMBERS

ᕶ The purity God demands is impossible unless we can be remade from within, and that is what Jesus Christ undertakes to do through the Atonement. BE 10

ᕶ He will keep your heart so pure that you would tremble with amazement if you knew how pure the Atonement of the Lord Jesus can make the vilest human heart, if we will but keep in the light, as God is in the light. BP 124

ᕶ "Blessed are the pure in heart," literally, 'Blessed are the God in heart,' i.e. in whom the nature of God is. HG 115

ᕶ The possiblity of being impure means that there is some value to Jesus Christ in our being pure. God gives us His supernatural life, but we have to keep entirely free from the world with a purity which is of value to God; we have to grow in purity. LG 72

ᕶ Purity is not innocence; it is much more. Purity means stainlessness, an unblemishedness that has stood the test. Purity is learned in private, never in public. Jesus Christ demands purity of mind and imagination, chastity of bodily and mental habits. The only men and women it is safe to trust are those who have been tried and have stood the test; purity is the outcome of conflict, not of necessity. MFL 88

238

❧ What do we mean by "pure in heart"? We mean nothing less and nothing else than what the Son of God was and is. When God raises us up into the heavenly places, He imparts to us the very purity that is Jesus Christ's. That is what the sanctified life means— the undisturbable range of His peace, the unshakable, indefatigable power of His strength, and the unfathomable, crystalline purity of His holiness. There is plenty of room in the heavenly places to grow into the realization of the unfathomable depths of the purity of Christ's heart. OBH 36

❧ Purity is not a question of doing things rightly, but of the doer on the inside being right. SSM 26

❧ Jesus Christ demands that the heart of a disciple be fathomlessly pure, and unless He can give me His disposition, His teaching is tantalizing. If all He came to do was to mock me by telling me to be what I know I never can be, I can afford to ignore Him; but if He can give me His own disposition of holiness, then I begin to see how I can lay my account with purity. SSM 27

---

a. Or *learn to live with his own wife;* or *learn to acquire a wife*

59

BE READY FOR THE LORD'S COMING

ow, brothers, about times and dates we do not need to write to you, for you know very well that the day of the Lord will come like a thief in the night. While people are saying, "Peace and safety," destruction will come on them suddenly, as labor pains on a pregnant woman, and they will not escape.

But you, brothers, are not in darkness so that this day should surprise you like a thief. You are all sons of the light and sons of the day. We do not belong to the night or to the darkness. So then, let us not be like others, who are asleep, but let us be alert and self-controlled. For those who sleep, sleep at night, and those who get drunk, get drunk at night. But since we belong to the day, let us be self-controlled, putting on faith and love as a breastplate, and the hope of salvation as a helmet. For God did not appoint us to suffer wrath but to receive salvation through our Lord Jesus Christ. He died for us so that, whether we are awake or asleep, we may live together with him. Therefore encourage one another and build each other up, just as in fact you are doing.

FINAL INSTRUCTIONS

Now we ask you, brothers, to respect those who work hard among you, who are over you in the Lord and who admonish you. Hold them in the highest regard in love because of their work. Live in peace with each other. And we urge you, brothers, warn those who are idle, encourage the timid, help the weak, be patient with everyone. Make sure that nobody pays back wrong for wrong, but always try to be kind to each other and to everyone else.

Be joyful always; pray continually; give thanks in all circumstances, for this is God's will for you in Christ Jesus.

Do not put out the Spirit's fire; do not treat prophecies with contempt. Test everything. Hold on to the good. Avoid every kind of evil.

May God himself, the God of peace, sanctify you through and through. May your whole spirit, soul and body be kept blameless at the coming of our Lord Jesus Christ. The one who calls you is faithful and he will do it.

Brothers, pray for us. Greet all the brothers with a holy kiss. I charge you before the Lord to have this letter read to all the brothers.

The grace of our Lord Jesus Christ be with you.

> *"Be joyful always; pray continually;*
> *give thanks in all circumstances,*
> *for this is God's will for you in Christ Jesus."*

FROM OSWALD CHAMBERS

⁊ It is never the big things that disturb us but the trivial things. Do I believe in the circumstances that are apt to bother me just now, that Jesus Christ is not perplexed at all? If I do, His peace is mine. If I try to worry it out, I obliterate Him and deserve what I get. CD VOL. 1, 153

⁊ When we know that nothing can separate us from the love of Christ, it does not matter what calamities may occur; we are as unshakable as God's throne. CD VOL. 1, 157

⁊ That God engineers our circumstances for us if we accept His purpose in Christ Jesus is a thought of great practical moment. CD VOL. 2, 55

⁊ We are not responsible for the circumstances we are in, but we are responsible for the way we allow those circumstances to affect us; we can either allow them to get on top of us, or we can allow them to transform us into what God wants us to be. CHI 40

⁊ God will bring us into circumstances and make us learn the particular lessons He wants us to learn, and slowly and surely we will work out all that He works in. CHI 55

≫ God engineers circumstances to see what we will do. HG 16

≫ The things we are going through are either making us sweeter, better, nobler men and women, or they are making us more captious and fault-fainding, more insistent on our own way. We are either getting more like our Father in heaven, or we are getting more mean and intensely selfish. IYA 55

≫ The circumstances of a saint's life are ordained by God, and not by happy-go-lucky chance. IYA 107

≫ A Christian is one who can live in the midst of the trouble and turmoil with the glory of God indwelling him, while he steadfastly looks not at the things which are seen, but at the things which are not seen. We have to learn to think only of things which are seen as a glorious chance of enabling us to concentrate on the things which are not seen. LG 89

≫ If you are a child of God and there is some part of your circumstances which is tearing you, if you are living in the heavenly places, you will thank God for the tearing things. If you are not in the heavenly places, you cry to God over and over again—"O Lord, remove this thing from me. If only I could live in golden streets and be surrounded with angels, and have the Spirit of God consciously indwelling me all the time and have everything wonderfully sweet, then I think I might be a Christian." That is not being a Christian! LG 89

≫ No matter what your circumstances may be, don't try to shield yourself from things God is bringing into your life. We have the idea sometimes that we ought to shield ourselves from some of the circumstances God brings round us. Never! God engineers circumstances; we have to see that we face them abiding continually with Him in His temptations. They are His temptations, they are not temptations to us, but to the Son of God in us. LG 156

60

2 THESSALONIANS 1–2:12

FAITH IN PERSECUTIONS

aul, Silas[a] and Timothy, To the church of the Thessalonians in God our Father and the Lord Jesus Christ: Grace and peace to you from God the Father and the Lord Jesus Christ.

THANKSGIVING AND PRAYER

We ought always to thank God for you, brothers, and rightly so, because your faith is growing more and more, and the love every one of you has for each other is increasing. Therefore, among God's churches we boast about your perseverance and faith in all the persecutions and trials you are enduring.

All this is evidence that God's judgment is right, and as a result you will be counted worthy of the kingdom of God, for which you are suffering. God is just: He will pay back trouble to those who trouble you and give relief to you who are troubled, and to us as well. This will happen when the Lord Jesus is revealed from heaven in blazing fire with his powerful angels. He will punish those who do not know God and do not obey the gospel of our Lord Jesus. They will be punished with everlasting destruction and shut out from the presence of the Lord and from the majesty of his power on the day he comes to be glorified in his holy people and to be marveled at among all those who have believed. This includes you, because you believed our testimony to you.

With this in mind, we constantly pray for you, that our God may count you worthy of his calling, and that by his power he may fulfill every good purpose of yours and every act prompted by your faith. We pray this so that the name of our Lord Jesus may be glorified in you, and you in him, according to the grace of our God and the Lord Jesus Christ.[b]

THE MAN OF LAWLESSNESS

Concerning the coming of our Lord Jesus Christ and our being gathered to him, we ask you, brothers, not to become easily unsettled or alarmed by some prophecy, report or letter supposed to have come from us, saying that the day of the Lord has already come. Don't let anyone deceive you in any way, for [that day will not come] until the rebellion occurs and the man of lawlessness[c] is revealed, the man doomed to destruction. He will oppose and will exalt himself over everything that is called God or is worshiped, so that he sets himself up in God's temple, proclaiming himself to be God.

Don't you remember that when I was with you I used to tell you these things? And now you know what is holding him back, so that he may be revealed at the proper time. For the secret power of lawlessness is already at work; but the one who now holds it back will continue to do so till he is taken out of the way. And then the lawless one will be revealed, whom the Lord Jesus will overthrow with the breath of his mouth and destroy by the splendor of his coming. The coming of the lawless one will be in accordance with the work of Satan displayed in all kinds of counterfeit miracles, signs and wonders, and in every sort of evil that deceives those who are perishing. They perish because they refused to love the truth and so be saved. For this reason God sends them a powerful delusion so that they will believe the lie and so that all will be condemned who have not believed the truth but have delighted in wickedness.

"Your faith is growing more and more . . .
[and] we boast about your perseverance and faith
in all the persecutions and trials you are enduring."

From Oswald Chambers

   God's Book reveals all through that holiness will bring persecution from those who are not holy. PS 80

❧ Persecution is not only met with at the threshold, it increases as we go on in the Christian life. A man may get through persecution from his own crowd, but when it comes to persecution from principalities and powers, that is a domain he knows nothing about. SHL 15

❧ Jesus Christ not only warned that persecution would come, He went further and said that it was profitable to go through persecution. "Blessed are ye, when men shall . . . persecute you" (Matt. 5:11). The way the world treats me is the exhibition of my inner disposition. "Whosoever maketh himself a friend of the world is the enemy of God." SHL 16

❧ To have brickbats and rotten eggs flung at you is not persecution; it simply makes you feel good and does you no harm at all. But when your own crowd cuts you dead and systematically vexes you, then says Jesus, "Count it all joy." "Blessed are ye when men shall hate you, and when they shall separate you from their company, and shall reproach you, and cast out your name as evil, *for the Son of man's sake"* (Luke 6:22) – not for the sake of some crotchety notion of our own. SHL 16

❧ Persecution is systematic vexation. It does not leave you alone, it is something that throngs you; but to be boycotted means to be left alone, destitute of the comrades you used to have – "They think it strange that ye run not with them to the same excess of riot, speaking evil of you" (1 Peter 4:4). But they don't know that you carry a wonderful kingdom within, a kingdom full of light and peace and joy no matter how destitute and alone you may be on the outside. That is the wonderful work of the Lord in a man's soul. "Rejoice in that day, and leap for joy" (Luke 6:23). SHL 21

❧ Huge waves that would frighten an ordinary swimmer produce a tremendous thrill for the surfer who has ridden them. Let's apply that to our own circumstances. The things we try to avoid and fight against – tribulation, suffering, and persecution – are the very things that produce abundant joy in us. "We are more than conquerors through Him" . . . *"in* all these things" (Rom. 8:37); not in spite of them, but in the midst of them. A saint doesn't know the joy of the Lord in spite of tribulation, but *because* of it. Paul said,

a. Greek *Silvanus,* a variant of *Silas*
b. Or *God and Lord, Jesus Christ*
c. Some manuscripts *sin*

61

2 THESSALONIANS 2:13–3

STAND FIRM

But we ought always to thank God for you, brothers loved by the Lord, because from the beginning God chose you[a] to be saved through the sanctifying work of the Spirit and through belief in the truth. He called you to this through our gospel, that you might share in the glory of our Lord Jesus Christ. So then, brothers, stand firm and hold to the teachings[b] we passed on to you, whether by word of mouth or by letter.

May our Lord Jesus Christ himself and God our Father, who loved us and by his grace gave us eternal encouragement and good hope, encourage your hearts and strengthen you in every good deed and word.

REQUEST FOR PRAYER

Finally, brothers, pray for us that the message of the Lord may spread rapidly and be honored, just as it was with you. And pray that we may be delivered from wicked and evil men, for not everyone has faith. But the Lord is faithful, and he will strengthen and protect you from the evil one. We have confidence in the Lord that you are doing and will continue to do the things we command. May the Lord direct your hearts into God's love and Christ's perseverance.

WARNING AGAINST IDLENESS

In the name of the Lord Jesus Christ, we command you, brothers, to keep away from every brother who is idle and does not live according to the teaching[c] you received from us. For you yourselves know how you ought to follow our example. We were not idle when we were with you, nor did we eat anyone's food without paying for it. On the contrary, we worked night and day, laboring and toiling so that we would not be a burden to any of you. We did this, not because we do not have the right to such help, but in order to make ourselves a model for you to follow. For even when we were with you, we gave you this rule: "If a man will not work, he shall not eat."

We hear that some among you are idle. They are not busy; they are busybodies. Such people we command and urge in the Lord Jesus Christ to settle down and earn the bread they eat. And as for you, brothers, never tire of doing what is right.

If anyone does not obey our instruction in this letter, take special note of him. Do not associate with him, in order that he may feel ashamed. Yet do not regard him as an enemy, but warn him as a brother.

FINAL GREETINGS

Now may the Lord of peace himself give you peace at all times and in every way. The Lord be with all of you.

I, Paul, write this greeting in my own hand, which is the distinguishing mark in all my letters. This is how I write.

The grace of our Lord Jesus Christ be with you all.

"Never tire of doing what is right."

FROM OSWALD CHAMBERS

⌘ God's "ought's" never alter; we never grow out of them. Our difficulty is that we find in ourselves this attitude—"I ought to do this, but I won't"; "I ought to do that, but I don't want to." That puts out of court the idea that if you teach men what is right, they will do it—they won't; what is needed is a power which will enable a man to do what he knows is right. BE 8

⌘ If you remain true to your relationship to Jesus Christ, the things that are either right or wrong are never the problem; it is the things that are right but which would impair what He wants you to be that are the problem. DI 35

248

⁊ If I try to be right, it is a sure sign I am wrong; the only way to be right is by stopping the humbug of trying to be and remaining steadfast in faith in Jesus Christ. "He that doeth righteousness is righteous, even as He is righteous" (1 John 3:7). GW 46

⁊ If I am a child of God, distress will lead me to Him for direction. The distress comes not because I have done wrong; it is part of the inevitable result of not being at home in the world, of being in contact with those who reason and live from a different standpoint. HG 8

⁊ Judge everything in the light of Jesus Christ, who is the Truth, and you will never do the wrong thing however right it looks. OPG 28

⁊ We must be right ourselves before we can help others to be right. PH 79

⁊ "Except your righteousness shall exceed the righteousness of the scribes and Pharisees" (Matt. 4:20) — not be different from but "exceed," that is, we have to be all they are and infinitely more! We have to be right in our external behavior, but we have to be as right, and "righter" in our internal behavior. We have to be right in our words and actions, but we have to be right in our thoughts and feelings. RTR 59

⁊ No man can do wrong in his heart and see right afterward. If I am going to approach the holy ground, I must get into the right frame of mind — the excellency of a broken heart. SA 13

⁊ If you stand true to the purity of Christ, you will have to meet problems connected with the margins of your bodily life, and if you turn for one second in public or in secret from walking in the light as God is in the light, you will lose the distinction between absolute right and wrong and make the word affinity an excuse to further orders. Test every emotional affinity in this way — If I let this thing have its way, what will it mean? If you can see the end of it to be wrong, grip it on the threshold of your mind, and at the peril of your soul never let it encroach again upon your attention.

Whenever you meet with difficulties, whether they are intellectual or circumstantial or physical, remain loyal to God. Don't compromise. If you do, everyone around you will suffer from your faithlessness, because you are disloyal to Jesus Christ and His way of looking at things. Never run away with the idea that you can ever do a thing or have an attitude of mind before God which no one else need know anything about. A man is what he is in the dark. Remain loyal to God and to His saints in private and in public, and you will find that not only are you continually with God, but that God is counting on you. PH 75

---

a. Some manuscripts *because God chose you as his firstfruits*
b. Or *traditions*
c. Or *tradition*

WARNING AGAINST FALSE TEACHERS OF THE LAW

aul, an apostle of Christ Jesus by the command of God our Savior and Christ Jesus our hope,
To Timothy my true son in the faith:
Grace, mercy and peace from God the Father and Christ Jesus our Lord.

As I urged you when I went into Macedonia, stay there in Ephesus so that you may command certain men not to teach false doctrines any longer nor to devote themselves to myths and endless genealogies. These promote controversies rather than God's work—which is by faith. The goal of this command is love, which comes from a pure heart and a good conscience and a sincere faith. Some have wandered away from these and turned to meaningless talk. They want to be teachers of the law, but they do not know what they are talking about or what they so confidently affirm.

We know that the law is good if one uses it properly. We also know that law[a] is made not for the righteous but for lawbreakers and rebels, the ungodly and sinful, the unholy and irreligious; for those who kill their fathers or mothers, for murderers, for adulterers and perverts, for slave traders and liars and perjurers— and for whatever else is contrary to the sound doctrine that conforms to the glorious gospel of the blessed God, which he entrusted to me.

THE LORD'S GRACE TO PAUL

I thank Christ Jesus our Lord, who has given me strength, that he considered me faithful, appointing me to his service. Even though I was once a blasphemer and a persecutor and a violent man, I was shown mercy because I acted in ignorance and unbelief. The grace of our Lord was poured out on me abundantly, along with the faith and love that are in Christ Jesus.

Here is a trustworthy saying that deserves full acceptance: Christ Jesus came into the world to save sinners — of whom I am the worst. But for that very reason I was shown mercy so that in me, the worst of sinners, Christ Jesus might display his unlimited patience as an example for those who would believe on him and receive eternal life. Now to the King eternal, immortal, invisible, the only God, be honor and glory for ever and ever. Amen.

Timothy, my son, I give you this instruction in keeping with the prophecies once made about you, so that by following them you may fight the good fight, holding on to faith and a good conscience. Some have rejected these and so have shipwrecked their faith. Among them are Hymenaeus and Alexander, whom I have handed over to Satan to be taught not to blaspheme.

INSTRUCTIONS ON WORSHIP

I urge, then, first of all, that requests, prayers, intercession and thanksgiving be made for everyone — for kings and all those in authority, that we may live peaceful and quiet lives in all godliness and holiness. This is good, and pleases God our Savior, who wants all men to be saved and to come to a knowledge of the truth. For there is one God and one mediator between God and men, the man Christ Jesus, who gave himself as a ransom for all men — the testimony given in its proper time. And for this purpose I was appointed a herald and an apostle — I am telling the truth, I am not lying — and a teacher of the true faith to the Gentiles.

I want men everywhere to lift up holy hands in prayer, without anger or disputing.

I also want women to dress modestly, with decency and propriety, not with braided hair or gold or pearls or expensive clothes, but with good deeds, appropriate for women who profess to worship God.

A woman should learn in quietness and full submission. I do not permit a woman to teach or to have authority over a man; she must be silent. For Adam was formed first, then Eve. And

Adam was not the one deceived; it was the woman who was deceived and became a sinner. But women[b] will be saved[c] through childbearing—if they continue in faith, love and holiness with propriety.

"Christ Jesus came into the world to save sinners —
of whom I am the worst."

FROM OSWALD CHAMBERS

⁊ God made His own Son to be sin that He might make the sinner a saint. The Bible reveals all through that Jesus Christ bore the sin of the world by *identification,* not by sympathy. He deliberately took upon Himself and bore in His own person the whole massed sin of the human race, and by so doing He rehabilitated the human race, that is, put it back to where God designed it to be, and anyone can enter into union with God on the ground of what our Lord did on the cross. AUG 71

⁊ Sin is not measured by a creed or a constitution or a society, but by a person. AUG 106

⁊ The New Testament says Jesus became literally identified with the sin of the human race. "Him who knew no sin" (here language almost fails) "He made Him to be sin for us for one purpose only— "that we might become the righteousness of God in Him" (2 Cor. 5:21). BSG 26

⁊ What our Lord Jesus Christ wants us to present to Him is not our goodness, or our honesty, or our endeavor, but our real solid sin; that is all He can take. "For He hath made Him to be sin for us, who knew no sin" (2 Cor. 5:21). And what does He give in exchange for our solid sin? Great solid righteousness—"that we might be made the righteousness of God in Him"; but we must relinquish all pretence of being anything; we must relinquish in every way all claim to being worthy of God's consideration. That is the meaning of conviction of sin. CD VOL. 1, 129

⁊ Sin is a revelation fact, not a commonsense fact. No natural man is ever bothered about sin; it is the saint, not the sinner, who knows what sin is. If you confound *sin* with *sins,* you belittle the redemption, make it "much ado about nothing." It is nonsense to talk

253

about the need of redemption to enable a man to stop committing sins—his own will power enables him to do that; a decent education will prevent him from breaking out into sinful acts. But to deny that there is *a heredity of sin* running straight through the human race aims a blasphemous blow at the redemption. The only word that expresses the enormity of sin is "Calvary." CHI 16

ॐ Measure your growth in grace by your sensitiveness to sin. DI 65

ॐ This is the greatest revelation that ever struck the human life, viz., that God loves the sinner. God so loved the world when it was sinful that He sent His Son to die for it. Our Lord has no illusions about any of us. He sees every man and woman as the descendants of Adam who sinned, and with capacities in our hearts of which we have no idea. PH 54

ॐ In our mental outlook, we have to reconcile ourselves to the fact that sin is the only explanation as to why Jesus Christ came, the only explanation of the grief and the sorrow that there is in life. There may be a great deal that is pathetic in a man's condition, but there is also a lot that is bad and wrong. There is the downright spiteful thing, as wrong as wrong can be, without a strand of good in it, in you and in me and in other people by nature, and we have to reconcile ourselves to the fact that there *is* sin. That does not mean that we compromise with sin; it means that we face the fact that it is there. PH 189

ॐ The revelation in the Bible is not that Jesus Christ was punished for our sins; but that He took on Him the sin of the human race and put it away—an infinitely profounder revelation. PH 49

ॐ Jesus Christ came to save us so that there should be no "sinner" left in us. PS 25

---

a. Or *that the law*
b. Greek *she*
c. Or *restored*

63

1 TIMOTHY 3–4

OVERSEERS AND DEACONS

Here is a trustworthy saying: If anyone sets his heart on being an overseer,[a] he desires a noble task. Now the overseer must be above reproach, the husband of but one wife, temperate, self-controlled, respectable, hospitable, able to teach, not given to drunkenness, not violent but gentle, not quarrelsome, not a lover of money. He must manage his own family well and see that his children obey him with proper respect. (If anyone does not know how to manage his own family, how can he take care of God's church?) He must not be a recent convert, or he may become conceited and fall under the same judgment as the devil. He must also have a good reputation with outsiders, so that he will not fall into disgrace and into the devil's trap.

Deacons, likewise, are to be men worthy of respect, sincere, not indulging in much wine, and not pursuing dishonest gain. They must keep hold of the deep truths of the faith with a clear conscience. They must first be tested; and then if there is nothing against them, let them serve as deacons.

In the same way, their wives[b] are to be women worthy of respect, not malicious talkers but temperate and trustworthy in everything.

A deacon must be the husband of but one wife and must manage his children and his household well. Those who have served well gain an excellent standing and great assurance in their faith in Christ Jesus.

Although I hope to come to you soon, I am writing you these instructions so that, if I am delayed, you will know how people ought to conduct themselves in God's household, which is the church of the living God, the pillar and foundation of the truth. Beyond all question, the mystery of godliness is great:

He[c] appeared in a body,[d]
was vindicated by the Spirit,
was seen by angels,
was preached among the nations,
was believed on in the world,
was taken up in glory.

INSTRUCTIONS TO TIMOTHY

The Spirit clearly says that in later times some will abandon the faith and follow deceiving spirits and things taught by demons. Such teachings come through hypocritical liars, whose consciences have been seared as with a hot iron. They forbid people to marry and order them to abstain from certain foods, which God created to be received with thanksgiving by those who believe and who know the truth. For everything God created is good, and nothing is to be rejected if it is received with thanksgiving, because it is consecrated by the word of God and prayer.

If you point these things out to the brothers, you will be a good minister of Christ Jesus, brought up in the truths of the faith and of the good teaching that you have followed. Have nothing to do with godless myths and old wives' tales; rather, train yourself to be godly. For physical training is of some value, but godliness has value for all things, holding promise for both the present life and the life to come.

This is a trustworthy saying that deserves full acceptance (and for this we labor and strive), that we have put our hope in the living God, who is the Savior of all men, and especially of those who believe.

Command and teach these things. Don't let anyone look down on you because you are young, but set an example for the believers in speech, in life, in love, in faith and in purity. Until I come, devote yourself to the public reading of Scripture, to preaching and to teaching. Do not neglect your gift, which was given you through a prophetic message when the body of elders laid their hands on you.

Be diligent in these matters; give yourself wholly to them, so that everyone may see your progress. Watch your life and doctrine closely. Persevere in them, because if you do, you will save both yourself and your hearers.

*"Set an example for the believers in speech,
in life, in love, in faith and in purity."*

FROM OSWALD CHAMBERS

ᔍ It is a great thing to be a believer but easy to misunderstand what the New Testament means by it. It is not that we believe Jesus Christ can *do* things, or that we believe in a plan of salvation; it is that we believe *Him;* whatever happens we will hang on to the fact that He is true. If we say, "I am going to believe He will put things right," we shall lose our confidence when we see things go wrong. AUG 114

ᔍ The problems of life get hold of a man and make it difficult for him to know whether in the face of these things he really is confident in Jesus Christ. The attitude of a believer must be, "Things do look black, but I believe Him; and when the whole thing is told I am confident my belief will be justified and God will be revealed as a God of love and justice." It does not mean that we won't have problems, but it does mean that our problems will never come in between us and our faith in Him. AUG 114

ᔍ To be "a believer in Jesus Christ" means we are committed to His way of looking at everything, not that we are open to discuss what people say He taught; that is the way difficulties have arisen with regard to Christian faith. AUG 116

ᔍ I have no right to say I believe in God unless I order my life as under His all-seeing eye. DI 1

ᔍ A believer is one whose whole being is based on the finished work of redemption. DI 1

ᔍ Believe what you do believe and stick to it, but don't profess to believe more than you intend to stick to. If you say you believe God is love, stick to it, [despite] a pandemonium shouting that God is cruel to allow what He does. DI 12

ᔍ The believer is one who bases all on Jesus Christ's sacrifice, and is so identified with Him that he is made broken bread and poured-out wine in the hands of his Lord. HG 105

❧ The gift of the Holy Spirit is the impartation of a personal Spirit that blends the historic Son of God and the individual believer into one, and the characteristic of the life is devotion to God, so much so that you don't even know you are devoted to Him until a crisis comes. HGM 18

❧ The test of a Christian, according to the New Testament, is not that a man believes aright, but that he lives as he believes, i.e., he is able to manifest that he has a power which, apart from his personal relationship to Jesus Christ, he would not have. We all know about the power that spoils our sin but does not take away our appetite for it. SA 69

---

a. Traditionally *bishop;* also in verse 2
b. Or *way, deaconesses*
c. Some manuscripts *God*
d. Or *in the flesh*

64

ADVICE ABOUT WIDOWS, ELDERS, AND SLAVES

Do not rebuke an older man harshly, but exhort him as if he were your father. Treat younger men as brothers, older women as mothers, and younger women as sisters, with absolute purity.

Give proper recognition to those widows who are really in need. But if a widow has children or grandchildren, these should learn first of all to put their religion into practice by caring for their own family and so repaying their parents and grandparents, for this is pleasing to God. The widow who is really in need and left all alone puts her hope in God and continues night and day to pray and to ask God for help. But the widow who lives for pleasure is dead even while she lives. Give the people these instructions, too, so that no one may be open to blame. If anyone does not provide for his relatives, and especially for his immediate family, he has denied the faith and is worse than an unbeliever.

No widow may be put on the list of widows unless she is over sixty, has been faithful to her husband,[a] and is well known for her good deeds, such as bringing up children, showing hospitality, washing the feet of the saints, helping those in trouble and devoting herself to all kinds of good deeds.

As for younger widows, do not put them on such a list. For when their sensual desires overcome their dedication to Christ, they want to marry. Thus they bring judgment on themselves, because they have broken their first pledge. Besides, they get into the habit of being idle and going about from house to house. And not only do they become idlers, but also gossips and busybodies, saying things they ought not to. So I counsel younger widows to marry, to have children, to manage their homes and to give the enemy no opportunity for slander. Some have in fact already turned away to follow Satan.

If any woman who is a believer has widows in her family, she should help them and not let the church be burdened with them, so that the church can help those widows who are really in need.

The elders who direct the affairs of the church well are worthy of double honor, especially those whose work is preaching and teaching. For the Scripture says, "Do not muzzle the ox while it is treading out the grain,"[b] and "The worker deserves his wages."[c] Do not entertain an accusation against an elder unless it is brought by two or three witnesses. Those who sin are to be rebuked publicly, so that the others may take warning.

I charge you, in the sight of God and Christ Jesus and the elect angels, to keep these instructions without partiality, and to do nothing out of favoritism.

Do not be hasty in the laying on of hands, and do not share in the sins of others. Keep yourself pure.

Stop drinking only water, and use a little wine because of your stomach and your frequent illnesses.

The sins of some men are obvious, reaching the place of judgment ahead of them; the sins of others trail behind them. In the same way, good deeds are obvious, and even those that are not cannot be hidden.

> *"The elders who direct the affairs of the church well*
> *are worthy of double honor,*
> *especially those whose work is*
> *preaching and teaching."*

From Oswald Chambers

⁊ The church is a separated band of people who are united to God by the regenerating power of the Spirit, and the bedrock of membership in the church is that we know who Jesus is by a personal revelation of Him. The indwelling Spirit is the supreme guide, and He keeps us absorbed with our Lord. The emphasis today is placed on the furtherance of an organization; the note is, "We must keep this thing going." If we are in God's order, the thing will go; if we are not in His order, it won't. CHI 50

ஐ The church is called to deliver God's message and to be for the praise of His glory, not to be a socialistic institution under the patronage of God. GW 73

ஐ The gifts of the Spirit are not for individual exaltation, but for the good of the whole body of Christ. The body of Christ is an organism, not an organization. How patient God is in forming the body of Christ. HGM 11

ஐ The church of Jesus Christ is built on these two things: the divine revelation of who Jesus Christ is, and the public confession of it. PR 76

ஐ All our Lord succeeded in doing during His life on earth was to gather together a group of fishermen—the whole church of God and the enterprise of our Lord on earth in a fishing boat! PH 180

ஐ The church of Jesus Christ is an organism; we are built up into Him, baptized by one Spirit into one body. Churchianity is an organization; Christianity is an organism. Organization is an enormous benefit until it is mistaken for the life. God has no concern about our organizations. When their purpose is finished, He allows them to be swept aside, and if we are attached to the organization, we shall go with it. Organization is a great necessity, but not an end in itself, and to live for any organization is a spiritual disaster. SA 118

ஐ Our word *church* is connected with civilized organizations of religious people; our Lord's attitude to the church is different. He says it is composed of those who have had a personal revelation from God as to who Jesus Christ is, and have made a public declaration of the same. SA 119

---

a. Or *has had but one husband*
b. Deut. 25:4
c. Luke 10:7

65

1 TIMOTHY 6

LOVE OF MONEY

All who are under the yoke of slavery should consider their masters worthy of full respect, so that God's name and our teaching may not be slandered. Those who have believing masters are not to show less respect for them because they are brothers. Instead, they are to serve them even better, because those who benefit from their service are believers, and dear to them. These are the things you are to teach and urge on them.

If anyone teaches false doctrines and does not agree to the sound instruction of our Lord Jesus Christ and to godly teaching, he is conceited and understands nothing. He has an unhealthy interest in controversies and quarrels about words that result in envy, strife, malicious talk, evil suspicions and constant friction between men of corrupt mind, who have been robbed of the truth and who think that godliness is a means to financial gain.

But godliness with contentment is great gain. For we brought nothing into the world, and we can take nothing out of it. But if we have food and clothing, we will be content with that. People who want to get rich fall into temptation and a trap and into many foolish and harmful desires that plunge men into ruin and destruction. For the love of money is a root of all kinds of evil. Some people, eager for money, have wandered from the faith and pierced themselves with many griefs.

PAUL'S CHARGE TO TIMOTHY

But you, man of God, flee from all this, and pursue righteousness, godliness, faith, love, endurance and gentleness. Fight the good fight of the faith. Take hold of the eternal life to which you were called when you made your good confession in the presence of many witnesses. In the sight of God, who gives life to everything, and of Christ Jesus, who while testifying before Pontius Pilate made the good confession, I charge you to keep this command without spot or blame until the appearing of our Lord Jesus Christ, which God will bring about in his own time—God, the blessed and only ruler, the King of kings and Lord of lords, who alone is immortal and who lives in unapproachable light, whom no one has seen or can see. To him be honor and might forever. Amen.

Command those who are rich in this present world not to be arrogant nor to put their hope in wealth, which is so uncertain, but to put their hope in God, who richly provides us with everything for our enjoyment. Command them to do good, to be rich in good deeds, and to be generous and willing to share. In this way they will lay up treasure for themselves as a firm foundation for the coming age, so that they may take hold of the life that is truly life.

Timothy, guard what has been entrusted to your care. Turn away from godless chatter and the opposing ideas of what is falsely called knowledge, which some have professed and in so doing have wandered from the faith.

Grace be with you.

"The love of money is a root of all kinds of evil."

From Oswald Chambers

❧ The two things around which our Lord centered His most scathing teaching were money and marriage, because they are the two things that make men and women devils or saints. Covetousness is the root of all evil, whether it shows itself in money matters or in any way. HG 23

❧ Jesus saw in money a much more formidable enemy of the kingdom of God than we are apt to recognize it to be. Money is one of the touchstones of reality. People say, "We must lay up for a rainy day." We must, if we do not know God. How many of us are willing to go the length of Jesus Christ's teaching? Ask yourself, how does the advocacy of insurance agree with the Sermon on the Mount, and you will soon see how unchristian we are in spite of all our Christian jargon. The more we try to reconcile modern principles of economy with the teachings of Jesus, the more we shall have to disregard Jesus. HG 42

❧ One of the most besmirching impurities lies in money matters. LG 72

❧ No man can stand in front of Jesus Christ and say, "I want to make money." MFL 11

❧ If we listen to what our Lord says about money, we shall see how we disbelieve Him. We quietly ignore all He says; He is so unpractical, so utterly stupid from the modern standpoint. MFL 125

❧ Money is one of the touchstones in our Lord's teaching. Nowadays we are taken up with our ideas of economy and thrift, and never see that those ideas are not God's ideas. The very nature of God is extravagance. PH 141

❧ "Money answereth all things" (Eccl. 10:19). Although money may cover up defects, yet ultimately it may lead to disaster. SHH 139

❧ "Give to him that asketh thee" (Matt. 5:42). Why do we always make this mean money? Our Lord makes no mention of money. The blood of most of us seems to run in gold. The reason we make it mean money is because that is where our heart is. SSM 46

❧ The Holy Spirit teaches us to fasten our thinking upon God, then when we come to deal with property and money and everything to do with the matters of earth, He reminds us that our real treasure is in heaven. Every effort to persuade myself that my treasure is in heaven is a sure sign that it is not. When my motive has been put right, it will put my thinking right. SSM 62

66

ENCOURAGEMENT TO BE FAITHFUL

Paul, an apostle of Christ Jesus by the will of God, according to the promise of life that is in Christ Jesus, To Timothy, my dear son: Grace, mercy and peace from God the Father and Christ Jesus our Lord.

I thank God, whom I serve, as my forefathers did, with a clear conscience, as night and day I constantly remember you in my prayers. Recalling your tears, I long to see you, so that I may be filled with joy. I have been reminded of your sincere faith, which first lived in your grandmother Lois and in your mother Eunice and, I am persuaded, now lives in you also. For this reason I remind you to fan into flame the gift of God, which is in you through the laying on of my hands. For God did not give us a spirit of timidity, but a spirit of power, of love and of self-discipline.

So do not be ashamed to testify about our Lord, or ashamed of me his prisoner. But join with me in suffering for the gospel, by the power of God, who has saved us and called us to a holy life — not because of anything we have done but because of his own purpose and grace. This grace was given us in Christ Jesus before the beginning of time, but it has now been revealed through the appearing of our Savior, Christ Jesus, who has destroyed death and has brought life and immortality to light through the gospel. And of this gospel I was appointed a herald and an apostle and a teacher. That is why I am suffering as I am. Yet I am not ashamed, because I know whom I have believed, and am convinced that he is able to guard what I have entrusted to him for that day.

What you heard from me, keep as the pattern of sound teaching, with faith and love in Christ Jesus. Guard the good deposit that was entrusted to you—guard it with the help of the Holy Spirit who lives in us.

You know that everyone in the province of Asia has deserted me, including Phygelus and Hermogenes.

May the Lord show mercy to the household of Onesiphorus, because he often refreshed me and was not ashamed of my chains. On the contrary, when he was in Rome, he searched hard for me until he found me. May the Lord grant that he will find mercy from the Lord on that day! You know very well in how many ways he helped me in Ephesus.

> *"I am not ashamed, because I know whom I have believed,*
> *and am convinced that he is able to guard*
> *what I have entrusted to him for that day."*

FROM OSWALD CHAMBERS

❧ The one thing that tells is the great fundamental rock: "Believe also in Me" (John 14:1). Many know a good deal about salvation, but not much about this intense patience of "hanging in" in perfect certainty to the fact that what Jesus Christ says is true. AUG 117

❧ Belief is a wholesome committal; it means making things inevitable, cutting off every possible retreat. Belief is as irrevocable as bereavement. DI 1

❧ Belief is the abandonment of all claim to merit. That is why it is so difficult to believe. DI 1

❧ The further we get away from Jesus, the more dogmatic we become over what we call our religious beliefs, while the nearer we live to Jesus, the less we have of certitude and the more of confidence in Him. DI 2

❧ It is easy to say we believe in God as long as we remain in the little world we choose to live in; but get out into the great world of facts, the noisy world where people are absolutely indifferent to you, where your message is nothing more than a crazy tale belonging to a bygone age, can you believe God there? GW 92

❧ Jesus did not say, "He that believeth on Me, shall experience the fullness of the blessing of God"; but "He that believeth on Me, out of him shall escape everything he receives" (John 7:38). It is a picture of the unfathomable, incalculable benediction which will flow from the one great sovereign source, belief in Jesus. HGM 18

❧ Belief is not that God can do the thing, but belief *in God.* HGM 71

❧ If we really believed some phases of our Lord's teaching, it would make us a laughing stock in the eyes of the world. It requires the miracle of God's grace for us to believe as Jesus taught us to. OBH 118

❧ To believe is literally to commit. Belief is a moral act, and Jesus makes an enormous demand of a man when He asks him to believe in Him. PH 222

❧ To believe in Jesus means much more than the experience of salvation in any form. It entails a mental and moral commitment to our Lord's view of the world, of the flesh, of the devil, of God, of man, and of the Scriptures. To "believe also in Me" means that we submit our intelligence to Jesus Christ our Lord as He submitted His intelligence to His Father. This does not mean that we do not exercise our reason, but it does mean that we exercise it in submission to reason incarnate. PR 131

❧ The devil likes to deceive us and limit us in our practical belief as to what Jesus Christ can do. There is no limit to what He can do, absolutely none. *"All things are possible to him that believeth"* (Mark 9:23). Jesus says that faith in Him is omnipotent. God grant we may get hold of this truth. SHL 31

❧ If you do not believe practically in your heart that the Lord Jesus Christ can alter and save the man you are talking to, you limit Jesus Christ in that life. WG 25

67

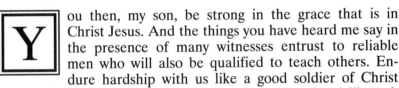

BE STRONG IN CHRIST'S GRACE

You then, my son, be strong in the grace that is in Christ Jesus. And the things you have heard me say in the presence of many witnesses entrust to reliable men who will also be qualified to teach others. Endure hardship with us like a good soldier of Christ Jesus. No one serving as a soldier gets involved in civilian affairs—he wants to please his commanding officer. Similarly, if anyone competes as an athlete, he does not receive the victor's crown unless he competes according to the rules. The hardworking farmer should be the first to receive a share of the crops. Reflect on what I am saying, for the Lord will give you insight into all this.

Remember Jesus Christ, raised from the dead, descended from David. This is my gospel, for which I am suffering even to the point of being chained like a criminal. But God's word is not chained. Therefore I endure everything for the sake of the elect, that they too may obtain the salvation that is in Christ Jesus, with eternal glory.

Here is a trustworthy saying:

If we died with him,
  we will also live with him;
if we endure,
  we will also reign with him.
If we disown him,
  he will also disown us;
if we are faithless,
  he will remain faithful,
  for he cannot disown himself.

A Workman Approved by God

Keep reminding them of these things. Warn them before God against quarreling about words; it is of no value, and only ruins those who listen. Do your best to present yourself to God as one approved, a workman who does not need to be ashamed and who correctly handles the word of truth. Avoid godless chatter, because those who indulge in it will become more and more ungodly. Their teaching will spread like gangrene. Among them are Hymenaeus and Philetus, who have wandered away from the truth. They say that the resurrection has already taken place, and they destroy the faith of some. Nevertheless, God's solid foundation stands firm, sealed with this inscription: "The Lord knows those who are his,"[a] and, "Everyone who confesses the name of the Lord must turn away from wickedness."

In a large house there are articles not only of gold and silver, but also of wood and clay; some are for noble purposes and some for ignoble. If a man cleanses himself from the latter, he will be an instrument for noble purposes, made holy, useful to the Master and prepared to do any good work.

Flee the evil desires of youth, and pursue righteousness, faith, love and peace, along with those who call on the Lord out of a pure heart. Don't have anything to do with foolish and stupid arguments, because you know they produce quarrels. And the Lord's servant must not quarrel; instead, he must be kind to everyone, able to teach, not resentful. Those who oppose him he must gently instruct, in the hope that God will grant them repentance leading them to a knowledge of the truth, and that they will come to their senses and escape from the trap of the devil, who has taken them captive to do his will.

"Be strong in the grace that is in Christ Jesus. . . .
Endure hardship with us
like a good soldier of Christ Jesus."

From Oswald Chambers

   ⁊ If we keep practicing, what we practice becomes our second nature; then in a crisis and in the details of life we shall find that not only will the grace of God stand by us, but also our own nature. Whereas if we refuse to practice, it is not God's grace but our own nature that fails when the crisis comes, because we have not been practicing in actual life. We may ask God to help us, but He cannot, unless we have made our nature our ally. The practicing is ours, not God's. He puts the Holy Spirit into us, He regenerates us, and puts us in contact with all His divine resources; but He cannot make us walk and decide in the way He wants — we must do that ourselves. AUG 123

❧ The day we live in is a day of wild imaginations everywhere — unchecked imaginations in music, in literature, and, worst of all, in the interpretation of Scripture. People are going off on wild speculations; they get hold of one line and run clean off at a tangent and try to explain everything on that line. Then they go off on another line: none of it is in accordance with the Spirit of God. There is no royal road for bringing our brains into harmony with the Spirit God has put in our hearts; we do not get there all at once, but only by steady discipline. BP 237

❧ The culture of the entirely sanctified life is often misunderstood. The discipline of that life consists of suffering, loneliness, patience, and prayer. How many who started with the high ecstasy of vision have ended in the disasters of shallowness! Time, the world, and God fire out the fools. CD VOL. 2, 68

❧ We must be willing to do in the spiritual domain what we have to do in the natural domain if we want to develop, viz., discipline ourselves. DI 70

❧ The discipline of negatives is the hardest discipline in the spiritual life, and if you are going through it you ought to shout "Hallelujah," for it is a sign that God is getting your mind and heart where the mind and heart of Jesus Christ was. IWP 44

❧ It is never God's will for us to be dummies or babies spiritually. It is God's will for us to be sons and daughters of God, but He does not prevent us paying the price of being sons and daughters. He makes us sons and daughters potentially, and then sends us out to be sons and daughters actually. IYA 89

---

a. Num. 16:5 (see Septuagint)

68

2 TIMOTHY 3–4

GODLESSNESS IN THE LAST DAYS

But mark this: There will be terrible times in the last days. People will be lovers of themselves, lovers of money, boastful, proud, abusive, disobedient to their parents, ungrateful, unholy, without love, unforgiving, slanderous, without self-control, brutal, not lovers of the good, treacherous, rash, conceited, lovers of pleasure rather than lovers of God—having a form of godliness but denying its power. Have nothing to do with them.

They are the kind who worm their way into homes and gain control over weak-willed women, who are loaded down with sins and are swayed by all kinds of evil desires, always learning but never able to acknowledge the truth. Just as Jannes and Jambres opposed Moses, so also these men oppose the truth—men of depraved minds, who, as far as the faith is concerned, are rejected. But they will not get very far because, as in the case of those men, their folly will be clear to everyone.

PAUL'S CHARGE TO TIMOTHY

You, however, know all about my teaching, my way of life, my purpose, faith, patience, love, endurance, persecutions, sufferings—what kinds of things happened to me in Antioch, Iconium and Lystra, the persecutions I endured. Yet the Lord rescued me from all of them. In fact, everyone who wants to live a godly life in Christ Jesus will be persecuted, while evil men and impostors will go from bad to worse, deceiving and being deceived. But as for you, continue in what you have learned and have become convinced of, because you know those from whom you learned it, and how from infancy you have known the holy

Scriptures, which are able to make you wise for salvation through faith in Christ Jesus. All Scripture is God-breathed and is useful for teaching, rebuking, correcting and training in righteousness, so that the man of God may be thoroughly equipped for every good work.

In the presence of God and of Christ Jesus, who will judge the living and the dead, and in view of his appearing and his kingdom, I give you this charge: Preach the Word; be prepared in season and out of season; correct, rebuke and encourage—with great patience and careful instruction. For the time will come when men will not put up with sound doctrine. Instead, to suit their own desires, they will gather around them a great number of teachers to say what their itching ears want to hear. They will turn their ears away from the truth and turn aside to myths. But you, keep your head in all situations, endure hardship, do the work of an evangelist, discharge all the duties of your ministry.

For I am already being poured out like a drink offering, and the time has come for my departure. I have fought the good fight, I have finished the race, I have kept the faith. Now there is in store for me the crown of righteousness, which the Lord, the righteous Judge, will award to me on that day—and not only to me, but also to all who have longed for his appearing.

PERSONAL REMARKS

Do your best to come to me quickly, for Demas, because he loved this world, has deserted me and has gone to Thessalonica. Crescens has gone to Galatia, and Titus to Dalmatia. Only Luke is with me. Get Mark and bring him with you, because he is helpful to me in my ministry. I sent Tychicus to Ephesus. When you come, bring the cloak that I left with Carpus at Troas, and my scrolls, especially the parchments.

Alexander the metalworker did me a great deal of harm. The Lord will repay him for what he has done. You too should be on your guard against him, because he strongly opposed our message.

At my first defense, no one came to my support, but everyone deserted me. May it not be held against them. But the Lord stood at my side and gave me strength, so that through me the message might be fully proclaimed and all the Gentiles might hear it. And I was delivered from the lion's mouth. The Lord will rescue me from every evil attack and will bring me safely to his heavenly kingdom. To him be glory for ever and ever. Amen.

FINAL GREETINGS

Greet Priscilla[a] and Aquila and the household of Onesiphorus. Erastus stayed in Corinth, and I left Trophimus sick in Miletus. Do your best to get here before winter. Eubulus greets you, and so do Pudens, Linus, Claudia and all the brothers.
   The Lord be with your spirit. Grace be with you.

"All Scripture is God-breathed and is useful
for teaching, rebuking, correcting and training in righteousness,
so that the man of God may be thoroughly equipped
for every good work."

FROM OSWALD CHAMBERS

❧ How one wishes that people who read books about the Bible would read the Bible itself! BE 116

❧ The Bible is the only Book that throws light on our physical condition, on our soul condition, and on our spiritual condition. In the Bible the sense of smell and sight, etc., are not used as metaphors only; they are identified with the nature of the soul's life. This accounts for what people are apt to call the vulgar teaching of the Bible. BP 53

❧ The Bible not only explains God; it explains the world in which we live; it explains not only things that are right, but things that are wrong. BP 235

❧ When a man's heart is right with God, the mysterious utterances of the Bible are "spirit and life" to him. BSG 42

❧ Beware of the trick of exposition which externalizes Scripture so that we teach but never learn its lessons. CD VOL. 2, 19

❧ The Bible states and affirms facts for the benefit of those who believe in God; those who don't believe in God can tear it to bits if they choose. DI 6

⁊ In the Bible there is no twilight, but intense light and intense darkness. HGM 39

⁊ The context of the Bible is our Lord Jesus Christ, and personal relationship to Him. The *words* of God and the *Word* of God stand together; to separate them is to render both powerless. Any expounder of the words of God is likely to go off at a tangent if he or she does not remember this stern undeviating standard of exposition, viz., that no individual experience is of the remotest value unless it is up to the standard of the Word of God. GW 70

⁊ There is a wrong use of God's Word and a right one. The wrong use is this sort of thing—someone comes to you, and you cast about in your mind what sort of man he is, then hurl a text at him like a projectile, either in prayer or in talking as you deal with him. That is a use of the Word of God that kills your own soul and the souls of the people you deal with. The Spirit of God is not in that. Jesus said, "The words I speak unto you, they are spirit, and they are life" (John 6:63). "Who also hath made us able ministers of the new testament; not of the letter, but of the spirit: for the letter killeth, but the spirit giveth life." Do remember to keep your soul in unsullied touch with the directions of the Spirit. WG 16

⁊ Never drag down the Word of God to anybody's understanding. Hammer at it, keep at it, and drive at it, till the laziness is taken out of people's hearts and brains and bodies, and they are willing to face what this Book has to say about their condition, and face it with the sterling earnestness they use to see what the newspapers have to say when they are on the hunt for a new situation. God grant we may learn the imperativeness of getting at what the Word of God has to say about our particular need; then perhaps we will begin to understand why we have that need. WG 78

⁊ Learn to get into the quiet place where you can hear God's voice speak through the words of the Bible, and never be afraid that you will run dry. He will simply pour the Word until you have no room to contain it. It won't be a question of hunting for messages or texts, but of opening the mouth wide and He fills it. IWP 93

---

a. Greek *Prisca*, a variant of *Priscilla*

69

TITUS 1–2

TITUS' TASK ON CRETE

Paul, a servant of God and an apostle of Jesus Christ for the faith of God's elect and the knowledge of the truth that leads to godliness—a faith and knowledge resting on the hope of eternal life, which God, who does not lie, promised before the beginning of time, and at his appointed season he brought his word to light through the preaching entrusted to me by the command of God our Savior,

To Titus, my true son in our common faith:

Grace and peace from God the Father and Christ Jesus our Savior.

The reason I left you in Crete was that you might straighten out what was left unfinished and appoint[a] elders in every town, as I directed you. An elder must be blameless, the husband of but one wife, a man whose children believe and are not open to the charge of being wild and disobedient. Since an overseer[b] is entrusted with God's work, he must be blameless—not overbearing, not quick-tempered, not given to drunkenness, not violent, not pursuing dishonest gain. Rather he must be hospitable, one who loves what is good, who is self-controlled, upright, holy and disciplined. He must hold firmly to the trustworthy message as it has been taught, so that he can encourage others by sound doctrine and refute those who oppose it.

For there are many rebellious people, mere talkers and deceivers, especially those of the circumcision group. They must be silenced, because they are ruining whole households by teaching things they ought not to teach—and that for the sake of dishonest gain. Even one of their own prophets has said, "Cretans are always liars, evil brutes, lazy gluttons." This testimony is true.

277

Therefore, rebuke them sharply, so that they will be sound in the faith and will pay no attention to Jewish myths or to the commands of those who reject the truth. To the pure, all things are pure, but to those who are corrupted and do not believe, nothing is pure. In fact, both their minds and consciences are corrupted. They claim to know God, but by their actions they deny him. They are detestable, disobedient and unfit for doing anything good.

What Must Be Taught to Various Groups

You must teach what is in accord with sound doctrine. Teach the older men to be temperate, worthy of respect, self-controlled, and sound in faith, in love and in endurance.

Likewise, teach the older women to be reverent in the way they live, not to be slanderers or addicted to much wine, but to teach what is good. Then they can train the younger women to love their husbands and children, to be self-controlled and pure, to be busy at home, to be kind, and to be subject to their husbands, so that no one will malign the word of God.

Similarly, encourage the young men to be self-controlled. In everything set them an example by doing what is good. In your teaching show integrity, seriousness and soundness of speech that cannot be condemned, so that those who oppose you may be ashamed because they have nothing bad to say about us.

Teach slaves to be subject to their masters in everything, to try to please them, not to talk back to them, and not to steal from them, but to show that they can be fully trusted, so that in every way they will make the teaching about God our Savior attractive.

For the grace of God that brings salvation has appeared to all men. It teaches us to say "No" to ungodliness and worldly passions, and to live self-controlled, upright and godly lives in this present age, while we wait for the blessed hope—the glorious appearing of our great God and Savior, Jesus Christ, who gave himself for us to redeem us from all wickedness and to purify for himself a people that are his very own, eager to do what is good.

These, then, are the things you should teach. Encourage and rebuke with all authority. Do not let anyone despise you.

"For the grace of God that brings salvation . . .
teaches us . . . to live self-controlled, upright and godly lives . . .

*while we wait for the blessed hope — the glorious appearing
of our great God and Savior, Jesus Christ."*

From Oswald Chambers

❧ The whole purpose of the redemption is to give back to man the original source of life, and in a regenerated man this means "Christ formed in you." BE 80

❧ The New Testament never says that Jesus Christ came primarily to teach men: it says that He came to reveal that He has put the basis of human life on redemption, that is, He has made it possible for any and every person to be born into the kingdom where He lives. BFB 19

❧ Redemption is the great outside fact of the Christian faith; it has to do not only with a person's experience of salvation, but with the basis of his thinking. The revelation of redemption means that Jesus Christ came here in order that by means of His death on the cross, He might put the whole human race on a redemptive basis, so making it possible for every man to get back into perfect communion with God. "I have finished the work which Thou gavest Me to do" (John 17:4). What was finished? The redemption of the world. CHI 8

❧ Through the redemption we have deliverance from the disposition of sin which is within us, and severance from the body of sin to which we are connected by our "old man"; that is, we are absolutely and completely delivered from sin both in disposition and domination. CHI 10

❧ If you look upon Jesus Christ from the commonsense standpoint, you will never discern who He is; but if you look upon Him as God "manifested in the flesh" for the purpose of putting the whole human race back to where God designed it to be, you get the meaning of redemption. CHI 11

❧ We can never expound the redemption, but we must have strong unshaken faith in it so that we are not swept off our feet by actual things. That the devil and man are allowed to do as they like is a mere episode in the providence of God. Everything that has been touched by sin and the devil has been redeemed; we are to live in the world immovably banked in that faith. HG 95

279

❧ Jesus Christ is not working out the redemption, it is complete; we are working it out, and beginning to realize it by obedience. HG 95

❧ The basis of human life is redemption. There is nothing more certain in time or eternity than what Jesus Christ did on the cross. He switched the whole of the human race back into right relationship to God, and any one of us can get into touch with God *now*, not presently. HGM 105

❧ Redemption means that Jesus Christ can give me His own disposition, and all the standards He gives are based on that disposition. *Jesus Christ's teaching is for the life He puts in.* LG 125

❧ When I realize what Jesus Christ has done for me, then I am a debtor to every human being until they know Him too, not for their sake, not because they will otherwise be lost, but because of Jesus Christ's redemption. SSY 23

---

a. Or *ordain*
b. Traditionally *bishop*

70

TITUS 3

DOING WHAT IS GOOD

Remind the people to be subject to rulers and authorities, to be obedient, to be ready to do whatever is good, to slander no one, to be peaceable and considerate, and to show true humility toward all men.

At one time we too were foolish, disobedient, deceived and enslaved by all kinds of passions and pleasures. We lived in malice and envy, being hated and hating one another. But when the kindness and love of God our Savior appeared, he saved us, not because of righteous things we had done, but because of his mercy. He saved us through the washing of rebirth and renewal by the Holy Spirit, whom he poured out on us generously through Jesus Christ our Savior, so that, having been justified by his grace, we might become heirs having the hope of eternal life. This is a trustworthy saying. And I want you to stress these things, so that those who have trusted in God may be careful to devote themselves to doing what is good. These things are excellent and profitable for everyone.

But avoid foolish controversies and genealogies and arguments and quarrels about the law, because these are unprofitable and useless. Warn a divisive person once, and then warn him a second time. After that, have nothing to do with him. You may be sure that such a man is warped and sinful; he is self-condemned.

FINAL REMARKS

As soon as I send Artemas or Tychicus to you, do your best to come to me at Nicopolis, because I have decided to winter there. Do everything you can to help Zenas the lawyer and Apollos on their way and see that they have everything they need. Our people must learn to devote themselves to doing what is good, in order that they may provide for daily necessities and not live unproductive lives.

Everyone with me sends you greetings. Greet those who love us in the faith.

Grace be with you all.

> *"[God] saved us through the washing of rebirth and*
> *renewal by the Holy Spirit, whom he poured out on us*
> *generously through Jesus Christ our Savior,*
> *so that, having been justified by his grace,*
> *we might become heirs having the hope of eternal life."*

FROM OSWALD CHAMBERS

๛ Jesus Christ's salvation works first at the center, not at the circumference. No one is capable of thinking about being born, or of how they will live when they are born, until they are born; we have to be born into this world first before we can think about it. "Marvel not that I said unto thee, Ye must be born again—you must be born into a new world first, and if you want to know My doctrine, do My will," (John 3:7; see 7:17), said Jesus. A right relation to God first is essential. BP 144

๛ What takes place at new birth is an "explosion" on the inside (a literal explosion, not a theoretical one) that opens all the doors which have been closed and life becomes larger; there is the incoming of a totally new point of view. BSG 62

๛ It is the "preaching of the cross" that produces the crisis we call new birth. We are in danger of preaching the new birth instead of proclaiming that which produces the new birth, viz., the preaching of Jesus Christ, and Him crucified. GW 17

๛ The creation performed by God is what the Apostle Paul calls it—a *new* creation; it is not the bringing out of something already there, but the creating of something which was never there before, an entirely new creation, as unlike anything born in a man by nature, as Jesus Christ is unlike anything produced by the human race throughout its history. GW 63

282

❧ New birth refers not only to a man's eternal salvation, but to his being of value to God in this order of things; it means infinitely more than being delivered from sin and from hell. The gift of the essential nature of God is made efficacious in us by the entering in of the Holy Spirit; He imparts to us the quickening life of the Son of God, and we are lifted into the domain where Jesus lives. LG 114

❧ In new birth God does three impossible things, impossible, that is, from the rational standpoint. The first is to make a man's past as though it had never been; the second, to make a man all over again, and the third, to make a man as certain of God as God is of Himself. New birth does not mean merely salvation from hell, but something more radical, something which tells in a man's actual life. PH 183

❧ We make the blunder of imagining that when we are born from above we cease to be ordinary human beings, whereas we become much more ordinary human beings than we were before. Our human nature goes on all the time. PR 38

❧ We make character out of our disposition. Character is what we make; disposition is what we are born with; and when we are born again we are given a new disposition. A man must make his own character, but he cannot make his disposition; that is a gift. Our natural disposition is gifted to us by heredity; by regeneration God gives us the disposition of His Son. SSM 28

71

PHILEMON

PAUL'S PLEA FOR ONESIMUS

aul, a prisoner of Christ Jesus, and Timothy our brother,

To Philemon our dear friend and fellow worker, to Apphia our sister, to Archippus our fellow soldier and to the church that meets in your home:

Grace to you and peace from God our Father and the Lord Jesus Christ.

I always thank my God as I remember you in my prayers, because I hear about your faith in the Lord Jesus and your love for all the saints. I pray that you may be active in sharing your faith, so that you will have a full understanding of every good thing we have in Christ. Your love has given me great joy and encouragement, because you, brother, have refreshed the hearts of the saints.

Therefore, although in Christ I could be bold and order you to do what you ought to do, yet I appeal to you on the basis of love. I then, as Paul — an old man and now also a prisoner of Christ Jesus — I appeal to you for my son Onesimus,[a] who became my son while I was in chains. Formerly he was useless to you, but now he has become useful both to you and to me.

I am sending him — who is my very heart — back to you. I would have liked to keep him with me so that he could take your place in helping me while I am in chains for the gospel. But I did not want to do anything without your consent, so that any favor you do will be spontaneous and not forced. Perhaps the reason he was separated from you for a little while was that you might have him back for good — no longer as a slave, but better than a slave, as a dear brother. He is very dear to me but even dearer to you, both as a man and as a brother in the Lord.

So if you consider me a partner, welcome him as you would welcome me. If he has done you any wrong or owes you anything, charge it to me. I, Paul, am writing this with my own hand. I will pay it back—not to mention that you owe me your very self. I do wish, brother, that I may have some benefit from you in the Lord; refresh my heart in Christ. Confident of your obedience, I write to you, knowing that you will do even more than I ask.

And one thing more: Prepare a guest room for me, because I hope to be restored to you in answer to your prayers.

Epaphras, my fellow prisoner in Christ Jesus, sends you greetings. And so do Mark, Aristarchus, Demas and Luke, my fellow workers.

The grace of the Lord Jesus Christ be with your spirit.

"I always thank my God as I remember you in my prayers,
because I hear about your faith in the Lord Jesus
and your love for all the saints."

FROM OSWALD CHAMBERS

❧ The proof that we have a healthy, vigorous faith is that we are expressing it in our lives, and bearing testimony with our lips as to how it came about. CHI 55

❧ The life of faith is the life of a soul who has given over every other life but the life of faith. Faith is not an action of the mind, nor of the heart, nor of the will, nor of the sentiment; it is the centering of the entire man in God. CD VOL. 2, 149

❧ We begin our Christian life by believing what we are told to believe, then we have to go on to so assimilate our beliefs that they work out in a way that redounds to the glory of God. The danger is in multiplying the acceptation of beliefs we do not make our own. CHI 125

❧ To be able to state explicitly in words what you know by faith is an impossibility; if you can state it in words, it is not faith. GW 108

❧ No one is surprised over what God does when once he has faith in Him. LG 149

➤ Every time you venture out in the life of faith, you will find something in your commonsense circumstances that flatly contradicts your faith. Common sense is not faith, and faith is not common sense; they stand in the relation of the natural and the spiritual. MUH 242

➤ When we go through the trial of faith, we gain so much wealth in our heavenly banking account, and the more we go through the trial of faith the wealthier we become in the heavenly regions. OBH 103

➤ Unless we are willing to give up good things for Jesus Christ, we have no realization of whom He is. "But really I cannot give up things that are quite legitimate!" Then never mention the word *love* again in connection with Jesus Christ if you cannot give up the best you have for Him. This is the essential nature of love in the natural life; otherwise it is a farce to call it love. It is not love, but lust; and when we come to our relationship with Jesus Christ, this is the love He demands of us. PR 103

➤ "Love never faileth!" (1 Cor. 13:1) What a wonderful phrase that is! But what a still more wonderful thing the reality of that love must be; greater than prophecy—that vast forthtelling of the mind and purpose of God; greater than philanthropic self-sacrifice; greater than the extraordinary gifts of emotions and ecstacies and all eloquence; and it is this love that is shed abroad in our hearts by the Holy Ghost which is given unto us. RTR 67

➤ In the Cross we may see the dimensions of divine love. The Cross is not the cross of man, but an exhibition of the heart of God. At the back of the wall of the world stands God with His arms outstretched, and every man driven there is driven into the arms of God. The Cross of Jesus is the supreme evidence of the love of God. RTR 88

➤ Love cannot be defined. Try to define your love for Jesus Christ, and you will find you cannot do it. Love is the sovereign preference of my person for another person, and Jesus Christ demands that that other person be Himself. That does not mean we have no preference for anyone else, but that Jesus Christ has the sovereign preference; within that sovereign preference come all other loving preferences, down to flowers and animals. The Bible makes no distinction between divine love and human love; it speaks only of love. SSY 158

---

a. *Onesimus* means *useful.*

THE SON SUPERIOR TO ANGELS

n the past God spoke to our forefathers through the prophets at many times and in various ways, but in these last days he has spoken to us by his Son, whom he appointed heir of all things, and through whom he made the universe. The Son is the radiance of God's glory and the exact representation of his being, sustaining all things by his powerful word. After he had provided purification for sins, he sat down at the right hand of the Majesty in heaven. So he became as much superior to the angels as the name he has inherited is superior to theirs.

For to which of the angels did God ever say,

"You are my Son;
today I have become your Father[a]"[b]?

Or again,

"I will be his Father,
and he will be my Son"[c]?

And again, when God brings his firstborn into the world, he says,

"Let all God's angels worship him."[d]

In speaking of the angels he says,

"He makes his angels winds,
his servants flames of fire."[e]

But about the Son he says,

"Your throne, O God, will last for ever and ever,
and righteousness will be the scepter of your kingdom.
You have loved righteousness and hated wickedness;
therefore God, your God, has set you above
your companions
by anointing you with the oil of joy."[f]

He also says,

"In the beginning, O Lord, you laid the foundations
of the earth,
and the heavens are the work of your hands.
They will perish, but you remain;
they will all wear out like a garment.
You will roll them up like a robe;
like a garment they will be changed.
But you remain the same,
and your years will never end."[g]

To which of the angels did God ever say,

"Sit at my right hand
until I make your enemies
a footstool for your feet"[h]?

Are not all angels ministering spirits sent to serve those who will inherit salvation?

WARNING TO PAY ATTENTION

We must pay more careful attention, therefore, to what we have heard, so that we do not drift away. For if the message spoken by angels was binding, and every violation and disobedience received its just punishment, how shall we escape if we ignore such a great salvation? This salvation, which was first announced by the Lord, was confirmed to us by those who heard him. God also testified to it by signs, wonders and various miracles, and gifts of the Holy Spirit distributed according to his will.

288

JESUS MADE LIKE HIS BROTHERS

It is not to angels that he has subjected the world to come, about which we are speaking. But there is a place where someone has testified:

"What is man that you are mindful of him,
   the son of man that you care for him?
You made him a little[i] lower than the angels;
   you crowned him with glory and honor
   and put everything under his feet."[j]

In putting everything under him, God left nothing that is not subject to him. Yet at present we do not see everything subject to him. But we see Jesus, who was made a little lower than the angels, now crowned with glory and honor because he suffered death, so that by the grace of God he might taste death for everyone.

In bringing many sons to glory, it was fitting that God, for whom and through whom everything exists, should make the author of their salvation perfect through suffering. Both the one who makes men holy and those who are made holy are of the same family. So Jesus is not ashamed to call them brothers. He says,

"I will declare your name to my brothers;
   in the presence of the congregation I will sing
         your praises."[k]

And again,

"I will put my trust in him."[l]

And again he says,

"Here am I, and the children God has given me."[m]

Since the children have flesh and blood, he too shared in their humanity so that by his death he might destroy him who holds the power of death—that is, the devil—and free those who all

289

their lives were held in slavery by their fear of death. For surely it is not angels he helps, but Abraham's descendants. For this reason he had to be made like his brothers in every way, in order that he might become a merciful and faithful high priest in service to God, and that he might make atonement[n] for the sins of the people. Because he himself suffered when he was tempted, he is able to help those who are being tempted.

"The Son is the radiance of God's glory
and the exact representation of his being,
sustaining all things by his powerful word."

FROM OSWALD CHAMBERS

❧ The mainspring of the heart of Jesus Christ was the mainspring of the heart of God the Father; consequently, the words Jesus Christ spoke were the exact expression of God's thought. In our Lord the tongue was in its right place; He never spoke from His head, but always from His heart. BP 126

❧ The words of the Bible express the inner soul; the words we use today are nearly all technical, borrowed from somewhere else, and our most modern words do not express the spirit at all, but cunningly cloak it over and give no expression. BP 246

❧ The stupendous profundities of God's will, surging with unfathomable mysteries, come down to the shores of our common life, not in emotions and fires, nor in aspirations and vows, and agonies and visions, but in a way so simple that the wayfaring men, yea fools, cannot make a mistake, viz., in words. CD VOL. 1, 16

❧ Words are full of revelation when we do not simply recall or memorize them but receive them. Receive these words from Jesus—"Father," "heaven," "Hallowed be Thy Name," "kingdom," "will"; there is all the vocabulary of the Deity and Dominion and Disposition of Almighty God in relation to men in these words. Or take the words—"bread," "forgiveness," "debts," "temptations," "deliverance," "evil"; in these words the primary psychological colors which portray the perplexing puzzles and problems of personal life are all spelled out before our Father.
    Or, lastly, look at such words as "power," "glory," "forever," "Amen"—in them there sounds the transcendant triumphant truth

that all is well, that God reigns and rules and rejoices, and His joy is our strength. CD VOL. 2, 26

> To take God at His word may mean expecting God to come up to my standard, whereas true faith does not so much take God at His word as to take the word of God as it is, in the face of all difficulties, and act upon it, with no attempt to explain or expound it. NKW 120

> When we take Jesus Christ's words about His Cross, the least thing we can do is to endeavor to get at His mind behind His words. Jesus says things from a different point of view from ours, and unless we receive His Spirit, we do not even begin to see what He is driving at. PH 218

> The administering of the word is not ministering it where we think it is needed; the word has to be sown in living touch with the Lord of the harvest, sown in touch with Him in solitude and prayer, and He will bring the folks round — black and white, educated and uneducated, rich and poor. They are all there, "white already to harvest," but most of us are so keen on our own notions that we do not recognize that they are ripe for reaping. If we are in touch with Jesus Christ, He says all the time — This is the moment; this one here, that one there, is ready to be reaped. We say — "Oh, but I want to go and get scores of heathen saved; I do not want to be the means of reaping my brother." But your brother happens to be the one who is white to harvest. The commission is to teach, to disciple — that is, to administer the word. SSY 139

---

a. Or *have begotten you*
b. Psalm 2:7
c. 2 Samuel 7:14; 1 Chron. 17:13
d. Deut. 32:43 (see Dead Sea Scrolls and Septuagint)
e. Psalm 104:4
f. Psalm 45:6-7
g. Psalm 102:25-27
h. Psalm 110:1
i. Or *him for a little while;* also in verse 9
j. Psalm 8:4-6
k. Psalm 22:22
l. Isaiah 8:17
m. Isaiah 8:18
n. Or *and that he might turn aside God's wrath, taking away*

73

JESUS GREATER THAN MOSES

T herefore, holy brothers, who share in the heavenly calling, fix your thoughts on Jesus, the apostle and high priest whom we confess. He was faithful to the one who appointed him, just as Moses was faithful in all God's house. Jesus has been found worthy of greater honor than Moses, just as the builder of a house has greater honor than the house itself. For every house is built by someone, but God is the builder of everything. Moses was faithful as a servant in all God's house, testifying to what would be said in the future. But Christ is faithful as a son over God's house. And we are his house, if we hold on to our courage and the hope of which we boast.

WARNING AGAINST UNBELIEF

So, as the Holy Spirit says:

"Today, if you hear his voice,
   do not harden your hearts
as you did in the rebellion,
   during the time of testing in the desert,
where your fathers tested and tried me
   and for forty years saw what I did.
That is why I was angry with that generation,
   and I said, 'Their hearts are always going astray,
   and they have not known my ways.'
So I declared on oath in my anger,
   'They shall never enter my rest.' "[a]

See to it, brothers, that none of you has a sinful, unbelieving heart that turns away from the living God. But encourage one another daily, as long as it is called Today, so that none of you may be hardened by sin's deceitfulness. We have come to share in Christ if we hold firmly till the end the confidence we had at first. As has just been said:

"Today, if you hear his voice,
do not harden your hearts
as you did in the rebellion."[b]

Who were they who heard and rebelled? Were they not all those Moses led out of Egypt? And with whom was he angry for forty years? Was it not with those who sinned, whose bodies fell in the desert? And to whom did God swear that they would never enter his rest if not to those who disobeyed[c]? So we see that they were not able to enter, because of their unbelief.

"Therefore, holy brothers,
who share in the heavenly calling,
fix your thoughts on Jesus,
the apostle and high priest whom we confess."

FROM OSWALD CHAMBERS

ꝫ Call is the inner motive of having been gripped by God—spoilt for every aim in life saving that of disciplining men to Jesus. DI 10

ꝫ No experience on earth is sufficient to be taken as a call of God; you must know that the call is from God for whom you care more than for all your experiences; then nothing can daunt you. DI 10

ꝫ If I hear the call of God and refuse to obey, I become the dullest, most commonplace of Christians because I have seen and heard and refused to obey. DI 10

ꝫ We need no call of God to help our fellowmen; that is the natural call of humanity. But we do need the supernatural work of God's grace before we are fit for God to help Himself through us. DI 11

꙯ The call of God can never be stated explicitly; it is implicit. The call of God is like the call of the sea, or of the mountains; no one hears these calls but the one who has the nature of the sea or of the mountains. And no one hears the call of God who has not the nature of God in him. It cannot be definitely stated what the call of God is to, because it is a call into comradeship with God Himself for His own purposes, and the test of faith is to believe that God knows what He is after. The call of God becomes clear only as we obey, never as we weigh the pros and cons and try to reason it out. The call is God's idea, not our idea, and only on looking back over the path of obedience do we realize what is the idea of God; God sanctifies memory. When we hear the call of God, it is not for us to dispute with God, and arrange to obey Him if He will expound the meaning of His call to us. As long as we insist on having the call expounded to us, we will never obey; but when we obey, it is expounded, and in looking back there comes a chuckle of confidence — "He doeth all things well." Before us there is nothing, but overhead there is God, and we have to trust Him. If we insist on explanations before we obey, we lie like clogs on God's plan and put ourselves clean athwart His purpose. NKW 12

꙯ One man or woman called of God is worth a hundred who have elected to work for God. RTR 41

---

a. Psalm 95:7-11
b. Psalm 95:7-8
c. Or *disbelieved*

74

━━━━━ ❧❀❧ ━━━━━

A SABBATH-REST
FOR THE PEOPLE OF GOD

Therefore, since the promise of entering his rest still stands, let us be careful that none of you be found to have fallen short of it. For we also have had the gospel preached to us, just as they did; but the message they heard was of no value to them, because those who heard did not combine it with faith.[a] Now we who have believed enter that rest, just as God has said,

"So I declared on oath in my anger,
'They shall never enter my rest.' "[b]

And yet his work has been finished since the creation of the world. For somewhere he has spoken about the seventh day in these words: "And on the seventh day God rested from all his work."[c] And again in the passage above he says, "They shall never enter my rest."

It still remains that some will enter that rest, and those who formerly had the gospel preached to them did not go in, because of their disobedience. Therefore God again set a certain day, calling it Today, when a long time later he spoke through David, as was said before:

"Today, if you hear his voice,
do not harden your hearts."[d]

For if Joshua had given them rest, God would not have spoken later about another day. There remains, then, a Sabbath-rest for the people of God; for anyone who enters God's rest also rests from his own work, just as God did from his. Let us, therefore, make every effort to enter that rest, so that no one will fall by following their example of disobedience.

For the word of God is living and active. Sharper than any double-edged sword, it penetrates even to dividing soul and spirit, joints and marrow; it judges the thoughts and attitudes of the heart. Nothing in all creation is hidden from God's sight Everything is uncovered and laid bare before the eyes of him to whom we must give account.

JESUS THE GREAT HIGH PRIEST

Therefore, since we have a great high priest who has gone through the heavens,e Jesus the Son of God, let us hold firmly to the faith we profess. For we do not have a high priest who is unable to sympathize with our weaknesses, but we have one who has been tempted in every way, just as we are—yet was without sin. Let us then approach the throne of grace with confidence, so that we may receive mercy and find grace to help us in our time of need.

"The word of God is living and active.
Sharper than any double-edged sword,
it penetrates even to dividing soul and spirit, joints and
marrow; it judges the thoughts and attitudes of the heart."

FROM OSWALD CHAMBERS

 Why should I believe a thing because it is in the Bible? That is a perfectly legitimate question. There is no reason why you should believe it; it is only when the Spirit of God applies the Scriptures to the inward consciousness that a man begins to understand their living efficacy. If we try from the outside to fit the Bible to an external standard, or to a theory of verbal inspiration or any other theory, we are wrong. "Ye search the Scriptures because ye think that in them ye have eternal life; and these are they which bear witness of Me; and ye will not come to Me, that ye may have life" (John 5:39-40).

There is another dangerous tendency, that of closing all questions by saying, "Let us get back to the external authority of the Bible." That attitude lacks courage and the power of the Spirit of God; it is a literalism that does not produce "written epistles," but persons who are more or less incarnate dictionaries; it produces not saints but fossils; people without life, with none of the living reality of the Lord Jesus. There must be the Incarnate Word and the interpreting word, i.e., people whose lives back up what they preach, "written epistles, known and read of all men" (see 2 Cor. 3:2). Only when we receive the Holy Spirit and are lifted into a total readjustment to God do the words of God become "quick and powerful" to us. The only way the words of God can be understood is by contact with the Word of God. The connection between our Lord Himself, who is the Word, and His spoken words is so close that to divorce them is fatal. "The words that I speak unto you, they are spirit, and they are life" (John 6:63). BE 122

꙳ Thinking takes place in the heart, not in the brain. The real spiritual powers of a man reside in the heart, which is the center of the physical life, of the soul life, and of the spiritual life. The expression of thinking is referred to the brain and the lips because through these organs thinking becomes articulate.

According to the Bible, thinking exists in the heart, and that is the region with which the Spirit of God deals. We may take it as a general rule that Jesus Christ never answers any questions that spring from a man's head, because the questions which spring from our brains are always borrowed from some book we have read, or from someone we have heard speak; but the questions that spring from our hearts, the real problems that vex us, Jesus Christ answers those. The questions He came to deal with are those that spring from the implicit center. These problems may be difficult to state in words, but they are the problems Jesus Christ will solve. BP 122

---

a. Many manuscripts *because they did not share in the faith of those who obeyed*
b. Psalm 95:11; also in verse 5
c. Gen. 2:2
d. Psalm 95:7-8
e. Or *gone into heaven*

297

75

A PRIEST FOREVER

very high priest is selected from among men and is appointed to represent them in matters related to God, to offer gifts and sacrifices for sins. He is able to deal gently with those who are ignorant and are going astray, since he himself is subject to weakness. This is why he has to offer sacrifices for his own sins, as well as for the sins of the people.

No one takes this honor upon himself; he must be called by God, just as Aaron was. So Christ also did not take upon himself the glory of becoming a high priest. But God said to him,

> "You are my Son;
> today I have become your Father.ᵃ"ᵇ

And he says in another place,

> "You are a priest forever,
> in the order of Melchizedek."ᶜ

During the days of Jesus' life on earth, he offered up prayers and petitions with loud cries and tears to the one who could save him from death, and he was heard because of his reverent submission. Although he was a son, he learned obedience from what he suffered and, once made perfect, he became the source of eternal salvation for all who obey him and was designated by God to be high priest in the order of Melchizedek.

WARNING AGAINST FALLING AWAY

We have much to say about this, but it is hard to explain because you are slow to learn. In fact, though by this time you ought to be teachers, you need someone to teach you the elementary truths of God's word all over again. You need milk, not solid food! Anyone who lives on milk, being still an infant, is not acquainted with the teaching about righteousness. But solid food is for the mature, who by constant use have trained themselves to distinguish good from evil.

> *"Solid food is for the mature, who by constant use have trained themselves to distinguish good from evil."*

FROM OSWALD CHAMBERS

~ Knowledge of evil broadens a man's mind, makes him tolerant, but paralyzes his action. Knowledge of good broadens a man's mind, makes him intolerant of all sin, and shows itself in intense activity. A bad man, an evil-minded man, is amazingly tolerant of everything and everyone, no matter whether they are good or bad, Christian or not, but his power of action is paralyzed entirely; he is tolerant of everything—the devil, the flesh, the world, sin, and everything else. BP 57

~ The most staggering thing about Jesus Christ is that He makes human destiny depend not on goodness or badness, not on things done or not done, but on who we say He is. IWP 116

~ There are some things of which we must be ignorant, because knowledge of them comes in no other way than by disobedience to God. In the life originally designed for Adam, it was not intended that he should be ignorant of evil, but that he should know evil through understanding good. Instead, he ate of the fruit of the tree of knowledge of good and evil and thereby knew evil positively and good negatively; consequently, none of us knows the order God intended. The knowledge of evil that comes through the Fall has given human nature a bias of insatiable curiosity about the bad, and only when we have been introduced into the kingdom of God do we know good and evil in the way God constituted man to know them. SHL 61–62

~ The knowledge of evil that came through the Fall gives a man a broad mind, but instead of instigating him to action, it paralyzes his action. Men and women whose minds are poisoned by gross experence of evil are marvelously generous with regard to other people's sins; they argue in this way—"To know all is to pardon all." Every bit of their broadmindedness paralyzes their power to *do* anything. They know good only by contrast with evil, which is the exact opposite of God's order. SHL 65

ॐ When a man knows good and evil in the way God intended he should, he becomes intolerant of evil, and this intolerance shows itself in an intense activity against evil. SHL 65

ॐ If we know good only by contrast with evil, we shall have the devilishness of the serpent through gross experience. But when we know good and evil in the way Jesus Christ knew them, all our subtle wisdom is on the side of the good and our dovelike nature is toward evil. SHL 69

---

a. Or *have begotten you*
b. Psalm 2:7
c. Psalm 110:4

76

HEBREWS 6

LET US GO ON TO MATURITY

Therefore let us leave the elementary teachings about Christ and go on to maturity, not laying again the foundation of repentance from acts that lead to death,[a] and of faith in God, instruction about baptisms, the laying on of hands, the resurrection of the dead, and eternal judgment. And God permitting, we will do so.

It is impossible for those who have once been enlightened, who have tasted the heavenly gift, who have shared in the Holy Spirit, who have tasted the goodness of the word of God and the powers of the coming age, if they fall away, to be brought back to repentance, because[b] to their loss they are crucifying the Son of God all over again and subjecting him to public disgrace.

Land that drinks in the rain often falling on it and that produces a crop useful to those for whom it is farmed receives the blessing of God. But land that produces thorns and thistles is worthless and is in danger of being cursed. In the end it will be burned.

Even though we speak like this, dear friends, we are confident of better things in your case — things that accompany salvation. God is not unjust; he will not forget your work and the love you have shown him as you have helped his people and continue to help them. We want each of you to show this same diligence to the very end, in order to make your hope sure. We do not want you to become lazy, but to imitate those who through faith and patience inherit what has been promised.

THE CERTAINTY OF GOD'S PROMISE

When God made his promise to Abraham, since there was no one greater for him to swear by, he swore by himself, saying, "I will surely bless you and give you many descendants."[c] And so after waiting patiently, Abraham received what was promised.

Men swear by someone greater than themselves, and the oath confirms what is said and puts an end to all argument. Because God wanted to make the unchanging nature of his purpose very clear to the heirs of what was promised, he confirmed it with an oath. God did this so that, by two unchangeable things in which it is impossible for God to lie, we who have fled to take hold of the hope offered to us may be greatly encouraged. We have this hope as an anchor for the soul, firm and secure. It enters the inner sanctuary behind the curtain, where Jesus, who went before us, has entered on our behalf. He has become a high priest forever, in the order of Melchizedek.

"We have this hope as an anchor for the soul, firm and secure."

From Oswald Chambers

> ❧ The term *soul* generally is used in three distinct ways. First, as applied to men and animals alike as distinct from all other creations; second, the more particular use of the word as applied to men distinguished from animals; and third, as applied to one man as distinct from another. BP 44

> ❧ The Bible nowhere says that God has a soul; the only way in which the soul of God is referred to is prophetically in anticipation of the Incarnation. Angels are never spoken of as having souls, because soul has reference to this order of creation, and angels belong to another order. Our Lord emphatically had a soul, but of God and of angels the term *soul* is not used. The term *soul* is never applied to plants. A plant has life, but the Bible never speaks of it as having soul. BP 44

> ❧ Nothing can enter the soul but through the senses. God enters the soul through the senses. BP 51

> ❧ In the life of Jesus Christ there was no division into secular and sacred, but with us when this power begins to be realized, it always manifests itself in a line of cleavage. There are certain things we won't do; certain things we won't look at; certain things we won't

eat; certain hours we won't sleep. It is not wrong; it is the Spirit of God in a soul beginning to utilize the powers of the soul for God. And as the soul goes on, it comes to a full-orbed condition, where it manifests itself as in the life of the Lord Jesus and all is sacred. BP 61

꙳ The Bible nowhere says the soul sleeps; it says that the body sleeps but never the personality. The moment after death, unhindered consciousness is the state. BP 94

꙳ The human soul is so mysterious that in the moment of a great tragedy men get face to face with things they never gave heed to before, and in the moment of death it is extraordinary what takes place in the human heart toward God. CD VOL. 1 110

꙳ "Soul" refers to the way a personal spirit reasons and thinks in a human body. We talk about a man exhibiting "soul" in singing or in painting, that is, he is expressing his personal spirit. HGM 74

꙳ Soul is "me," my personal spirit, manifesting itself in my body, my way of estimating things. OBH 77

꙳ Soul is the expression of my personal spirit in my body, the way I reason and think and act, and Jesus taught that a man must lose his soul in order to gain it; he must lose absolutely his own way of reasoning and looking at things, and begin to estimate from an entirely different standpoint. PH 64

꙳ "Soul" in the Bible nearly always refers to the fleshly nature; it is the only power a man has for expressing his true spirit. PS 15

꙳ The soul . . . is simply the spirit of a man expressing itself. The spirit of a child can rarely express itself; the soul has not become articulate. PS 15

---

a. Or *from useless rituals*
b. Or *repentance while*
c. Gen. 22:17

77

MELCHIZEDEK THE PRIEST

This Melchizedek was king of Salem and priest of God Most High. He met Abraham returning from the defeat of the kings and blessed him, and Abraham gave him a tenth of everything. First, his name means "king of righteousness"; then also, "king of Salem" means "king of peace." Without father or mother, without genealogy, without beginning of days or end of life, like the Son of God he remains a priest forever.

Just think how great he was: Even the patriarch Abraham gave him a tenth of the plunder! Now the law requires the descendants of Levi who become priests to collect a tenth from the people—that is, their brothers—even though their brothers are descended from Abraham. This man, however, did not trace his descent from Levi, yet he collected a tenth from Abraham and blessed him who had the promises. And without doubt the lesser person is blessed by the greater. In the one case, the tenth is collected by men who die; but in the other case, by him who is declared to be living. One might even say that Levi, who collects the tenth, paid the tenth through Abraham, because when Melchizedek met Abraham, Levi was still in the body of his ancestor.

JESUS LIKE MELCHIZEDEK

If perfection could have been attained through the Levitical priesthood (for on the basis of it the law was given to the people), why was there still need for another priest to come—one in the order of Melchizedek, not in the order of Aaron? For when there is a change of the priesthood, there must also be a change of the law. He of whom these things are said belonged to a different tribe, and no one from that tribe has ever served at the altar. For it is clear that our Lord descended from Judah, and in regard to that tribe Moses said nothing about priests. And what we have said is even more clear if another priest like Melchizedek appears, one who has become a priest not on the basis of a regulation as to his ancestry but on the basis of the power of an indestructible life. For it is declared:

"You are a priest forever,
　in the order of Melchizedek."[a]

The former regulation is set aside because it was weak and useless (for the law made nothing perfect), and a better hope is introduced, by which we draw near to God.

And it was not without an oath! Others became priests without any oath, but he became a priest with an oath when God said to him:

"The Lord has sworn
　and will not change his mind:
'You are a priest forever.' "[b]

Because of this oath, Jesus has become the guarantee of a better covenant.

Now there have been many of those priests, since death prevented them from continuing in office; but because Jesus lives forever, he has a permanent priesthood. Therefore he is able to save completely[c] those who come to God through him, because he always lives to intercede for them.

Such a high priest meets our need—one who is holy, blameless, pure, set apart from sinners, exalted above the heavens. Unlike the other high priests, he does not need to offer sacrifices day after day, first for his own sins, and then for the sins of the people. He sacrificed for their sins once for all when he offered himself. For the law appoints as high priests men who are weak; but the oath, which came after the law, appointed the Son, who has been made perfect forever.

"Unlike the other high priests,
[Jesus] does not need to offer sacrifices day after day,

first for his own sins, and then for the sins of the people.
He sacrificed for their sins once for all when he offered himself."

From Oswald Chambers

ಜ It is easy to be thrilled by the sacrifices men make: it takes the Spirit of Almighty God to get us even interested in the cost of our redemption to God. BE 60

ಜ We talk about the sacrifice of the Son of God and forget that it was the sacrifice of God Himself. *"God was in Christ* reconciling the world unto Himself"* (2 Cor. 5:19). BSG 47

ಜ He deliberately laid down His life without any possibility of deliverance. There was no compulsion; it was a sacrifice made with a free mind. Nor was there anything of the impulsive about it; He laid down His life with a clear knowledge of what He was doing. Jesus understood what was coming; it was not a foreboding, but a certainty — not a catastrophe which might happen, but an ordained certainty in the decrees of God, and He knew it. GW 113

ಜ There is no room for the pathetic in our Lord's attitude; it is we who take the pathetic view and look at His sacrifice from a point of view the Spirit of God never once uses. The Spirit of God never bewitches men with the strange pathos of the sacrifice of Jesus: the Spirit of God keeps us at the passion of the sacrifice of Jesus. The great passion at the back of His heart and mind in all Jesus did was devotion to His Father. GW 113

ಜ When we are identified with Jesus Christ, the Spirit of God would have us sacrifice ourselves for Him, point for point, as He did for His Father. We pray and wait, and need urging, and want the thrilling vision; but Jesus wants us to narrow and limit ourselves to one thing — clearly and intelligently knowing what we are doing. We deliberately lay down our lives for Him as He laid down His life for us in the purpose of God. GW 114

ಜ Jesus sacrificed His natural life and made it spiritual by obeying His Father's voice, and we have any number of glorious opportunities of proving how much we love God by the delighted way we sacrifice for Him. IWP 82

ॐ Jesus Christ laid down His holy life for His Father's purposes. Then if we are God's children we have to lay down our lives for His sake, not for the sake of a truth, not for the sake of devotion to a doctrine, but for Jesus Christ's sake — the personal relationship all through. IWP 85

---

a. Psalm 110:4
b. Psalm 110:4
c. Or *forever*

78

THE HIGH PRIEST OF A NEW COVENANT

he point of what we are saying is this: We do have such a high priest, who sat down at the right hand of the throne of the Majesty in heaven, and who serves in the sanctuary, the true tabernacle set up by the Lord, not by man.

Every high priest is appointed to offer both gifts and sacrifices, and so it was necessary for this one also to have something to offer. If he were on earth, he would not be a priest, for there are already men who offer the gifts prescribed by the law. They serve at a sanctuary that is a copy and shadow of what is in heaven. This is why Moses was warned when he was about to build the tabernacle: "See to it that you make everything according to the pattern shown you on the mountain."[a] But the ministry Jesus has received is as superior to theirs as the covenant of which he is mediator is superior to the old one, and it is founded on better promises.

For if there had been nothing wrong with that first covenant, no place would have been sought for another. But God found fault with the people and said:[b]

"The time is coming, declares the Lord,
when I will make a new covenant
    with the house of Israel and with the house of Judah.
It will not be like the covenant
    I made with their forefathers
when I took them by the hand
    to lead them out of Egypt,
because they did not remain
    faithful to my covenant,

and I turned away from them, declares the Lord.
This is the covenant I will make
  with the house of Israel after that time, declares the Lord.
I will put my laws in their minds
  and write them on their hearts.
I will be their God,
  and they will be my people.
No longer will a man teach his neighbor,
  or a man his brother, saying,
    'Know the Lord,'
because they will all know me,
  from the least of them to the greatest.
For I will forgive their wickedness
  and will remember their sins no more."[c]

By calling this covenant "new," he has made the first one obsolete; and what is obsolete and aging will soon disappear.

*"I will put my laws in their minds
and write them on their hearts.
I will be their God, and they will be my people."*

FROM OSWALD CHAMBERS

❧ God's laws are not watered down to suit anyone; if God did that He would cease to be God. The moral law never alters for the noblest or the weakest; it remains abidingly and eternally the same. BE 8

❧ The moral law is not imperative, because it can be disobeyed and immediate destruction does not follow. And yet the moral law never alters, however much men disobey it; it can be violated, but it never alters. Remember, at the back of all human morality stands God. BE 7

❧ The moral law ordained by God does not make itself weak to the weak. It does not palliate our shortcomings; it takes no account of our heredity and our infirmities; it demands that we be absolutely moral. Not to recognize this is to be less than alive. BE 7

309

❧ The inexorable Law of God is laid down that I shall be held responsible for the wrong that I do; I shall smart for it and be punished for it, no matter who I am. The Atonement has made provision for what I am not responsible for, viz., the disposition of sin. BP 157

❧ Man has to fulfill God's laws in his physical life, in his mental and moral life, in his social and spiritual life, and to offend in one point is to be guilty of all. BE 15

❧ As there is a law in the natural world whereby we reason and think and argue about natural things, so there is a law in the spiritual world, but the law which runs through the natural world is not the same as in the spiritual world. BP 210

❧ We transgress a law of God and expect an experience akin to death, but exactly the opposite happens; we feel enlarged, more broad-minded, more tolerant of evil, but we are more powerless, knowledge which comes from eating of the tree of the knowledge of good and evil, instead of instigating to action, paralyzes. OPG 7

---

a. Exodus 25:40
b. Some manuscripts may be translated *fault and said to the people.*
c. Jer. 31:31-34

79

WORSHIP IN THE EARTHLY TABERNACLE

N ow the first covenant had regulations for worship and also an earthly sanctuary. A tabernacle was set up. In its first room were the lampstand, the table and the consecrated bread; this was called the Holy Place. Behind the second curtain was a room called the Most Holy Place, which had the golden altar of incense and the gold-covered ark of the covenant. This ark contained the gold jar of manna, Aaron's staff that had budded, and the stone tablets of the covenant. Above the ark were the cherubim of the Glory, overshadowing the atonement cover.[a] But we cannot discuss these things in detail now.

When everything had been arranged like this, the priests entered regularly into the outer room to carry on their ministry. But only the high priest entered the inner room, and that only once a year, and never without blood, which he offered for himself and for the sins the people had committed in ignorance. The Holy Spirit was showing by this that the way into the Most Holy Place had not yet been disclosed as long as the first tabernacle was still standing. This is an illustration for the present time, indicating that the gifts and sacrifices being offered were not able to clear the conscience of the worshiper. They are only a matter of food and drink and various ceremonial washings — external regulations applying until the time of the new order.

THE BLOOD OF CHRIST

When Christ came as high priest of the good things that are already here,[b] he went through the greater and more perfect tabernacle that is not man-made, that is to say, not a part of this creation. He did not enter by means of the blood of goats and calves; but he entered the Most Holy Place once for all by his own blood, having obtained eternal redemption. The blood of goats and bulls and the ashes of a heifer sprinkled on those who are ceremonially unclean sanctify them so that they are outwardly clean. How much more, then, will the blood of Christ, who through the eternal Spirit offered himself unblemished to God, cleanse our consciences from acts that lead to death,[c] so that we may serve the living God!

For this reason Christ is the mediator of a new covenant, that those who are called may receive the promised eternal inheritance — now that he has died as a ransom to set them free from the sins committed under the first covenant.

In the case of a will,[d] it is necessary to prove the death of the one who made it, because a will is in force only when somebody has died; it never takes effect while the one who made it is living. This is why even the first covenant was not put into effect without blood. When Moses had proclaimed every commandment of the law to all the people, he took the blood of calves, together with water, scarlet wool and branches of hyssop, and sprinkled the scroll and all the people. He said, "This is the blood of the covenant, which God has commanded you to keep."[e] In the same way, he sprinkled with the blood both the tabernacle and everything used in its ceremonies. In fact, the law requires that nearly everything be cleansed with blood, and without the shedding of blood there is no forgiveness.

It was necessary, then, for the copies of the heavenly things to be purified with these sacrifices, but the heavenly things themselves with better sacrifices than these. For Christ did not enter a man-made sanctuary that was only a copy of the true one; he entered heaven itself, now to appear for us in God's presence. Nor did he enter heaven to offer himself again and again, the way the high priest enters the Most Holy Place every year with blood that is not his own. Then Christ would have had to suffer many times since the creation of the world. But now he has appeared once for all at the end of the ages to do away with sin by the sacrifice of himself. Just as man is destined to die once, and after that to face judgment, so Christ was sacrificed once to take away the sins of many people; and he will appear a second time, not to bear sin, but to bring salvation to those who are waiting for him.

312

"Christ was sacrificed once to take away the sins of many people;
and he will appear a second time, not to bear sin,
but to bring salvation to those
who are waiting for him. "

FROM OSWALD CHAMBERS

≈ Forgiveness is the divine miracle of grace. AUG 47

≈ The forgiveness of God penetrates to the very heart of His nature and to the very heart of man's nature. That is why God cannot forgive until a man realizes what sin is. DI 65

≈ Think what God's forgiveness means: it means that He forgets away every sin. GW 11

≈ Forgiveness is a miracle, because in forgiving a man God imparts to him the power to be exactly the opposite of what he has been. God transmutes the sinner who sinned into the saint who does not sin; consequently, the only true repentant man is the holy man. GW 53

≈ Forgiveness is the great message of the Gospel, and it satisfies a man's sense of justice completely. The fundamental factor of Christianity is "the forgivness of sins." HGM 100

≈ We may talk as much as we like about forgiveness, but it will never make any difference to us unless we realize that we need it. HGM 101

≈ God can never forgive the man who does not want to be forgiven. HGM 101

≈ There is no such thing as God overlooking sin. That is where people make a great mistake with regard to God's love. They say, "God is love and of course He will forgive sin." God is *holy* love and, of course, He *cannot* forgive sin. Therefore if God does forgive, there must be a reason that justifies Him in doing it. HGM 102

≈ When we turn to God and say we are sorry, Jesus Christ has pledged His word that we will be forgiven, but the forgiveness is not

313

operative unless we turn, because our turning is the proof that we know we need forgiveness. HGM 104

---

a. Traditionally *the mercy seat*
b. Some early manuscripts *are to come*
c. Or *from useless rituals*
d. Same Greek word as *covenant;* also in verse 17
e. Exodus 24:8

80

HEBREWS 10

CHRIST'S SACRIFICE ONCE FOR ALL

T he law is only a shadow of the good things that are coming—not the realities themselves. For this reason it can never, by the same sacrifices repeated endlessly year after year, make perfect those who draw near to worship. If it could, would they not have stopped being offered? For the worshipers would have been cleansed once for all, and would no longer have felt guilty for their sins. But those sacrifices are an annual reminder of sins, because it is impossible for the blood of bulls and goats to take away sins.

Therefore, when Christ came into the world, he said:

"Sacrifice and offering you did not desire,
　　but a body you prepared for me;
with burnt offerings and sin offerings
　　you were not pleased.
Then I said, 'Here I am—it is written about me
　　in the scroll—
I have come to do your will, O God.' "[a]

First he said, "Sacrifices and offerings, burnt offerings and sin offerings you did not desire, nor were you pleased with them" (although the law required them to be made). Then he said, "Here I am, I have come to do your will." He sets aside the first to establish the second. And by that will, we have been made holy through the sacrifice of the body of Jesus Christ once for all.

Day after day every priest stands and performs his religious duties; again and again he offers the same sacrifices, which can never take away sins. But when this priest had offered for all time one sacrifice for sins, he sat down at the right hand of God.

Since that time he waits for his enemies to be made his footstool, because by one sacrifice he has made perfect forever those who are being made holy.

The Holy Spirit also testifies to us about this. First he says:

> "This is the covenant I will make with them
> after that time, says the Lord.
> I will put my laws in their hearts,
> and I will write them on their minds."[b]

Then he adds:

> "Their sins and lawless acts
> I will remember no more."[c]

And where these have been forgiven, there is no longer any sacrifice for sin.

A CALL TO PERSEVERE

Therefore, brothers, since we have confidence to enter the Most Holy Place by the blood of Jesus, by a new and living way opened for us through the curtain, that is, his body, and since we have a great priest over the house of God, let us draw near to God with a sincere heart in full assurance of faith, having our hearts sprinkled to cleanse us from a guilty conscience and having our bodies washed with pure water. Let us hold unswervingly to the hope we profess, for he who promised is faithful. And let us consider how we may spur one another on toward love and good deeds. Let us not give up meeting together, as some are in the habit of doing, but let us encourage one another—and all the more as you see the Day approaching.

If we deliberately keep on sinning after we have received the knowledge of the truth, no sacrifice for sins is left, but only a fearful expectation of judgment and of raging fire that will consume the enemies of God. Anyone who rejected the law of Moses died without mercy on the testimony of two or three witnesses. How much more severely do you think a man deserves to be punished who has trampled the Son of God under foot, who has treated as an unholy thing the blood of the covenant that sanctified him, and who has insulted the Spirit of grace? For we know him who said, "It is mine to avenge; I will repay,"[d] and again, "The Lord will judge his people."[e] It is a dreadful thing to fall into the hands of the living God.

Remember those earlier days after you had received the light, when you stood your ground in a great contest in the face of suffering. Sometimes you were publicly exposed to insult and persecution; at other times you stood side by side with those who were so treated. You sympathized with those in prison and joyfully accepted the confiscation of your property, because you knew that you yourselves had better and lasting possessions.

So do not throw away your confidence; it will be richly rewarded. You need to persevere so that when you have done the will of God, you will receive what he has promised. For in just a very little while,

"He who is coming will come and will not delay.
But my righteous one[f] will live by faith.
And if he shrinks back,
I will not be pleased with him."[g]

But we are not of those who shrink back and are destroyed, but of those who believe and are saved.

"You need to persevere so that when you have done the will of God, you will receive what he has promised."

FROM OSWALD CHAMBERS

❧ There is a distinct period in our experience when we cease to say — "Lord, show me Thy will," and the realization begins to dawn that we *are* God's will, and He can do with us what He likes. We wake up to the knowledge that we have the privilege of giving ourselves over to God's will. It is a question of being yielded to God. AUG 108

❧ The will of God is the gladdest, brightest, most bountiful thing possible to conceive, and yet some of us talk of the will of God with a terrific sigh — "Oh well, I suppose it is the will of God," as if His will were the most calamitous thing that could befall us. IWP 19

ᕗ How are we going to find out the will of God? "God will communicate it to us." He will not. His will is there all the time, but we have to discover it by being renewed in our minds, by taking heed to His Word and obeying it. MFL 80

ᕗ At first we pray, "Teach me Thy ways, O Lord," then we pray, "Teach me to do Thy will," and step by step God teaches us what is His will. Then comes a great burst of joy, "I delight to do Thy will! There is nothing on earth I delight in more than in Thy will." MFL 127

ᕗ The joy of Jesus lay in knowing that every power of His nature was in such harmony with His Father that He did His Father's will with delight. Some of us are slow to do God's will. We do it as if our shoes were iron and lead; we do it with a great sigh and with the corners of our mouths down, as if His will were the most arduous thing on earth. But when our wills are rectified and brought into harmony with God, it is a delight, a superabounding joy, to do God's will. MFL 127

ᕗ *Do* God's will. God not only expects me to do His will, but He is in me to do it. OBH 130

ᕗ Doing God's will is never hard. The only thing that is hard is *not* doing His will. All the forces of nature and of grace are at the back of the man who does God's will because in obedience we let God have His amazing way with us. OBH 130

ᕗ We ought to be superabounding with joy and delight because God is working in us to will and to do of His good pleasure. The "goodest" thing there is is the will of God. God's will is hard only when it comes up against our stubbornness; then it is as cruel as a ploughshare and as devastating as an earthquake. God is merciless with the thing that tells against the relationship of a man to Himself. When once God does have His way, we are emancipated into the very life of God, i.e., into the life that Jesus lived. The only estimate of a consistent Christian character is that the life of the Son of God is being manifested in the bodily life. OBH 130

---

a. Psalm 40:6-8 (see Septuagint)
b. Jer. 31:33
c. Jer. 31:34
d. Deut. 32:35
e. Deut. 32:36; Psalm 135:14
f. One early manuscript *But the righteous*
g. Hab. 2:3-4

81

BY FAITH

N ow faith is being sure of what we hope for and certain of what we do not see. This is what the ancients were commended for.

By faith we understand that the universe was formed at God's command, so that what is seen was not made out of what was visible.

By faith Abel offered God a better sacrifice than Cain did. By faith he was commended as a righteous man, when God spoke well of his offerings. And by faith he still speaks, even though he is dead.

By faith Enoch was taken from this life, so that he did not experience death; he could not be found, because God had taken him away. For before he was taken, he was commended as one who pleased God. And without faith it is impossible to please God, because anyone who comes to him must believe that he exists and that he rewards those who earnestly seek him.

By faith Noah, when warned about things not yet seen, in holy fear built an ark to save his family. By his faith he condemned the world and became heir of the righteousness that comes by faith.

By faith Abraham, when called to go to a place he would later receive as his inheritance, obeyed and went, even though he did not know where he was going. By faith he made his home in the promised land like a stranger in a foreign country; he lived in tents, as did Isaac and Jacob, who were heirs with him of the same promise. For he was looking forward to the city with foundations, whose architect and builder is God.

By faith Abraham, even though he was past age — and Sarah herself was barren — was enabled to become a father because he[a]

319

considered him faithful who had made the promise. And so from this one man, and he as good as dead, came descendants as numerous as the stars in the sky and as countless as the sand on the seashore.

All these people were still living by faith when they died. They did not receive the things promised; they only saw them and welcomed them from a distance. And they admitted that they were aliens and strangers on earth. People who say such things show that they are looking for a country of their own. If they had been thinking of the country they had left, they would have had opportunity to return. Instead, they were longing for a better country—a heavenly one. Therefore God is not ashamed to be called their God, for he has prepared a city for them.

By faith Abraham, when God tested him, offered Isaac as a sacrifice. He who had received the promises was about to sacrifice his one and only son, even though God had said to him, "It is through Isaac that your offspring[b] will be reckoned."[c] Abraham reasoned that God could raise the dead, and figuratively speaking, he did receive Isaac back from death.

By faith Isaac blessed Jacob and Esau in regard to their future.

By faith Jacob, when he was dying, blessed each of Joseph's sons, and worshiped as he leaned on the top of his staff.

By faith Joseph, when his end was near, spoke about the exodus of the Israelites from Egypt and gave instructions about his bones.

By faith Moses' parents hid him for three months after he was born, because they saw he was no ordinary child, and they were not afraid of the king's edict.

By faith Moses, when he had grown up, refused to be known as the son of Pharaoh's daughter. He chose to be mistreated along with the people of God rather than to enjoy the pleasures of sin for a short time. He regarded disgrace for the sake of Christ as of greater value than the treasures of Egypt, because he was looking ahead to his reward. By faith he left Egypt, not fearing the king's anger; he persevered because he saw him who is invisible. By faith he kept the Passover and the sprinkling of blood, so that the destroyer of the firstborn would not touch the firstborn of Israel.

By faith the people passed through the Red Sea[d] as on dry land; but when the Egyptians tried to do so, they were drowned.

By faith the walls of Jericho fell, after the people had marched around them for seven days.

By faith the prostitute Rahab, because she welcomed the spies, was not killed with those who were disobedient.[e]

And what more shall I say? I do not have time to tell about Gideon, Barak, Samson, Jephthah, David, Samuel and the prophets, who through faith conquered kingdoms, administered justice, and gained what was promised; who shut the mouths of lions, quenched the fury of the flames, and escaped the edge of the sword; whose weakness was turned to strength; and who became powerful in battle and routed foreign armies. Women received back their dead, raised to life again. Others were tortured and refused to be released, so that they might gain a better resurrection. Some faced jeers and flogging, while still others were chained and put in prison. They were stoned;[f] they were sawed in two; they were put to death by the sword. They went about in sheepskins and goatskins, destitute, persecuted and mistreated — the world was not worthy of them. They wandered in deserts and mountains, and in caves and holes in the ground.

These were all commended for their faith, yet none of them received what had been promised. God had planned something better for us so that only together with us would they be made perfect.

*"Now faith is being sure of what we hope for
and certain of what we do not see."*

From Oswald Chambers

~ Naturally, we are inclined to be so mathematical and calculating that we look upon uncertainty as a bad thing. We imagine that we have to reach some end, but that is not the nature of spiritual life. The nature of spiritual life is that we are certain in our uncertainty; consequently, we do not make our nests anywhere. Common sense says,"Well, suppose I were in that condition. . . . " We cannot suppose ourselves in any condition we have never been in. MUH 120

~ Certainty is the mark of the commonsense life: gracious uncertainty is the mark of the spiritual life. To be certain of God means that we are uncertain in all our ways; we do not know what a day may bring forth. This is generally said with a sigh of sadness; it should be rather an expression of breathless expectation. We are uncertain of the next step, but we are certain of God. Immediately, we abandon to God, and do the duty that lies nearest; He packs our life with surprises all the time. MUH 120

❧ When we become advocates of a creed, something dies; we do not believe God; we only believe our belief about Him. Jesus said, "Except ye . . . become as little children" (Matt. 18:3). Spiritual life is the life of a child. We are not uncertain of God but uncertain of what He is going to do next. If we are only certain in our beliefs, we get dignified and severe and have the ban of finality about our views; but when we are rightly related to God, life is full of spontaneous, joyful uncertainty and expectancy. MUH 120

❧ "Believe also in Me," said Jesus, not—"Believe certain things about Me" (John 14:1). Leave the whole thing to Him; it is gloriously uncertain how He will come in, but He will come. Remain loyal to Him.

MUH 120

---

a. Or *By faith even Sarah, who was past age, was enabled to bear children because she*
b. Greek *seed*
c. Gen. 21:12
d. That is, Sea of Reeds
e. Or *unbelieving*
f. Some early manuscripts *stoned; they were put to the test;*

82

HEBREWS 12

GOD DISCIPLINES HIS SONS

T herefore, since we are surrounded by such a great cloud of witnesses, let us throw off everything that hinders and the sin that so easily entangles, and let us run with perseverance the race marked out for us. Let us fix our eyes on Jesus, the author and perfecter of our faith, who for the joy set before him endured the cross, scorning its shame, and sat down at the right hand of the throne of God. Consider him who endured such opposition from sinful men, so that you will not grow weary and lose heart.

In your struggle against sin, you have not yet resisted to the point of shedding your blood. And you have forgotten that word of encouragement that addresses you as sons:

"My son, do not make light of the Lord's discipline,
and do not lose heart when he rebukes you,
because the Lord disciplines those he loves,
and he punishes everyone he accepts as a son."[a]

Endure hardship as discipline; God is treating you as sons. For what son is not disciplined by his father? If you are not disciplined (and everyone undergoes discipline), then you are illegitimate children and not true sons. Moreover, we have all had human fathers who disciplined us and we respected them for it. How much more should we submit to the Father of our spirits and live! Our fathers disciplined us for a little while as they thought best; but God disciplines us for our good, that we may share in his holiness. No discipline seems pleasant at the time, but painful. Later on, however, it produces a harvest of righteousness and peace for those who have been trained by it.

Therefore, strengthen your feeble arms and weak knees. "Make level paths for your feet,"[b] so that the lame may not be disabled, but rather healed.

WARNING AGAINST REFUSING GOD

Make every effort to live in peace with all men and to be holy; without holiness no one will see the Lord. See to it that no one misses the grace of God and that no bitter root grows up to cause trouble and defile many. See that no one is sexually immoral, or is godless like Esau, who for a single meal sold his inheritance rights as the oldest son. Afterward, as you know, when he wanted to inherit this blessing, he was rejected. He could bring about no change of mind, though he sought the blessing with tears.

You have not come to a mountain that can be touched and that is burning with fire; to darkness, gloom and storm; to a trumpet blast or to such a voice speaking words that those who heard it begged that no further word be spoken to them, because they could not bear what was commanded: "If even an animal touches the mountain, it must be stoned."[c] The sight was so terrifying that Moses said, "I am trembling with fear."[d]

But you have come to Mount Zion, to the heavenly Jerusalem, the city of the living God. You have come to thousands upon thousands of angels in joyful assembly, to the church of the firstborn, whose names are written in heaven. You have come to God, the judge of all men, to the spirits of righteous men made perfect, to Jesus the mediator of a new covenant, and to the sprinkled blood that speaks a better word than the blood of Abel.

See to it that you do not refuse him who speaks. If they did not escape when they refused him who warned them on earth, how much less will we, if we turn away from him who warns us from heaven? At that time his voice shook the earth, but now he has promised, "Once more I will shake not only the earth but also the heavens."[e] The words "once more" indicate the removing of what can be shaken—that is, created things—so that what cannot be shaken may remain.

Therefore, since we are receiving a kingdom that cannot be shaken, let us be thankful, and so worship God acceptably with reverence and awe, for our "God is a consuming fire."[f]

"No discipline seems pleasant at the time, but painful.
Later on, however, it produces a harvest of righteousness
and peace for those who have been trained by it."

From Oswald Chambers

- We can all see God in exceptional things, but it requires the culture of spiritual discipline to see God in every detail. MUH 319

- God will not discipline us; we must discipline ourselves. God will not bring every thought and imagination into captivity; we have to do it. MUH 323

- The element of discipline in the life of faith must never be lost sight of, because only by means of the discipline are we taught the difference between the natural interpretation of what we call good and what God means by "good." NKW 22

- God disciplines us by disappointment. Life may have been going on like a torrent; then suddenly down comes a barrier of disappointment, until slowly we learn that the disappointment was His appointment. PH 84

- It may be that in our inner life Jesus is teaching us by the disciplining force of His delays. "I expected God to answer my prayer, but He has not." He is bringing us to the place where by obedience we shall see what it is He is after. PH 221

- The resentment of discipline of any kind will warp the whole life away from God's purpose. RTR 11

- There are many things that are perfectly legitimate, but if you are going to concentrate on God, you cannot do them. Your right hand is one of the best things you have, but Jesus says if it hinders you in following His precepts, cut it off. This line of discipline is the sternest one that ever struck mankind. RTR 91

- The reason for the need of discipline is that our bodies have been used by the wrong disposition, and when the new disposition is put in, the old physical case is not taken away; it is left there for us to discipline and turn into an obedient servant to the new disposition. SSM 35

❧ God puts us through discipline, not for our own sake, but for the sake of His purpose and His call. Never debate about anything God is putting you through, and never try to find out why you are going through it. Keep right with God and let Him do what He likes in your circumstances, and you will find He is producing the kind of bread and wine that will be a benefit to others. SSY 20

❧ Nothing and no one can detect us saving God. We are in the quarry now and God is hewing us out. God's Spirit gathers and marks the stones; then they have to be blasted out of their holdings by the dynamite of the Holy Ghost, to be chiseled and shaped, and then lifted into the heavenly places. SSY 41

❧ The stern discipline that looks like distress and chastisement turns out to be the biggest benediction; it is the shadow of God's hand that keeps us perfectly fitted in Him. SSY 109

---

a. Prov. 3:11-12
b. Prov. 4:26
c. Exodus 19:12-13
d. Deut. 9:19
e. Haggai 2:6
f. Deut. 4:24

83

HEBREWS 13

CONCLUDING EXHORTATIONS

 eep on loving each other as brothers. Do not forget to entertain strangers, for by so doing some people have entertained angels without knowing it. Remember those in prison as if you were their fellow prisoners, and those who are mistreated as if you yourselves were suffering.

Marriage should be honored by all, and the marriage bed kept pure, for God will judge the adulterer and all the sexually immoral. Keep your lives free from the love of money and be content with what you have, because God has said,

"Never will I leave you;
    never will I forsake you."[a]

So we say with confidence,

"The Lord is my helper; I will not be afraid.
    What can man do to me?"[b]

Remember your leaders, who spoke the word of God to you. Consider the outcome of their way of life and imitate their faith. Jesus Christ is the same yesterday and today and forever.

Do not be carried away by all kinds of strange teachings. It is good for our hearts to be strengthened by grace, not by ceremonial foods, which are of no value to those who eat them. We have an altar from which those who minister at the tabernacle have no right to eat.

The high priest carries the blood of animals into the Most Holy Place as a sin offering, but the bodies are burned outside the camp. And so Jesus also suffered outside the city gate to make the people holy through his own blood. Let us, then, go to him outside the camp, bearing the disgrace he bore. For here we do not have an enduring city, but we are looking for the city that is to come.

Through Jesus, therefore, let us continually offer to God a sacrifice of praise—the fruit of lips that confess his name. And do not forget to do good and to share with others, for with such sacrifices God is pleased.

Obey your leaders and submit to their authority. They keep watch over you as men who must give an account. Obey them so that their work will be a joy, not a burden, for that would be of no advantage to you.

Pray for us. We are sure that we have a clear conscience and desire to live honorably in every way. I particularly urge you to pray so that I may be restored to you soon.

May the God of peace, who through the blood of the eternal covenant brought back from the dead our Lord Jesus, that great Shepherd of the sheep, equip you with everything good for doing his will, and may he work in us what is pleasing to him, through Jesus Christ, to whom be glory for ever and ever. Amen.

Brothers, I urge you to bear with my word of exhortation, for I have written you only a short letter.

I want you to know that our brother Timothy has been released. If he arrives soon, I will come with him to see you.

Greet all your leaders and all God's people. Those from Italy send you their greetings.

Grace be with you all.

"Jesus Christ is the same yesterday and today and forever."

FROM OSWALD CHAMBERS

> Jesus never asks anyone to define his position or to understand a creed, but—"Who am I to you?" . . . Jesus Christ makes the whole of human destiny depend on a man's relationship to Himself. AUG 82

> The Great Life is to believe that Jesus Christ is not a fraud. AUG 114

> The Jesus who saves our souls and identifies us with Himself is "this same Jesus" who went to sleep as a babe on His mother's

bosom; and it is "this same Jesus," the almighty, powerful Christ, with all power in heaven and on earth, who is at work in the world today by His Spirit. BSG 72

❧ Get into the habit of recalling to your mind what Jesus was like when He was here; picture what He did and what He said. Recall His gentleness and tenderness as well as His strength and sternness, and then say, "That is what God is like." CHI 77

❧ Our Lord never worried, nor was He ever anxious, because He was not "out" to realize His own ideas. He was "out" to realize God's ideas. GW 81

❧ Jesus Christ is not only Savior, He is King, and He has the right to exact anything and everything from us at His own discretion. HGM 129

❧ Jesus Christ is the last word on God, on sin and death, on heaven and hell; the last word on every problem that human life has to face. IWP 125

❧ Our Lord was not a recluse nor an ascetic; He did not cut Himself off from society, but He was inwardly disconnected all the time. He was not aloof, but He lived in another world. He was so much in the ordinary world that the religious people of His day called Him a glutton and wine-bibber. MUH 332

❧ Jesus Christ is *Savior* and *Lord* in experience, and *Lord* and *Savior* in discernment. OBH 88

---

a. Deut. 31:6
b. Psalm 118:6-7

84

JAMES 1

TRIALS AND TEMPTATIONS

James, a servant of God and of the Lord Jesus Christ,
To the twelve tribes scattered among the nations:
Greetings.

Consider it pure joy, my brothers, whenever you face
trials of many kinds, because you know that the testing
of your faith develops perseverance. perseverance must finish its
work so that you may be mature and complete, not lacking anything. If any of you lacks wisdom, he should ask God, who gives
generously to all without finding fault, and it will be given to him.
But when he asks, he must believe and not doubt, because he who
doubts is like a wave of the sea, blown and tossed by the wind. That
man should not think he will receive anything from the Lord; he is
a double-minded man, unstable in all he does.

The brother in humble circumstances ought to take pride in
his high position. But the one who is rich should take pride in his
low position, because he will pass away like a wild flower. For the
sun rises with scorching heat and withers the plant; its blossom
falls and its beauty is destroyed. In the same way, the rich man
will fade away even while he goes about his business.

Blessed is the man who perseveres under trial, because when
he has stood the test, he will receive the crown of life that God
has promised to those who love him.

When tempted, no one should say, "God is tempting me." For
God cannot be tempted by evil, nor does he tempt anyone; but
each one is tempted when, by his own evil desire, he is dragged
away and enticed. Then, after desire has conceived, it gives birth
to sin; and sin, when it is full-grown, gives birth to death.

Don't be deceived, my dear brothers. Every good and perfect
gift is from above, coming down from the Father of the heavenly

lights, who does not change like shifting shadows. He chose to give us birth through the word of truth, that we might be a kind of firstfruits of all he created.

LISTENING AND DOING

My dear brothers, take note of this: Everyone should be quick to listen, slow to speak and slow to become angry, for man's anger does not bring about the righteous life that God desires. Therefore, get rid of all moral filth and the evil that is so prevalent and humbly accept the word planted in you, which can save you.

Do not merely listen to the word, and so deceive yourselves. Do what it says. Anyone who listens to the word but does not do what it says is like a man who looks at his face in a mirror and, after looking at himself, goes away and immediately forgets what he looks like. But the man who looks intently into the perfect law that gives freedom, and continues to do this, not forgetting what he has heard, but doing it—he will be blessed in what he does.

If anyone considers himself religious and yet does not keep a tight rein on his tongue, he deceives himself and his religion is worthless. Religion that God our Father accepts as pure and faultless is this: to look after orphans and widows in their distress and to keep oneself from being polluted by the world.

"Consider it pure joy . . . whenever you face trials of many kinds, because you know that the testing of your faith develops perseverance."

FROM OSWALD CHAMBERS

ᴈ Fortitude in trial comes from having the long view of God. No matter how closely I am imprisoned by poverty or tribulation, I see "the land that is very far off," and there is no drudgery on earth that is not turned divine by the very sight. CHI 86

ᴈ We have no faith at all until it is proved, proved through conflict and in no other way. HGM 58

ᴈ The very nature of faith is that it must be tried; faith untried is only ideally real, not actually real. Faith is not rational; therefore, it cannot be worked out on the basis of logical reason; it can be worked out only on the implicit line by living obedience. NKW 112

❧ Faith is not logical; it works on the line of life and by its very nature must be tried. Never confound the trial of faith with the ordinary discipline of life. Much that we call the trial of our faith is the inevitable result of being alive. NKW 117

❧ To walk with God means the perpetual realization of the nature of faith, viz., that it must be tried or it is mere fancy; faith untried has no character-value for the individual. OPG 18

❧ There is nothing akin to faith in the natural world. Defiant pluck and courage is not faith; it is the *trial* of faith that is "much more precious than of gold," and the trial of faith is never without the essentials of temptation. OPG 18

❧ The thing that is precious in the sight of God is faith that has been tried. Tried faith is spendable, it is so much wealth stored up in heaven, and the more we go through the trial of our faith, the wealthier we become in the heavenly regions. PH 83

❧ You cannot state definitely what the call of God is to; it is to be in comradeship with God for His own purposes, and the test of faith is to believe God knows what He is after. PH 181

❧ Faith must be tried or it is not faith; faith is not mathematics nor reason. Scriptural faith is not to be illustrated by the faith we exhibit in our commonsense life; it is trust in the character of one we have never seen, in the integrity of Jesus Christ, and it must be tried. PH 204

❧ It is the trial of our faith that makes us wealthy in heaven. We want the treasure on earth all the time. We interpret answers to prayer on the material plane only, and if God does not answer there, we say He does not answer at all. SSY 61

85

JAMES 2

FAVORITISM FORBIDDEN

My brothers, as believers in our glorious Lord Jesus Christ, don't show favoritism. Suppose a man comes into your meeting wearing a gold ring and fine clothes, and a poor man in shabby clothes also comes in. If you show special attention to the man wearing fine clothes and say, "Here's a good seat for you," but say to the poor man, "You stand there" or "Sit on the floor by my feet," have you not discriminated among yourselves and become judges with evil thoughts?

Listen, my dear brothers: Has not God chosen those who are poor in the eyes of the world to be rich in faith and to inherit the kingdom he promised those who love him? But you have insulted the poor. Is it not the rich who are exploiting you? Are they not the ones who are dragging you into court? Are they not the ones who are slandering the noble name of him to whom you belong?

If you really keep the royal law found in Scripture, "Love your neighbor as yourself,"[a] you are doing right. But if you show favoritism, you sin and are convicted by the law as lawbreakers. For whoever keeps the whole law and yet stumbles at just one point is guilty of breaking all of it. For he who said, "Do not commit adultery,"[b] also said, "Do not murder."[c] If you do not commit adultery but do commit murder, you have become a lawbreaker.

Speak and act as those who are going to be judged by the law that gives freedom, because judgment without mercy will be shown to anyone who has not been merciful. Mercy triumphs over judgment!

FAITH AND DEEDS

What good is it, my brothers, if a man claims to have faith but has no deeds? Can such faith save him? Suppose a brother or sister is without clothes and daily food. If one of you says to him, "Go, I wish you well; keep warm and well fed," but does nothing about his physical needs, what good is it? In the same way, faith by itself, if it is not accompanied by action, is dead.

But someone will say, "You have faith; I have deeds."

Show me your faith without deeds, and I will show you my faith by what I do. You believe that there is one God. Good! Even the demons believe that—and shudder.

You foolish man, do you want evidence that faith without deeds is useless[d]? Was not our ancestor Abraham considered righteous for what he did when he offered his son Isaac on the altar? You see that his faith and his actions were working together, and his faith was made complete by what he did. And the scripture was fulfilled that says, "Abraham believed God, and it was credited to him as righteousness,"[e] and he was called God's friend. You see that a person is justified by what he does and not by faith alone.

In the same way, was not even Rahab the prostitute considered righteous for what she did when she gave lodging to the spies and sent them off in a different direction? As the body without the spirit is dead, so faith without deeds is dead.

"If you show favoritism,
you sin and are convicted by the law as lawbreakers.
For whoever keeps the whole law and yet stumbles at just one point
is guilty of breaking all of it."

FROM OSWALD CHAMBERS

❧ Every man has an imperative something within him which makes him say "I ought," even in the most degraded specimens of humanity the "ought" is there, and the Bible tells us where it comes from—it comes from God. The modern tendency is to leave God out and make our standard what is most useful to man. The utilitarian says that these distinct laws of conduct have been evolved by man for the benefit of man—the greatest use to the greatest number. That is not the reason a thing is right; the reason a thing is right is that God is behind it. God's "ought's" never alter; we never grow out of them. Our difficulty is that we find in ourselves this attitude—"I ought to do this, but I won't"; "I ought to do that, but

I don't want to." That puts out of court the idea that if you teach men what is right they will do it—they won't; what is needed is a power which will enable a man to do what he knows is right. We may say, "Oh, I won't count this time," but every bit of moral wrong is counted by God. The moral law exerts no coercion, neither does it allow any compromise. "For whosoever shall keep the whole law, and yet offend in one point, he is guilty of all" (James 2:10). Once we realize this we see why it was necessary for Jesus Christ to come. The redemption is the reality which alters inability into ability. BE 8

❧ The moral law does not consider our weaknesses as human beings; in fact, it does not take into account our heredity or infirmities. It simply demands that we be absolutely moral. The moral law never changes, either for the highest of society or for the weakest in the world. It is enduring and eternally the same. The moral law, ordained by God, does not make itself weak to the weak by excusing our shortcomings. It remains absolute for all time and eternity. If we are not aware of this, it is because we are less than alive. Once we do realize it, our life immediately becomes a fatal tragedy. "I was alive once without the law, but when the commandment came, sin revived and I died" (Romans 7:9). The moment we realize this, the Spirit of God convicts us of sin. Until a person gets there and sees that there is no hope, the Cross of Christ remains absurd to him. Conviction of sin always brings a fearful, confining sense of the law. It makes a person hopeless—"sold under sin" (Romans 7:14). I, a guilty sinner, can never work to get right with God—it is impossible. There is only one way by which I can get right with God, and that is through the death of Jesus Christ. I must get rid of the underlying idea that I can ever be right with God because of my obedience. Who of us could ever obey God to absolute perfection! MUM-UE 12/1

a. Lev. 19:18
b. Exodus 20:14; Deut. 5:18
c. Exodus 20:13; Deut. 5:17
d. Some early manuscripts *dead*
e. Gen. 15:6

86

JAMES 3–4

TAMING THE TONGUE

ot many of you should presume to be teachers, my brothers, because you know that we who teach will be judged more strictly. We all stumble in many ways. If anyone is never at fault in what he says, he is a perfect man, able to keep his whole body in check.

When we put bits into the mouths of horses to make them obey us, we can turn the whole animal. Or take ships as an example. Although they are so large and are driven by strong winds, they are steered by a very small rudder wherever the pilot wants to go. Likewise the tongue is a small part of the body, but it makes great boasts. Consider what a great forest is set on fire by a small spark. The tongue also is a fire, a world of evil among the parts of the body. It corrupts the whole person, sets the whole course of his life on fire, and is itself set on fire by hell.

All kinds of animals, birds, reptiles and creatures of the sea are being tamed and have been tamed by man, but no man can tame the tongue. It is a restless evil, full of deadly poison.

With the tongue we praise our Lord and Father, and with it we curse men, who have been made in God's likeness. Out of the same mouth come praise and cursing. My brothers, this should not be. Can both fresh water and salt[a] water flow from the same spring? My brothers, can a fig tree bear olives, or a grapevine bear figs? Neither can a salt spring produce fresh water.

TWO KINDS OF WISDOM

Who is wise and understanding among you? Let him show it by his good life, by deeds done in the humility that comes from wisdom. But if you harbor bitter envy and selfish ambition in your hearts, do not boast about it or deny the truth. Such "wisdom" does not come down from heaven but is earthly, unspiritual, of the devil. For where you have envy and selfish ambition, there you find disorder and every evil practice.

But the wisdom that comes from heaven is first of all pure; then peace-loving, considerate, submissive, full of mercy and good fruit, impartial and sincere. Peacemakers who sow in peace raise a harvest of righteousness.

SUBMIT YOURSELVES TO GOD

What causes fights and quarrels among you? Don't they come from your desires that battle within you? You want something but don't get it. You kill and covet, but you cannot have what you want. You quarrel and fight. You do not have, because you do not ask God. When you ask, you do not receive, because you ask with wrong motives, that you may spend what you get on your pleasures.

You adulterous people, don't you know that friendship with the world is hatred toward God? Anyone who chooses to be a friend of the world becomes an enemy of God. Or do you think Scripture says without reason that the spirit he caused to live in us envies intensely?[b] But he gives us more grace. That is why Scripture says:

"God opposes the proud
  but gives grace to the humble."[c]

Submit yourselves, then, to God. Resist the devil, and he will flee from you. Come near to God and he will come near to you. Wash your hands, you sinners, and purify your hearts, you double-minded. Grieve, mourn and wail. Change your laughter to mourning and your joy to gloom. Humble yourselves before the Lord, and he will lift you up.

Brothers, do not slander one another. Anyone who speaks against his brother or judges him speaks against the law and judges it. When you judge the law, you are not keeping it, but sitting in judgment on it. There is only one Lawgiver and Judge, the one who is able to save and destroy. But you — who are you to judge your neighbor?

Boasting about Tomorrow

Now listen, you who say, "Today or tomorrow we will go to this or that city, spend a year there, carry on business and make money." Why, you do not even know what will happen tomorrow. What is your life? You are a mist that appears for a little while and then vanishes. Instead, you ought to say, "If it is the Lord's will, we will live and do this or that." As it is, you boast and brag. All such boasting is evil. Anyone, then, who knows the good he ought to do and doesn't do it, sins.

"Submit yourselves . . . to God.
Resist the devil, and he will flee from you."

From Oswald Chambers

~ Submission . . . means etymologically surrender to another, but in the evangelical sense it means that I conduct myself actually among men as the submissive child of my Father in heaven. CD VOL. 2, 28

~ Relief in the redemption is difficult because it needs surrender first. I never can believe until I have surrendered myself to God. HG 106

~ Take an absolute plunge into the love of God, and when you are there you will be amazed at your foolishness for not getting there before. IWP 48

~ We have dragged down the idea of surrender and of sacrifice; we have taken the life out of the words and made them mean something sad and weary and despicable. In the Bible they mean the very opposite. LG 148

~ Our Lord habitually submitted His will to His Father, that is, He engineered nothing but left room for God. The modern trend is dead against this submission; we do engineer, and engineer with all the sanctified ingenuity we have, and when God suddenly bursts in in an expected way, we are taken unawares. It is easier to engineer things than determinedly submit all our powers to God. We say we must do all we can: Jesus says we must let God do all He can. MFL 109

❧ In every degree in which you are not real, you will dispute rather than come; you will quibble rather than come; you will go through sorrow rather than come; you will do anything rather than come the last lap of unutterable foolishness—"Just as I am." As long as you have the tiniest bit of spiritual impertinence, it will always reveal itself in the fact that you are expecting God to tell you to do a big thing, and all He is telling you to do is to "come." MUH 282

❧ Submission does not mean that I submit to the power of God because I must. A stoic submits without passion; that is slavery. A saint sees God's will and submits to it with a passionate love, and in his daily life exhibits his love to God to whom he has submitted. PH 56

❧ We are much more ready to celebrate what Jesus Christ has done than to surrender to Him. I do not mean the initial surrender to God of a sinner, but the more glorious surrender to God of a saint. PH 86

❧ The tendency is strong to say—"Oh, God won't be so stern as to expect me to give up that!" *but He will;* "He won't expect me to walk in the light so that I have nothing to hide," *but He will;* "He won't expect me to draw on His grace for everything," *but He will.* RTR 3

❧ By surrendering ourselves to quiet communion with God, by resting for a while from all our thinking and acting and serving, by leaving all things for once in our Heavenly Father's hands, secret wounds are healed, gathering unbelief is dispelled, and displaced armor refixed. RTR 81

---

a. Greek *bitter* (see also verse 14)
b. Or *that God jealously longs for the spirit that he made to live in us;* or *that the Spirit he caused to live in us longs jealously*
c. Prov. 3:34

87

WARNING TO RICH OPPRESSORS

ow listen, you rich people, weep and wail because of the misery that is coming upon you. Your wealth has rotted, and moths have eaten your clothes. Your gold and silver are corroded. Their corrosion will testify against you and eat your flesh like fire. You have hoarded wealth in the last days. Look! The wages you failed to pay the workmen who mowed your fields are crying out against you. The cries of the harvesters have reached the ears of the Lord Almighty. You have lived on earth in luxury and self-indulgence. You have fattened yourselves in the day of slaughter.[a] You have condemned and murdered innocent men, who were not opposing you.

PATIENCE IN SUFFERING

Be patient, then, brothers, until the Lord's coming. See how the farmer waits for the land to yield its valuable crop and how patient he is for the autumn and spring rains. You too, be patient and stand firm, because the Lord's coming is near. Don't grumble against each other, brothers, or you will be judged. The Judge is standing at the door!

Brothers, as an example of patience in the face of suffering, take the prophets who spoke in the name of the Lord. As you know, we consider blessed those who have persevered. You have heard of Job's perseverance and have seen what the Lord finally brought about. The Lord is full of compassion and mercy.

Above all, my brothers, do not swear—not by heaven or by earth or by anything else. Let your "Yes" be yes, and your "No," no, or you will be condemned.

THE PRAYER OF FAITH

Is any one of you in trouble? He should pray. Is anyone happy? Let him sing songs of praise. Is any one of you sick? He should call the elders of the church to pray over him and anoint him with oil in the name of the Lord. And the prayer offered in faith will make the sick person well; the Lord will raise him up. If he has sinned, he will be forgiven. Therefore confess your sins to each other and pray for each other so that you may be healed. The prayer of a righteous man is powerful and effective.

Elijah was a man just like us. He prayed earnestly that it would not rain, and it did not rain on the land for three and a half years. Again he prayed, and the heavens gave rain, and the earth produced its crops.

My brothers, if one of you should wander from the truth and someone should bring him back, remember this: Whoever turns a sinner from the error of his way will save him from death and cover over a multitude of sins.

*"Confess your sins to each other
and pray for each other so that you may be healed.
The prayer of a righteous man is powerful and effective."*

FROM OSWALD CHAMBERS

> ✌ The essential meaning of prayer is that it nourishes the life of the Son of God in me and enables Him to manifest Himself in my mortal flesh. BE 46

> ✌ Intercessory prayer is part of the sovereign purpose of God. If there were no saints praying for us, our lives would be infinitely balder than they are; consequently, the responsibility of those who never intercede and who are withholding blessing from other lives is truly appalling. CD VOL. 2, 57

> ✌ We do not ask: we worry, whereas one minute in prayer will put God's decree at work, viz., that He answers prayer on the ground of Redemption. BFB 77

> ✌ Our prayers should be in accordance with the nature of God; therefore, the answers are not in accordance with our nature but with

His. We are apt to forget this and to say without thinking that God does not answer prayer; but He always answers prayer, and when we are in close communion with Him, we know that we have not been misled. CD VOL. 2, 45

꙳ We must have a selected place for prayer and when we get there the plague of flies begins—This must be done, and that. "Shut thy door" (Matt. 6:6). A secret silence means to shut the door deliberately on emotions and remember God. God is in secret, and He sees us from the secret place; He does not see us as other people see us, or as we see ourselves. MUH 236

꙳ The prayers of some people are more efficacious than those of others, the reason being that they are under no delusion. They do not rely on their own earnestness; they rely absolutely on the supreme authority of the Lord Jesus Christ. PR 126

꙳ Prayer means that we get into union with God's view of other people. Our devotion as saints is to identify ourselves with God's interests in other lives. God pays no attention to our personal affinities; He expects us to identify ourselves and *His* interests in others. PR 97

꙳ It is not so true that "Prayer changes things" as that prayer changes *me,* and then I change things; consequently, we must not ask God to do what He has created us to do. IYA 14

꙳ There is always a suitable place to pray, to lift up your eyes to God; there is no need to get to a place of prayer; pray wherever you are. HG 22

꙳ Prayer alters a man on the inside, alters his mind and his attitude to things. The point of praying is not that we get things from God, but that we learn by prayer to detect the difference between God's order and God's permissive will. God's order is—no pain, no sickness, no devil, no war, no sin: His permissive will is all these things, the "soup" we are in just now. What a man needs to do is to get hold of God's order in the kingdom on the inside, and then he will begin to see how to handle the riddle of the universe on the outside. SHH 19

---

a. Or *yourselves as in a day of feasting*

88

1 PETER 1

PRAISE TO GOD FOR A LIVING HOPE

Peter, an apostle of Jesus Christ,
To God's elect, strangers in the world, scattered throughout Pontus, Galatia, Cappadocia, Asia and Bithynia, who have been chosen according to the foreknowledge of God the Father, through the sanctifying work of the Spirit, for obedience to Jesus Christ and sprinkling by his blood:

Grace and peace be yours in abundance.

Praise be to the God and Father of our Lord Jesus Christ! In his great mercy he has given us new birth into a living hope through the resurrection of Jesus Christ from the dead, and into an inheritance that can never perish, spoil or fade — kept in heaven for you, who through faith are shielded by God's power until the coming of the salvation that is ready to be revealed in the last time. In this you greatly rejoice, though now for a little while you may have had to suffer grief in all kinds of trials. These have come so that your faith — of greater worth than gold, which perishes even though refined by fire — may be proved genuine and may result in praise, glory and honor when Jesus Christ is revealed. Though you have not seen him, you love him; and even though you do not see him now, you believe in him and are filled with an inexpressible and glorious joy, for you are receiving the goal of your faith, the salvation of your souls.

Concerning this salvation, the prophets, who spoke of the grace that was to come to you, searched intently and with the greatest care, trying to find out the time and circumstances to which the Spirit of Christ in them was pointing when he predicted the sufferings of Christ and the glories that would follow. It was revealed to them that they were not serving themselves but you, when they spoke of the things that have now been told you by those who have preached the gospel to you by the Holy Spirit sent from heaven. Even angels long to look into these things.

BE HOLY

Therefore, prepare your minds for action; be self-controlled; set your hope fully on the grace to be given you when Jesus Christ is revealed. As obedient children, do not conform to the evil desires you had when you lived in ignorance. But just as he who called you is holy, so be holy in all you do; for it is written: "Be holy, because I am holy."[a]

Since you call on a Father who judges each man's work impartially, live your lives as strangers here in reverent fear. For you know that it was not with perishable things such as silver or gold that you were redeemed from the empty way of life handed down to you from your forefathers, but with the precious blood of Christ, a lamb without blemish or defect. He was chosen before the creation of the world, but was revealed in these last times for your sake. Through him you believe in God, who raised him from the dead and glorified him, and so your faith and hope are in God.

Now that you have purified yourselves by obeying the truth so that you have sincere love for your brothers, love one another deeply, from the heart.[b] For you have been born again, not of perishable seed, but of imperishable, through the living and enduring word of God. For,

"All men are like grass,
   and all their glory is like the flowers of the field;
the grass withers and the flowers fall,
   but the word of the Lord stands forever."[c]

And this is the word that was preached to you.

"As he who called you is holy, so be holy in all you do;
for it is written: 'Be holy, because I am holy.' "

FROM OSWALD CHAMBERS

❧ What is holiness? Transfigured morality blazing with indwelling God. Any other kind of holiness is fictitious and dangerous. One of the dangers of dealing too much with the higher Christian life is that it is apt to fizzle off into abstractions. But when we see holiness in the Lord Jesus, we do know what it means; it means an unsullied walk with the feet, unsullied talk with the tongue, unsullied thinking of the mind, unsullied transactions of the bodily organs, unsullied life of the heart, unsullied dreams of the imagination—that is the actual holiness Jesus says He has given. This is the meaning of sanctification. PR 135

 Wherever Jesus comes, He reveals that man is away from God by reason of sin, and man is terrified at His presence. That is why men will put anything in the place of Jesus Christ, anything rather than let God come near in His startling purity, because immediately when God comes near, conscience records that God is holy and nothing unholy can live with Him; consequently, His presence hurts the sinner. "If I had not come and spoken unto them, they had not had sin: but now they have no cloak for their sin" (John 15:22). PS 62

 God's Book reveals all through that holiness will bring persecution from those who are not holy. PS 80

 You can never make yourself holy by external acts, but, if you are holy, your external acts will be the natural expression of holiness. RTR 23

 "The Son of man came eating and drinking" (Luke 7:34). One of the most staggering things in the New Testament is just this commonplace aspect. The curious difference between Jesus Christ's idea of holiness and that of other religions lies here. The one says holiness is not compatible with ordinary food and married life, but Jesus Christ represents a character lived straight down in the ordinary amalgam of human life, and His claim is that the character He manifested is possible for any man, if he will come in by the door provided for him. SA 33

 Jesus Christ's holiness has to do with human life as it is. It is not a mystical, aesthetic thing that cannot work in the ordinary things of life; it is a holiness which "can be achieved with an ordinary diet and a wife and five children." SA 74

---

a. Lev. 11:44-45; 19:2; 20:7
b. Some early manuscripts *from a pure heart*
c. Isaiah 40:6-8

89

1 PETER 2

THE LIVING STONE
AND A CHOSEN PEOPLE

herefore, rid yourselves of all malice and all deceit, hypocrisy, envy, and slander of every kind. Like new-born babies, crave pure spiritual milk, so that by it you may grow up in your salvation, now that you have tasted that the Lord is good.

As you come to him, the living Stone—rejected by men but chosen by God and precious to him—you also, like living stones, are being built into a spiritual house to be a holy priesthood, offering spiritual sacrifices acceptable to God through Jesus Christ. For in Scripture it says:

> "See, I lay a stone in Zion,
>   a chosen and precious cornerstone,
> and the one who trusts in him
>   will never be put to shame."[a]

Now to you who believe, this stone is precious. But to those who do not believe,

> "The stone the builders rejected
>   has become the capstone,[b]"[c]

and,

> "A stone that causes men to stumble
>   and a rock that makes them fall."[d]

They stumble because they disobey the message—which is also what they were destined for.

But you are a chosen people, a royal priesthood, a holy nation, a people belonging to God, that you may declare the praises of him who called you out of darkness into his wonderful light. Once you were not a people, but now you are the people of God; once you had not received mercy, but now you have received mercy.

Dear friends, I urge you, as aliens and strangers in the world, to abstain from sinful desires, which war against your soul. Live such good lives among the pagans that, though they accuse you of doing wrong, they may see your good deeds and glorify God on the day he visits us.

SUBMISSION TO RULERS AND MASTERS

Submit yourselves for the Lord's sake to every authority instituted among men: whether to the king, as the supreme authority, or to governors, who are sent by him to punish those who do wrong and to commend those who do right. For it is God's will that by doing good you should silence the ignorant talk of foolish men. Live as free men, but do not use your freedom as a cover-up for evil; live as servants of God. Show proper respect to everyone: Love the brotherhood of believers, fear God, honor the king.

Slaves, submit yourselves to your masters with all respect, not only to those who are good and considerate, but also to those who are harsh. For it is commendable if a man bears up under the pain of unjust suffering because he is conscious of God. But how is it to your credit if you receive a beating for doing wrong and endure it? But if you suffer for doing good and you endure it, this is commendable before God. To this you were called, because Christ suffered for you, leaving you an example, that you should follow in his steps.

> "He committed no sin,
>   and no deceit was found in his mouth."[e]

When they hurled their insults at him, he did not retaliate; when he suffered, he made no threats. Instead, he entrusted himself to him who judges justly. He himself bore our sins in his body on the tree, so that we might die to sins and live for righteousness; by his wounds you have been healed. For you were like sheep going astray, but now you have returned to the Shepherd and Overseer of your souls.

"You are a chosen people, a royal priesthood,
a holy nation, a people belonging to God,
that you may declare the praises of him who called you
out of darkness into his wonderful light."

FROM OSWALD CHAMBERS

❧ There is no variableness in God, no "shadow that is cast by turning." We are told that where there is light and substance, there must be shadow; but there is no shadow in God, none whatever. BP 219

❧ A searchlight illuminates only what it does and no more; but let daylight come, and you find there are a thousand and one things the searchlight had not revealed. Whenever you get the light of God on salvation, it acts like a searchlight. Everything you read in the Bible teaches salvation and you say, "Why, it is as simple as can be!" The same with sanctification and the Second Coming. When you come to the place where God is the dominant light, you find facts you never realized before, facts which no one is sufficient to explain, save the Lord Jesus Christ. BSG 62

❧ In actual life we must be always in the light, and we cease to be in the light when we want to explain why we did a thing. The significant thing about our Lord is that He never explained anything; He let mistakes correct themselves because He always lived in the light. There is so much in us that is folded and twisted, but the sign that we are following God is that we keep in the light. LG 66

❧ To walk in the light means that everything that is of the darkness drives me closer into the center of the light. MUH 361

❧ One step in the right direction in obedience to the light, and the manifestation of the Son of God in your mortal flesh is as certain as that God is on His throne. When once God's light has come to us through Jesus Christ, we must never hang back, but obey; and we shall not walk in darkness, but will have the light of life. OBH 43

ン "What I tell you in darkness"—watch where God puts you into darkness, and when you are there, keep your mouth shut. When you are in the dark, listen, and God will give you a very precious message for someone else when you get into the light. RTR 83

ン Light is the description of clear, beautiful, moral character from God's standpoint, and if we walk in the light, "the blood of Jesus Christ cleanses us from all sin" (1 John 1:7); God Almighty can find nothing to censure. SA 52

---

a. Isaiah 28:16
b. Or *cornerstone*
c. Psalm 118:22
d. Isaiah 8:14
e. Isaiah 53:9

WIVES AND HUSBANDS

ives, in the same way be submissive to your husbands so that, if any of them do not believe the word, they may be won over without words by the behavior of their wives, when they see the purity and reverence of your lives. Your beauty should not come from outward adornment, such as braided hair and the wearing of gold jewelry and fine clothes. Instead, it should be that of your inner self, the unfading beauty of a gentle and quiet spirit, which is of great worth in God's sight. For this is the way the holy women of the past who put their hope in God used to make themselves beautiful. They were submissive to their own husbands, like Sarah, who obeyed Abraham and called him her master. You are her daughters if you do what is right and do not give way to fear.

Husbands, in the same way be considerate as you live with your wives, and treat them with respect as the weaker partner and as heirs with you of the gracious gift of life, so that nothing will hinder your prayers.

SUFFERING FOR DOING GOOD

Finally, all of you, live in harmony with one another; be sympathetic, love as brothers, be compassionate and humble. Do not repay evil with evil or insult with insult, but with blessing, because to this you were called so that you may inherit a blessing. For,

> "Whoever would love life
> and see good days
> must keep his tongue from evil

and his lips from deceitful speech.
He must turn from evil and do good;
he must seek peace and pursue it.
For the eyes of the Lord are on the righteous
and his ears are attentive to their prayer,
but the face of the Lord is against those who do evil."[a]

Who is going to harm you if you are eager to do good? But even if you should suffer for what is right, you are blessed. "Do not fear what they fear[b]; do not be frightened."[c] But in your hearts set apart Christ as Lord. Always be prepared to give an answer to everyone who asks you to give the reason for the hope that you have. But do this with gentleness and respect, keeping a clear conscience, so that those who speak maliciously against your good behavior in Christ may be ashamed of their slander. It is better, if it is God's will, to suffer for doing good than for doing evil. For Christ died for sins once for all, the righteous for the unrighteous, to bring you to God. He was put to death in the body but made alive by the Spirit, through whom[d] also he went and preached to the spirits in prison who disobeyed long ago when God waited patiently in the days of Noah while the ark was being built. In it only a few people, eight in all, were saved through water, and this water symbolizes baptism that now saves you also—not the removal of dirt from the body but the pledge[e] of a good conscience toward God. It saves you by the resurrection of Jesus Christ, who has gone into heaven and is at God's right hand—with angels, authorities and powers in submission to him.

"Christ died for sins once for all,
the righteous for the unrighteous,
to bring you to God."

FROM OSWALD CHAMBERS

❧ The one who talked most about sin was our Lord Jesus Christ. We are apt to run off with the idea that in order to be saved from sin a man must have lived a vile life himself; but the One who has an understanding of the awful horror of sin is the spotlessly holy

Christ, who "knew no sin." The lower down we get into the experience of sin, the less conviction of sin we have. When we are regenerated and lifted into the light, we begin to know what sin means. HG 89

❧ Cleansing from all sin does not mean conscious deliverance from sin only; it means infinitely more than we are conscious of. The part we are conscious of is walking in the light. Cleansing from all sin means something infinitely more profound; it means cleansing from all sin in the sight of God. God never bases any of His work on our consciousness. MFL 44

❧ Many people are never guilty of gross sins. They are not brought up in that way; they are too refined, have too much good taste; but that does not mean that the disposition to sin is not there. The essence of sin is my claim to my right to myself. I may prefer to live morally because it is better for me. I am responsible to no one; my conscience is my god. That is the very essence of sin. MFL 22

❧ To be born of God means that I have the supernatural power of God to stop sinning. In the Bible it is never—Should a Christian sin? The Bible puts it emphatically—*a Christian must not sin.* The effective working of the new birth life in us is that we do not commit sin, not merely that we have the power not to sin, but that we have stopped sinning. MUH 228

❧ If God overlooked one sin in me, He would cease to be God. OPG 16

❧ *Sin* has to be cleansed; *sins* must be forgiven. The redemption of Jesus Christ deals with sin. BE 63

❧ Conviction of sin and being guilty of sins are not the same thing. Conviction of sin is produced by the incoming of the Holy Spirit, because conscience is promptly made to look at God's demands and the whole nature cries out, in some form or other, "What must I do to be saved?" BE 76

---

a. Psalm 34:12-16
b. Or *not fear their threats*
c. Isaiah 8:12
d. Or *alive in the spirit, through which*
e. Or *response*

91

1 PETER 4–5

LIVING FOR GOD

T herefore, since Christ suffered in his body, arm yourselves also with the same attitude, because he who has suffered in his body is done with sin. As a result, he does not live the rest of his earthly life for evil human desires, but rather for the will of God. For you have spent enough time in the past doing what pagans choose to do—living in debauchery, lust, drunkenness, orgies, carousing and detestable idolatry. They think it strange that you do not plunge with them into the same flood of dissipation, and they heap abuse on you. But they will have to give account to him who is ready to judge the living and the dead. For this is the reason the gospel was preached even to those who are now dead, so that they might be judged according to men in regard to the body, but live according to God in regard to the spirit.

The end of all things is near. Therefore be clear minded and self-controlled so that you can pray. Above all, love each other deeply, because love covers over a multitude of sins. Offer hospitality to one another without grumbling. Each one should use whatever gift he has received to serve others, faithfully administering God's grace in its various forms. If anyone speaks, he should do it as one speaking the very words of God. If anyone serves, he should do it with the strength God provides, so that in all things God may be praised through Jesus Christ. To him be the glory and the power for ever and ever. Amen.

SUFFERING FOR BEING A CHRISTIAN

Dear friends, do not be surprised at the painful trial you are suffering, as though something strange were happening to you.

But rejoice that you participate in the sufferings of Christ, so that you may be overjoyed when his glory is revealed. If you are insulted because of the name of Christ, you are blessed, for the Spirit of glory and of God rests on you. If you suffer, it should not be as a murderer or thief or any other kind of criminal, or even as a meddler. However, if you suffer as a Christian, do not be ashamed, but praise God that you bear that name. For it is time for judgment to begin with the family of God; and if it begins with us, what will the outcome be for those who do not obey the gospel of God? And,

"If it is hard for the righteous to be saved,
what will become of the ungodly and the sinner?"[a]

So then, those who suffer according to God's will should commit themselves to their faithful Creator and continue to do good.

To Elders and Young Men

To the elders among you, I appeal as a fellow elder, a witness of Christ's sufferings and one who also will share in the glory to be revealed: Be shepherds of God's flock that is under your care, serving as overseers—not because you must, but because you are willing, as God wants you to be; not greedy for money, but eager to serve; not lording it over those entrusted to you, but being examples to the flock. And when the Chief Shepherd appears, you will receive the crown of glory that will never fade away.

Young men, in the same way be submissive to those who are older. All of you, clothe yourselves with humility toward one another, because,

"God opposes the proud
but gives grace to the humble."[b]

Humble yourselves, therefore, under God's mighty hand, that he may lift you up in due time. Cast all your anxiety on him because he cares for you.

Be self-controlled and alert. Your enemy the devil prowls around like a roaring lion looking for someone to devour. Resist him, standing firm in the faith, because you know that your brothers throughout the world are undergoing the same kind of sufferings.

And the God of all grace, who called you to his eternal glory in Christ, after you have suffered a little while, will himself restore you and make you strong, firm and steadfast. To him be the power for ever and ever. Amen.

FINAL GREETINGS

With the help of Silas,[c] whom I regard as a faithful brother, I have written to you briefly, encouraging you and testifying that this is the true grace of God. Stand fast in it.

She who is in Babylon, chosen together with you, sends you her greetings, and so does my son Mark. Greet one another with a kiss of love.

Peace to all of you who are in Christ.

"If you suffer as a Christian, do not be ashamed,
but praise God that you bear that name."

FROM OSWALD CHAMBERS

- When we talk about suffering, we are apt to think only of bodily pain, or of suffering because we have given up something for God, which is paltry nonsense. AUG 28

- Why there should be suffering we do not know; but we have to remain loyal to the character of God as revealed by Jesus Christ in the face of it. BE 93

- The awful problem of suffering continually crops up in the Scriptures, and in life and remains a mystery. CD VOL. 1, 61

- To be able to explain suffering is the clearest indication of never having suffered. Sin, suffering, and sanctification are not problems of the mind, but facts of life—mysteries that awaken all other mysteries until the heart rests in God, and waiting patiently knows "He doeth all things well." CD VOL. 1, 61

- To suffer because of meekness is an exalting, refining, and God-glorifying suffering. And mark this and mark it well, to suffer "as a

357

Christian" is a shameful thing in the eyes of the societies of this world. The friends who in your hour of trial and slander gather round to support and stand with you, are first amazed, then dazed, and then disgusted, when they find that you really do not mean to stand up for yourself, but meekly to submit. CD VOL. 1, 68

~ To "suffer as a Christian" is not to be marked peculiar as of your views, or because you will not bend to conventionality. These things are not Christian but ordinary human traits from which all men suffer irrespective of creed or religion or no religion. To "suffer as a Christian" is to suffer because there is an essential difference between you and the world which rouses the contempt of the world and the disgust and hatred of the spirit that is in the world. To "suffer as a Christian" is to have no answer when the world's satire is turned on you, as it was turned on Jesus Christ when He hung upon the cross, when they turned His words into jest and jeer; they will do the same to you. He gave no answer; neither can you. CD VOL. 1, 69

~ Suffering is grand when the heart is right with God. But for the night "the moon and the stars, which Thou has ordained" (Ps. 8:3) would never be seen. And so God giveth to His own "the treasures of darkness" (Isa. 45:3). CD VOL. 1, 85

~ The saint knows not why he suffers as he does, yet he comprehends with a knowledge that passeth knowledge that all is well. CD VOL. 2, 105

~ We are called to fellowship with His sufferings, and some of the greatest suffering lies in remaining powerless where He remained powerless. LG 56

~ To choose to suffer means that there is something wrong; to choose God's will even if it means suffering is a very different thing. No healthy saint ever chooses suffering; He chooses God's will, as Jesus did, whether it means suffering or not. MUH 223

---

a. Prov. 11:31
b. Prov. 3:34
c. Greek *Silvanus*, a variant of *Silas*

92

2 PETER 1

MAKING ONE'S CALLING
AND ELECTION SURE

S imon Peter, a servant and apostle of Jesus Christ,
To those who through the righteousness of our God
and Savior Jesus Christ have received a faith as precious as ours:

Grace and peace be yours in abundance through the knowledge of God and of Jesus our Lord.

His divine power has given us everything we need for life and godliness through our knowledge of him who called us by his own glory and goodness. Through these he has given us his very great and precious promises, so that through them you may participate in the divine nature and escape the corruption in the world caused by evil desires.

For this very reason, make every effort to add to your faith goodness; and to goodness, knowledge; and to knowledge, self-control; and to self-control, perseverance; and to perseverance, godliness; and to godliness, brotherly kindness; and to brotherly kindness, love. For if you possess these qualities in increasing measure, they will keep you from being ineffective and unproductive in your knowledge of our Lord Jesus Christ. But if anyone does not have them, he is nearsighted and blind, and has forgotten that he has been cleansed from his past sins.

Therefore, my brothers, be all the more eager to make your calling and election sure. For if you do these things, you will never fall, and you will receive a rich welcome into the eternal kingdom of our Lord and Savior Jesus Christ.

PROPHECY OF SCRIPTURE

So I will always remind you of these things, even though you know them and are firmly established in the truth you now have. I think it is right to refresh your memory as long as I live in the tent of this body, because I know that I will soon put it aside, as our Lord Jesus Christ has made clear to me. And I will make every effort to see that after my departure you will always be able to remember these things.

We did not follow cleverly invented stories when we told you about the power and coming of our Lord Jesus Christ, but we were eyewitnesses of his majesty. For he received honor and glory from God the Father when the voice came to him from the Majestic Glory, saying, "This is my Son, whom I love; with him I am well pleased."[a] We ourselves heard this voice that came from heaven when we were with him on the sacred mountain.

And we have the word of the prophets made more certain, and you will do well to pay attention to it, as to a light shining in a dark place, until the day dawns and the morning star rises in your hearts. Above all, you must understand that no prophecy of Scripture came about by the prophet's own interpretation. For prophecy never had its origin in the will of man, but men spoke from God as they were carried along by the Holy Spirit.

"His divine power has given us everything we need
for life and godliness through our knowledge of him
who called us by his own glory and goodness."

FROM OSWALD CHAMBERS

- ⌘ The One who made the world and who upholds all things by the word of His power is the One who keeps His saints. GW 44

- ⌘ "Power from on high"—the words have a fascinating sound in the ears of men, but this power is not a magical power, not the power to work miracles; it is the power that transforms character, that sanctifies faculties. "But ye shall receive power, when the Holy Ghost is come upon you" (Acts 1:8), said Jesus to the disciples, and they did—the power that made them like their Lord. HGM 22

✋ We have a great deal more power than we know, and as we do the overcoming we find He is there all the time until it becomes the habit of our life. HGM 30

✋ There is only one "power from on high," a holy power that transfigures morality. Never yield to a power unless you know its character. LG 121

✋ As Son of man, Jesus Christ deliberately limited omnipotence, omnipresence, and omniscience in Himself, now they are His in absolute full power. As deity, they were always His; now as Son of man they are His in absolute full power. PR 124

✋ At the throne of God, Jesus Christ has all power as Son of man. That means He can do anything for any human being in keeping with His own character. PR 124

✋ While we are on this earth, living in alien territory, it is a marvelous emancipation to know that we are raised above it all through Jesus Christ, and that we have power over all the power of the enemy in and through Him. PS 75

✋ Can God keep me from stumbling this second? Yes. Can He keep me from sin this second? Yes. Well, that is the whole of life. You cannot live more than a second at a time. If God can keep you blameless this second, He can do it the next. No wonder Jesus Christ said, "Let not your heart be troubled!" (John 14:1) We do get troubled when we do not remember the amazing power of God. RTR 87

✋ The Bible characters fell on their strong points, never on their weak ones. "Kept by the power of God"—that is the only safeguard. RTR 47

✋ Before we were saved we had not the power to obey, but now He has planted in us on the ground of redemption the heredity of the Son of God, we have the power to obey, and, consequently, the power to disobey. SSM 104

---

a. Matt. 17:5; Mark 9:7; Luke 9:35

93

2 PETER 2

FALSE TEACHERS
AND THEIR DESTRUCTION

But there were also false prophets among the people, just as there will be false teachers among you. They will secretly introduce destructive heresies, even denying the sovereign Lord who bought them—bringing swift destruction on themselves. Many will follow their shameful ways and will bring the way of truth into disrepute. In their greed these teachers will exploit you with stories they have made up. Their condemnation has long been hanging over them, and their destruction has not been sleeping.

For if God did not spare angels when they sinned, but sent them to hell,[a] putting them into gloomy dungeons[b] to be held for judgment; if he did not spare the ancient world when he brought the flood on its ungodly people, but protected Noah, a preacher of righteousness, and seven others; if he condemned the cities of Sodom and Gomorrah by burning them to ashes, and made them an example of what is going to happen to the ungodly; and if he rescued Lot, a righteous man, who was distressed by the filthy lives of lawless men (for that righteous man, living among them day after day, was tormented in his righteous soul by the lawless deeds he saw and heard)—if this is so, then the Lord knows how to rescue godly men from trials and to hold the unrighteous for the day of judgment, while continuing their punishment.[c] This is especially true of those who follow the corrupt desire of the sinful nature[d] and despise authority.

Bold and arrogant, these men are not afraid to slander celestial beings; yet even angels, although they are stronger and more powerful, do not bring slanderous accusations against such beings in the presence of the Lord. But these men blaspheme in matters they do not understand. They are like brute beasts, creatures of instinct, born only to be caught and destroyed, and like beasts they too will perish.

They will be paid back with harm for the harm they have done. Their idea of pleasure is to carouse in broad daylight. They are blots and blemishes, reveling in their pleasures while they feast with you.[e] With eyes full of adultery, they never stop sinning; they seduce the unstable; they are experts in greed — an accursed brood! They have left the straight way and wandered off to follow the way of Balaam son of Beor, who loved the wages of wickedness. But he was rebuked for his wrongdoing by a donkey — a beast without speech — who spoke with a man's voice and restrained the prophet's madness.

These men are springs without water and mists driven by a storm. Blackest darkness is reserved for them. For they mouth empty, boastful words and, by appealing to the lustful desires of sinful human nature, they entice people who are just escaping from those who live in error. They promise them freedom, while they themselves are slaves of depravity — for a man is a slave to whatever has mastered him. If they have escaped the corruption of the world by knowing our Lord and Savior Jesus Christ and are again entangled in it and overcome, they are worse off at the end than they were at the beginning. It would have been better for them not to have known the way of righteousness, than to have known it and then to turn their backs on the sacred command that was passed on to them. Of them the proverbs are true: "A dog returns to its vomit,"[f] and, "A sow that is washed goes back to her wallowing in the mud."

"There were also false prophets among the people,
just as there will be false teachers among you . . .
denying the sovereign Lord."

From Oswald Chambers

❧ One of the most despairing things of our day is the shallow dogmatic competence of the people who tell us they believe in the teachings of Jesus but not in His Atonement. The most unmitigated piece of nonsense human ears ever listened to! Believe in the teachings of Jesus—what is the good of it? What is the good of telling me that I have to be what I know I never can be if I live for a million years—perfect as God is perfect? What is the good of telling me I have to be a child of my Father in heaven and be like Him? We must rid our minds of the idea that is being introduced by the modern trend of things that Jesus Christ came to teach. The world is sick of teachers. Teachers never can do any good unless they can interpret the teaching that is already here. HG 59

❧ Jesus Christ is not a great teacher alongside Plato and other great teachers; He stands absolutely alone. "Test your teachers," said Jesus; the teachers who come from God are those who clear the way to Jesus Christ, and keep it clear. We are estimated in God's sight as workers by whether or not we clear the way for people to see Jesus. HGM 125

❧ If a teacher fascinates with his doctrine, his teaching never came from God. The teacher sent from God is the one who clears the way to Jesus and keeps it clear; souls forget altogether about him because the vision of Jesus is the only abiding result. When people are attracted to Jesus Christ through you, see always that you stay on God all the time, and their hearts and affections will never stop at you. IWP 112

❧ If once you get the thought, "It is my winsome way of putting it, my presentation of the truth that attracts"—the only name for that is the ugly name of thief, stealing the hearts of the sheep of God who do not know why they stop at you. Keep the mind stayed on God, and I defy anyone's heart to stop at you, it will always go on to God. IWP 112

❧ The test for apostles and teachers is not that they talk wonderful stuff, not that they are able to expound God's Word, but that they edify the saints. OBH 42

---

a. Greek *Tartarus*
b. Some manuscripts *into chains of darkness*
c. Or *unrighteous for punishment until the day of judgment*
d. Or *the flesh*
e. Some manuscripts *in their love feasts*
f. Prov. 26:11

THE DAY OF THE LORD

Dear friends, this is now my second letter to you. I have written both of them as reminders to stimulate you to wholesome thinking. I want you to recall the words spoken in the past by the holy prophets and the command given by our Lord and Savior through your apostles.

First of all, you must understand that in the last days scoffers will come, scoffing and following their own evil desires. They will say, "Where is this 'coming' he promised? Ever since our fathers died, everything goes on as it has since the beginning of creation." But they deliberately forget that long ago by God's word the heavens existed and the earth was formed out of water and by water. By these waters also the world of that time was deluged and destroyed. By the same word the present heavens and earth are reserved for fire, being kept for the day of judgment and destruction of ungodly men.

But do not forget this one thing, dear friends: With the Lord a day is like a thousand years, and a thousand years are like a day. The Lord is not slow in keeping his promise, as some understand slowness. He is patient with you, not wanting anyone to perish, but everyone to come to repentance.

But the day of the Lord will come like a thief. The heavens will disappear with a roar; the elements will be destroyed by fire, and the earth and everything in it will be laid bare.[a]

Since everything will be destroyed in this way, what kind of people ought you to be? You ought to live holy and godly lives as you look forward to the day of God and speed its coming.[b] That day will bring about the destruction of the heavens by fire, and the elements will melt in the heat. But in keeping with his promise we are looking forward to a new heaven and a new earth, the home of righteousness.

So then, dear friends, since you are looking forward to this, make every effort to be found spotless, blameless and at peace with him. Bear in mind that our Lord's patience means salvation, just as our dear brother Paul also wrote you with the wisdom that God gave him. He writes the same way in all his letters, speaking in them of these matters. His letters contain some things that are hard to understand, which ignorant and unstable people distort, as they do the other Scriptures, to their own destruction.

Therefore, dear friends, since you already know this, be on your guard so that you may not be carried away by the error of lawless men and fall from your secure position. But grow in the grace and knowledge of our Lord and Savior Jesus Christ. To him be glory both now and forever! Amen.

> *"The Lord is not slow in keeping his promise,*
> *as some understand slowness. He is patient with you,*
> *not wanting anyone to perish,*
> *but everyone to come to repentance."*

FROM OSWALD CHAMBERS

ও The patience of God and the patience of our Lord is working to one grand divine event, and our Lord knows, as He did in the days of His flesh, how all His saints are straightened till it be accomplished. CD VOL. 2, 148

ও "The word of My patience" (Rev. 3:10) is a striking phrase. It cannot be the patience of pessimism because that was not the characteristic of the patience of our Lord; neither is it the patience of exhaustion, for "He shall not fail nor be discouraged" (Isa. 42:4). It is surely the patience of love, the patience of joyfulness, which knows that God reigns and rules and rejoices, and that His joy is our strength. CD VOL. 2, 155

ও The patience of the saints, like the patience of our Lord, puts the sovereignty of God over all the saint's career. And because the love of God is shed abroad in our hearts by the Holy Ghost, we choose by our free will what God predestinates, for the mind of God, the mind of the Holy Spirit, and the mind of the saint are all held together by a oneness of personal passionate devotion. CD VOL. 2, 156

    ∿ When we first become rightly related to God, we have the idea that we have to talk to everyone, until we get one or two well deserved snubs; then our Lord takes us aside and teaches us His way of dealing with them. How impatient we are in dealing with others! Our attitude implies that we think God is asleep. When we begin to reason and work in God's way, He reminds us first of all how long it took Him to get us where we are, and we realize His amazing patience, and we learn to come on other lives from above. As we learn to rely on the Spirit of God, He gives us the resourcefulness of Jesus. MFL 126

    ∿ Jesus says we are to keep the word of His patience. There are so many things in this life that it seems much better to be impatient about. The best illustration is that of an archer. He pulls the string farther and farther away from his bow with the arrow fixed; then, when it is adjusted, with his eye on the mark, he lets fly. The Christian's life is like that. God is the archer: He takes the saint like a bow which He stretches, and we get to a certain point and say, "I can't stand any more; I can't stand this test of patience any longer," but God goes on stretching. He is not aiming at our mark, but at His own, and the patience of the saints is that we hold on until He lets the arrow fly straight to His goal. PH 149

    ∿ We have to stop hesitating and take the first step; and the first step is to stop hestitating! "How long halt ye between two opinions?" (1 Kings 18:21) There are times when we wish that God would kick us right over the line and *make* us do the thing; but the remarkable thing about God's patience is that He waits until we stop hesitating. Some of us hesitate so long that we become like spiritual storks. We look elegant only as long as we stand on one leg; when we stand on two we look very ungraceful. OBH 52

---

a. Some manuscripts *be burned up*
b. Or *as you wait eagerly for the day of God to come*

95

1 JOHN 1

THE WORD OF LIFE

That which was from the beginning, which we have heard, which we have seen with our eyes, which we have looked at and our hands have touched—this we proclaim concerning the Word of life. The life appeared; we have seen it and testify to it, and we proclaim to you the eternal life, which was with the Father and has appeared to us. We proclaim to you what we have seen and heard, so that you also may have fellowship with us. And our fellowship is with the Father and with his Son, Jesus Christ. We write this to make our[a] joy complete.

WALKING IN THE LIGHT

This is the message we have heard from him and declare to you: God is light; in him there is no darkness at all. If we claim to have fellowship with him yet walk in the darkness, we lie and do not live by the truth. But if we walk in the light, as he is in the light, we have fellowship with one another, and the blood of Jesus, his Son, purifies us from all[b] sin.

If we claim to be without sin, we deceive ourselves and the truth is not in us. If we confess our sins, he is faithful and just and will forgive us our sins and purify us from all unrighteousness. If we claim we have not sinned, we make him out to be a liar and his word has no place in our lives.

"Therefore, my brothers, be all the more eager
to make your calling and election sure.
For if you do these things, you will never fall,

*and you will receive a rich welcome into the eternal kingdom
of our Lord and Savior Jesus Christ."*

FROM OSWALD CHAMBERS

- "Many are called, but few prove the choice ones" (see Matt. 20:16); that is, few of us take up the cross and follow Jesus, the reason being not that we are irreligious and bad, but we don't prefer that Jesus should be Lord. HBM 140

- The call of God is not for the special few; it is for everyone. Whether or not I hear God's call depends upon the state of my ears; and what I hear depends upon my disposition. "Many are called but few are chosen" (Matt. 20:16), that is, few prove themselves the chosen ones. MUH 14

- To ratify is to make sure of. I have to form the habit of assuring myself of my election, to bend the whole energy of my Christian powers to realize my calling, and to do that I must remember what I am saved for, viz., that the Son of God might be manifested in my mortal flesh. OBH 80

- Deliverance from sin is not a question of God's election, but of an experience in human life which God demands. The effective working of the new birth life in us is that we do not commit sin, not merely that we have the power not to sin, but that we have stopped sinning—a much more practical thing. PR 35

- "I have chosen you" (John 15:16). Keep that note of greatness in your creed. It is not that you have got God, but that He has got you. Why is God at work in me, bending, breaking, molding, doing just as He chooses?—for one purpose only—that He may be able to say, "This is My man, My woman." RTR 21

- When this election to God in Christ Jesus is realized by us individually, God begins to destroy our prejudices and our parochial notions and to turn us into the servants of His own purpose. The experience of salvation in individual lives means the incoming of this realization of the election of God. SSY 101

- The connection between the election of God and human free will is confusing to our Gentile type of mind, but the connection was an

371

essential element underlying all Hebrew thought. The predestinations of God cannot be experienced by individuals of their own free choice; but when we are born again, the fact that we do choose what has been predestined of God comes to us as a revelation. The rationalist says it is absurd to imagine that the purposes of Almighty God are furthered by an individual life, but it is true. God's predestinations are the voluntary, choosing of the sanctified soul. SSY 102

ॐ The realization by regeneration of the election of God, and of being made thereby perfectly fit for Him, is the most joyful realization on earth. When we are born from above we *realize* the election of God, our being regenerated does not *create* it. When once we realize that through the salvation of Jesus we are made perfectly fit for God, we understand why Jesus is apparently so ruthless in His claims, why He demands such absolute rectitude from the saint: He has given him the very nature of God. SSY 105

---

a. Some manuscripts *your*
b. Or *every*

96

1 JOHN 2

JESUS, OUR ATONING SACRIFICE

y dear children, I write this to you so that you will not sin. But if anybody does sin, we have one who speaks to the Father in our defense—Jesus Christ, the Righteous One. He is the atoning sacrifice for our sins, and not only for ours but also for[a] the sins of the whole world.

We know that we have come to know him if we obey his commands. The man who says, "I know him," but does not do what he commands is a liar, and the truth is not in him. But if anyone obeys his word, God's love[b] is truly made complete in him. This is how we know we are in him: Whoever claims to live in him must walk as Jesus did.

Dear friends, I am not writing you a new command but an old one, which you have had since the beginning. This old command is the message you have heard. Yet I am writing you a new command; its truth is seen in him and you, because the darkness is passing and the true light is already shining.

Anyone who claims to be in the light but hates his brother is still in the darkness. Whoever loves his brother lives in the light, and there is nothing in him[c] to make him stumble. But whoever hates his brother is in the darkness and walks around in the darkness; he does not know where he is going, because the darkness has blinded him.

I write to you, dear children,
   because your sins have been forgiven
      on account of his name.
I write to you, fathers,
   because you have known him who is from the beginning.

I write to you, young men,
   because you have overcome the evil one.
I write to you, dear children,
   because you have known the Father.
I write to you, fathers,
   because you have known him who is from the beginning.
I write to you, young men,
   because you are strong,
      and the word of God lives in you,
      and you have overcome the evil one.

DO NOT LOVE THE WORLD

Do not love the world or anything in the world. If anyone loves the world, the love of the Father is not in him. For everything in the world—the cravings of sinful man, the lust of his eyes and the boasting of what he has and does—comes not from the Father but from the world. The world and its desires pass away, but the man who does the will of God lives forever.

WARNING AGAINST ANTICHRISTS

Dear children, this is the last hour; and as you have heard that the antichrist is coming, even now many antichrists have come. This is how we know it is the last hour. They went out from us, but they did not really belong to us. For if they had belonged to us, they would have remained with us; but their going showed that none of them belonged to us.

But you have an anointing from the Holy One, and all of you know the truth.[d] I do not write to you because you do not know the truth, but because you do know it and because no lie comes from the truth. Who is the liar? It is the man who denies that Jesus is the Christ. Such a man is the antichrist—he denies the Father and the Son. No one who denies the Son has the Father; whoever acknowledges the Son has the Father also.

See that what you have heard from the beginning remains in you. If it does, you also will remain in the Son and in the Father. And this is what he promised us—even eternal life.

I am writing these things to you about those who are trying to lead you astray. As for you, the anointing you received from him remains in you, and you do not need anyone to teach you. But as his anointing teaches you about all things and as that anointing is real, not counterfeit—just as it has taught you, remain in him.

CHILDREN OF GOD

And now, dear children, continue in him, so that when he appears we may be confident and unashamed before him at his coming.

If you know that he is righteous, you know that everyone who does what is right has been born of him.

> *"We know that we have come to know him*
> *if we obey his commands.*
> *The man who says, 'I know him,'*
> *but does not do what he commands is a liar,*
> *and the truth is not in him."*

FROM OSWALD CHAMBERS

ه God will have us discern what He is doing, but it takes time because we are so slow to obey, and only as we obey do we perceive morally and spiritually. BFB 52

ه Weighing the *pros* and *cons* for and against a statement of Jesus Christ means that for the time being I refuse to obey Him. DI 71

ه It is not a question of being willing to go straight through, but of going straight through. Not a question of saying, "Lord, I will do it," but of doing it. There must be the reckless committal of everything to Him with no regard for the consequences. GW 79

ه "I am crucified with Christ; nevertheless I live; yet not I, but Christ liveth in me" (Gal. 2:20). These words mean the breaking of my independence and surrendering to the supremacy of the Lord Jesus. No one can do this for me; I must do it myself. There is no possibility of debate when once I am there. It is not that we have to do work for God; we have to be so loyal to Jesus Christ that He does His work through us. We learn His truth by obeying it. HGM 148

🕊 God never insists on our obedience; human authority does. Our Lord does not give us rules and regulations; He makes very clear what the standard is, and if the relation of my spirit to Him is that of love, I will do all He wants me to do without the slightest hesitation. If I begin to object, it is because I love someone else in competition with Him, viz., myself. HGM 148

🕊 Jesus Christ's first obedience was to the will of His Father, and our first obedience is to be to Him. The thing that detects where we live spiritually is the word *obey*. The natural heart of man hates the word, and that hatred is the essence of the disposition that will not let Jesus Christ rule. MFL 114

🕊 "Consider the lilies of the field" (Matt. 6:28) — they grow where they are put. Many of us refuse to grow where we are put; consequently, we take root nowhere. Jesus says that if we obey the life God has given us, He will look after all the other things. MUH 26

🕊 Our Lord never enforces obedience; He does not take means to make me do what He wants. At certain times I wish God would master me and make me do the things; but He will not; in other moods I wish He would leave me alone, but He does not. MUH 266

🕊 All God's revelations are sealed until they are opened to us by obedience. You will never get them open by philosophy or thinking. Immediately you obey, a flash of light comes. Let God's truth work in you by soaking in it, not by worrying into it. The only way you can get to know is to stop trying to find out and by being born again. Obey God in the thing He shows you, and instantly the next thing is opened up. One reads tomes on the work of the Holy Spirit, when one five minutes of drastic obedience would make things as clear as a sunbeam. MUH 284

---

a. Or *He is the one who turns aside God's wrath, taking away our sins, and not only ours but also*
b. Or *word, love for God*
c. Or *it*
d. Some manuscripts *and you know all things*

97

1 JOHN 3

CHILDREN OF GOD

H ow great is the love the Father has lavished on us, that we should be called children of God! And that is what we are! The reason the world does not know us is that it did not know him. Dear friends, now we are children of God, and what we will be has not yet been made known. But we know that when he appears,[a] we shall be like him, for we shall see him as he is. Everyone who has this hope in him purifies himself, just as he is pure.

Everyone who sins breaks the law; in fact, sin is lawlessness. But you know that he appeared so that he might take away our sins. And in him is no sin. No one who lives in him keeps on sinning. No one who continues to sin has either seen him or known him.

Dear children, do not let anyone lead you astray. He who does what is right is righteous, just as he is righteous. He who does what is sinful is of the devil, because the devil has been sinning from the beginning. The reason the Son of God appeared was to destroy the devil's work. No one who is born of God will continue to sin, because God's seed remains in him; he cannot go on sinning, because he has been born of God. This is how we know who the children of God are and who the children of the devil are: Anyone who does not do what is right is not a child of God; nor is anyone who does not love his brother.

LOVE ONE ANOTHER

This is the message you heard from the beginning: We should love one another. Do not be like Cain, who belonged to the evil one and murdered his brother. And why did he murder him?

Because his own actions were evil and his brother's were righteous. Do not be surprised, my brothers, if the world hates you. We know that we have passed from death to life, because we love our brothers. Anyone who does not love remains in death. Anyone who hates his brother is a murderer, and you know that no murderer has eternal life in him.

This is how we know what love is: Jesus Christ laid down his life for us. And we ought to lay down our lives for our brothers. If anyone has material possessions and sees his brother in need but has no pity on him, how can the love of God be in him? Dear children, let us not love with words or tongue but with actions and in truth. This then is how we know that we belong to the truth, and how we set our hearts at rest in his presence whenever our hearts condemn us. For God is greater than our hearts, and he knows everything.

Dear friends, if our hearts do not condemn us, we have confidence before God and receive from him anything we ask, because we obey his commands and do what pleases him. And this is his command: to believe in the name of his Son, Jesus Christ, and to love one another as he commanded us. Those who obey his commands live in him, and he in them. And this is how we know that he lives in us: We know it by the Spirit he gave us.

> *"Now we are children of God, and what we will be*
> *has not yet been made known."*

From Oswald Chambers

- When we are rightly related to God as Jesus was, the spiritual life becomes as natural as the life of a child. BSG 14

- The child-heart is open to any and all avenues; an angel would no more surprise it than a man. In dreams, in visions, in visible and invisible ways, God can talk and reveal Himself to a child; but this profound yet simple way is lost forever immediately when we lose the open, childlike nature. CD VOL. 1, 17

- When a little child becomes conscious of being a little child, the childlikeness is gone; and when a saint becomes conscious of being a saint, something has gone wrong. OBH 68

❧ The religion of Jesus Christ is the religion of a little child. There is no affectation about a disciple of Jesus; he is as a little child, amazingly simple but unfathomably deep. Many of us are not child-like enough; we are childish. Jesus said—"Except ye become as little children" (Matt. 18:3). OBH 97

❧ Jesus Christ uses the child-spirit as a touchstone for the character of a disciple. He did not put up a child before His disciples as an ideal, but as an expression of the simple-hearted life they would live when they were born again. The life of a little child is expectant, full of wonder, and free from self-consciousness, and Jesus said, "Except ye turn, and become as little children, ye shall in no wise enter into the kingdom of heaven" (Matt. 18:3). PH 185

❧ The Spirit of God creates the intuitions of a child in a man and keeps him in touch with the elemental and real, and the miracle of Christianity is that a man can be made young in heart and mind and spirit. PH 186

❧ As we bring the child mind to what Jesus says about things, we will begin to manifest the miracle of an undisturbed heart. In the Cross our Lord deals with everything that keeps a man's heart disturbed. PH 222

---

a. Or *when it is made known*

98

TEST THE SPIRITS

Dear friends, do not believe every spirit, but test the spirits to see whether they are from God, because many false prophets have gone out into the world. This is how you can recognize the Spirit of God: Every spirit that acknowledges that Jesus Christ has come in the flesh is from God, but every spirit that does not acknowledge Jesus is not from God. This is the spirit of the antichrist, which you have heard is coming and even now is already in the world.

You, dear children, are from God and have overcome them, because the one who is in you is greater than the one who is in the world. They are from the world and therefore speak from the viewpoint of the world, and the world listens to them. We are from God, and whoever knows God listens to us; but whoever is not from God does not listen to us. This is how we recognize the Spirit[a] of truth and the spirit of falsehood.

GOD'S LOVE AND OURS

Dear friends, let us love one another, for love comes from God. Everyone who loves has been born of God and knows God. Whoever does not love does not know God, because God is love. This is how God showed his love among us: He sent his one and only Son[b] into the world that we might live through him. This is love: not that we loved God, but that he loved us and sent his Son as an atoning sacrifice for[c] our sins. Dear friends, since God so loved us, we also ought to love one another. No one has ever seen God; but if we love one another, God lives in us and his love is made complete in us.

We know that we live in him and he in us, because he has given us of his Spirit. And we have seen and testify that the Father has sent his Son to be the Savior of the world. If anyone acknowledges that Jesus is the Son of God, God lives in him and he in God. And so we know and rely on the love God has for us.

God is love. Whoever lives in love lives in God, and God in him. In this way, love is made complete among us so that we will have confidence on the day of judgment, because in this world we are like him. There is no fear in love. But perfect love drives out fear, because fear has to do with punishment. The one who fears is not made perfect in love.

We love because he first loved us. If anyone says, "I love God," yet hates his brother, he is a liar. For anyone who does not love his brother, whom he has seen, cannot love God, whom he has not seen. And he has given us this command: Whoever loves God must also love his brother.

> *"Since God so loved us, we also ought to love one another. . . .*
> *If we love each other, God lives in us*
> *and his love is made complete in us."*

FROM OSWALD CHAMBERS

> ❧ If my love is first of all God, I shall take no account of the base ingratitude of others, because the mainspring of my service to my fellowmen is love to God. BP 181

> ❧ Most of us love other people for what they are to us instead of for what God wants them to be. CHI 69

> ❧ "Love is of God"; it never came from the devil and never can go to the devil. When I am rightly related to God, the more I love, the more blessing does He pour out on other lives. The reward of love is the capacity to pour out more love all the time, "hoping for nothing again." That is the essential nature of perfect love. GW 41

> ❧ When you are sentimentally interested in a person, you are conscious of it; when you are in love with a person, you are not conscious of it, because the love is deeper than consciousness and is only revealed in a crisis. When you love God, you become identified

with His interests in other people, and He will bring around you those He is interested in—the sinners, the mean, the ungrateful, and you will soon know by your attitude to them whether you love God. GW 41

❧ God's love for me is inexhaustible, and His love for me is the basis of my love for others. We have to love where we cannot respect and where we must not respect, and this can only be done on the basis of God's love for us. "This is My commandment, That ye love one another, *as I have loved you*" (John 13:34). OBH 59

❧ The greatest love of a man is his love for his friends; the greatest love of God is His love for His enemies; the highest Christian love is that a man will lay down his life for his Friend, the Lord Jesus Christ. OBH 60

❧ When the Holy Spirit has shed abroad the love of God in our hearts, then that love requires cultivation. No love on earth will develop without being cultivated. We have to dedicate ourselves to love, which means identifying ourselves with God's interests in other people, and God is interested in some funny people, viz., in you and in me! OBH 117

❧ Jesus has loved me to the end of all my meanness and selfishness and sin; now, He says, show that same love to others. PH 81

---

a. Or *spirit*
b. Or *his only begotten Son*
c. Or *as the one who would turn aside his wrath, taking away*

99

1 JOHN 5

FAITH IN THE SON OF GOD

Everyone who believes that Jesus is the Christ is born of God, and everyone who loves the father loves his child as well. This is how we know that we love the children of God: by loving God and carrying out his commands. This is love for God: to obey his commands. And his commands are not burdensome, for everyone born of God overcomes the world. This is the victory that has overcome the world, even our faith. Who is it that overcomes the world? Only he who believes that Jesus is the Son of God.

This is the one who came by water and blood—Jesus Christ. He did not come by water only, but by water and blood. And it is the Spirit who testifies, because the Spirit is the truth. For there are three that testify: the^a Spirit, the water and the blood; and the three are in agreement. We accept man's testimony, but God's testimony is greater because it is the testimony of God, which he has given about his Son. Anyone who believes in the Son of God has this testimony in his heart. Anyone who does not believe God has made him out to be a liar, because he has not believed the testimony God has given about his Son. And this is the testimony: God has given us eternal life, and this life is in his Son. He who has the Son has life; he who does not have the Son of God does not have life.

CONCLUDING REMARKS

I write these things to you who believe in the name of the Son of God so that you may know that you have eternal life. This is the confidence we have in approaching God: that if we ask anything according to his will, he hears us. And if we know that he hears us—

whatever we ask—we know that we have what we asked of him.

If anyone sees his brother commit a sin that does not lead to death, he should pray and God will give him life. I refer to those whose sin does not lead to death. There is a sin that leads to death. I am not saying that he should pray about that. All wrong-doing is sin, and there is sin that does not lead to death.

We know that anyone born of God does not continue to sin; the one who was born of God keeps him safe, and the evil one cannot harm him. We know that we are children of God, and that the whole world is under the control of the evil one. We know also that the Son of God has come and has given us under-standing, so that we may know him who is true. And we are in him who is true—even in his Son Jesus Christ. He is the true God and eternal life.

Dear children, keep yourselves from idols.

"I write these things to you who believe in
the name of the Son of God so that you may
know that you have eternal life."

FROM OSWALD CHAMBERS

- All we know about eternal life, about hell and damnation, the Bible alone tells us. BP 95

- The gift *of God* is eternal life" (Rom. 6:23), not the gift *from* God, as if eternal life were a present given by God: it is Himself. CD VOL. 1, 139

- Whenever our Lord speaks of "life" He means *eternal* life, and He says, "Ye have not [this] life in yourselves." Men have natural life and intellectual life apart from Jesus Christ. HG 110

- The life which Jesus Christ exhibited was eternal life, and He says—anyone who believes in Me, i.e., commits himself to Me, has that life. To commit myself to Jesus means there is nothing that is not committed. HG 110

- The upward look toward God for eternal life is an indication of the inherent nature of the life; that is, it is not attained by effort.

Natural characteristics, natural virtues, and natural attainments have nothing to do with the life itself. HG 111

❧ Our Lord's life is the exhibition of eternal life in time. Eternal life in the Christian is based on redemptive certainty; he is not working to redeem men; he is a fellow worker with God among men because they are redeemed. HG 111

❧ Eternal life has nothing to do with time; it is the life which Jesus lived when He was down here. The only source of life is the Lord Jesus Christ. MUH 103

❧ "Verily, verily, I say unto you, he that believeth on Me hath everlasting life" (John 6:47). The very life that was in Jesus is the life of the soul who believes in Him, because it is created in him by Jesus. This life is only in Jesus Christ, it is not in anyone else, and we cannot get it by obeying or by praying, by vowing, or by sacrificing. OBH 26

❧ "As He is, so are we." The sanctified life is a life that bears a strong family likeness to Jesus Christ, a life that exhibits His virtues, His patience, His love, His holiness. Slowly and surely we learn the great secret of eternal life, which is to know God. OBH 43

❧ Jesus Christ came to give us eternal life, a life in which there is neither time nor space, which cannot be marked with suffering or death; it is the life Jesus lived. PH 76

a. Late manuscripts of the Vulgate *testify in heaven: the Father, the Word and the Holy Spirit, and these three are one. And there are three that testify on earth: the* (not found in any Greek manuscript before the sixteenth century)

100

2 & 3 JOHN

WARNING ABOUT DECEIVERS

he elder,
To the chosen lady and her children, whom I love in the truth—and not I only, but also all who know the truth—because of the truth, which lives in us and will be with us forever:

Grace, mercy and peace from God the Father and from Jesus Christ, the Father's Son, will be with us in truth and love.

It has given me great joy to find some of your children walking in the truth, just as the Father commanded us. And now, dear lady, I am not writing you a new command but one we have had from the beginning. I ask that we love one another. And this is love: that we walk in obedience to his commands. As you have heard from the beginning, his command is that you walk in love.

Many deceivers, who do not acknowledge Jesus Christ as coming in the flesh, have gone out into the world. Any such person is the deceiver and the antichrist. Watch out that you do not lose what you have worked for, but that you may be rewarded fully. Anyone who runs ahead and does not continue in the teaching of Christ does not have God; whoever continues in the teaching has both the Father and the Son. If anyone comes to you and does not bring this teaching, do not take him into your house or welcome him. Anyone who welcomes him shares in his wicked work.

I have much to write to you, but I do not want to use paper and ink. Instead, I hope to visit you and talk with you face to face, so that our joy may be complete.

The children of your chosen sister send their greetings.

The elder,
To my dear friend Gaius, whom I love in the truth.
Dear friend, I pray that you may enjoy good health and that all

may go well with you, even as your soul is getting along well. It gave me great joy to have some brothers come and tell about your faithfulness to the truth and how you continue to walk in the truth. I have no greater joy than to hear that my children are walking in the truth.

Dear friend, you are faithful in what you are doing for the brothers, even though they are strangers to you. They have told the church about your love. You will do well to send them on their way in a manner worthy of God. It was for the sake of the Name that they went out, receiving no help from the pagans. We ought therefore to show hospitality to such men so that we may work together for the truth.

I wrote to the church, but Diotrephes, who loves to be first, will have nothing to do with us. So if I come, I will call attention to what he is doing, gossiping maliciously about us. Not satisfied with that, he refuses to welcome the brothers. He also stops those who want to do so and puts them out of the church.

Dear friend, do not imitate what is evil but what is good. Anyone who does what is good is from God. Anyone who does what is evil has not seen God. Demetrius is well spoken of by everyone — and even by the truth itself. We also speak well of him, and you know that our testimony is true.

I have much to write you, but I do not want to do so with pen and ink. I hope to see you soon, and we will talk face to face.

Peace to you. The friends here send their greetings. Greet the friends there by name.

"It has given me great joy
to find some of your children walking in the truth,
just as the Father commanded us."

FROM OSWALD CHAMBERS

 ⳩ Truth is moral, not intellectual. We perceive truth by doing the right thing, not by thinking it out. "If any man will do His will, he shall know of the doctrine" (John 7:17). BP 102

 ⳩ Amid all the whirling contentions and confusions produced in men's minds by what is called truth, again our Lord's word to

Thomas abides, "I am the truth" (John 14:6). CD VOL. 1, 138

ॐ Every partial truth has so much error in it that you can dispute it, but you can't dispute truth as it is in Jesus. DI 3

ॐ Allow nothing to take you away from Jesus Himself, and all other phases of truth will take their right place. GW 106

ॐ Truth is a person. *"I am the truth,"* said Jesus. OPG 1

ॐ Truth is not discerned intellectually; it is discerned spiritually. PR 116

ॐ Beware of making God's truth simpler than He has made it Himself. RTR 39

ॐ Beware of turning your back on what you know is true because you do not want it to be real. SHL 60

ॐ The central truth is not salvation, nor sanctification, nor the Second Coming; the central truth is nothing less than Jesus Christ Himself. "I, if I be lifted up from the earth, will draw all men unto Me" (John 12:32). Error always comes in when we take something Jesus Christ does and preach it as the truth. It is part of the truth, but if we take it to be the whole truth we become advocates of an idea instead of a person, the Lord Himself. SSM 83

ॐ Jesus Christ is the truth, an incarnate ideal; to be "in Christ" means that through regeneration and sanctification that ideal can become a reality, so that in my mortal flesh there is manifested that which is easily discerned to be "the life also of Jesus." We are to be incorporated into the truth. GW 34

ॐ "The truth" is our Lord Himself; "the whole truth" is the inspired Scripture interpreting the truth to us; and "nothing but the truth" is the Holy Spirit, "the Spirit of truth" efficaciously regenerating and sanctifying us, and guiding us into "all the truth." GW 35

ॐ The one great truth to keep steadfastly before us is the Lord Jesus Christ; He is the truth. Only the whole truth is the truth, and any part of the truth may become an error. If you have a ray of light on the truth, never call it the whole truth; follow it up and it will lead you to the central truth, the Lord Jesus Christ. BSG 69

101

JUDE

THE SIN AND DOOM OF GODLESS MEN

Jude, a servant of Jesus Christ and a brother of James,
To those who have been called, who are loved by
God the Father and kept by[a] Jesus Christ:

Mercy, peace and love be yours in abundance.

Dear friends, although I was very eager to write to
you about the salvation we share, I felt I had to write and urge
you to contend for the faith that was once for all entrusted to the
saints. For certain men whose condemnation was written about[b]
long ago have secretly slipped in among you. They are godless
men, who change the grace of our God into a license for immorality and deny Jesus Christ our only Sovereign and Lord.

Though you already know all this, I want to remind you that
the Lord[c] delivered his people out of Egypt, but later destroyed
those who did not believe. And the angels who did not keep their
positions of authority but abandoned their own home—these he
has kept in darkness, bound with everlasting chains for judgment
on the great Day. In a similar way, Sodom and Gomorrah and
the surrounding towns gave themselves up to sexual immorality
and perversion. They serve as an example of those who suffer the
punishment of eternal fire.

In the very same way, these dreamers pollute their own bodies,
reject authority and slander celestial beings. But even the archangel Michael, when he was disputing with the devil about the
body of Moses, did not dare to bring a slanderous accusation
against him, but said, "The Lord rebuke you!" Yet these men
speak abusively against whatever they do not understand; and
what things they do understand by instinct, like unreasoning animals—these are the very things that destroy them.

Woe to them! They have taken the way of Cain; they have

rushed for profit into Balaam's error; they have been destroyed in Korah's rebellion.

These men are blemishes at your love feasts, eating with you without the slightest qualm—shepherds who feed only themselves. They are clouds without rain, blown along by the wind; autumn trees, without fruit and uprooted—twice dead. They are wild waves of the sea, foaming up their shame; wandering stars, for whom blackest darkness has been reserved forever.

Enoch, the seventh from Adam, prophesied about these men: "See, the Lord is coming with thousands upon thousands of his holy ones to judge everyone, and to convict all the ungodly of all the ungodly acts they have done in the ungodly way, and of all the harsh words ungodly sinners have spoken against him." These men are grumblers and faultfinders; they follow their own evil desires; they boast about themselves and flatter others for their own advantage.

A Call to Persevere

But, dear friends, remember what the apostles of our Lord Jesus Christ foretold. They said to you, "In the last times there will be scoffers who will follow their own ungodly desires." These are the men who divide you, who follow mere natural instincts and do not have the Spirit.

But you, dear friends, build yourselves up in your most holy faith and pray in the Holy Spirit. Keep yourselves in God's love as you wait for the mercy of our Lord Jesus Christ to bring you to eternal life.

Be merciful to those who doubt; snatch others from the fire and save them; to others show mercy, mixed with fear—hating even the clothing stained by corrupted flesh.

Doxology

To him who is able to keep you from falling and to present you before his glorious presence without fault and with great joy—to the only God our Savior be glory, majesty, power and authority, through Jesus Christ our Lord, before all ages, now and forevermore! Amen.

*"Contend for the faith that was once for all
entrusted to the saints."*

From Oswald Chambers

- As saints, we should smart and suffer keenly whenever we see pride and covetousness and self-realization, because these are the things that go against the honor of God. BP 185

- Character in a saint means the disposition of Jesus Christ persistently manifested. BP 205

- The work of Jesus is the creation of saints; He can take the worst, the most misshapen material, and make a saint. BSG 55

- The production of a saint is the grandest thing earth can give to heaven. A saint is not a person with a saintly character: a saint *is* a saintly character. Character, not ecstatic moods, is the stuff of saintliness. A saint is a living epistle written by the finger of God, known and read of all men. CD VOL. 1, 99

- The vocation of a saint is to be in the thick of it "for Thy sake." Whenever Jesus Christ refers to discipleship or to suffering, it is always, "for My sake." The deep relationship of a saint is a personal one, and the reason a saint can be radiant is that he has lost interest in his own individuality and has become absolutely devoted to the person of the Lord Jesus Christ. CD VOL. 1, 156

- The Lord can never make a saint out of a good man; He can only make a saint out of three classes of people — the godless man, the weak man, and the sinful man, and no one else; and the marvel of the Gospel of God's grace is that Jesus Christ can make us naturally what He wants us to be. HG 76

- As saints we are called to go through the heroism of what we believe, not of stating what we believe, but of standing by it when the facts are dead against God. HGM 80

- The weakest saint can experience the power of the deity of the Son of God if once he is willing to "let go." Any strand of our own energy will blur the life of Jesus. We have to keep letting go, and slowly and surely the great full life of God will invade us in every

395

part, and men will take knowledge of us that we have been with Jesus. MUH 103

≈ If the saint is paying attention to the source, Jesus Christ, out of him and unconsciously to him are flowing the rivers of living water wherever he goes. Men are either getting better or worse because of us. PR 44

≈ The saints who satisfy the heart of Jesus are the imperial people of God forever; nothing deflects them. They are super-conquerors, and in the future they will be side by side with Jesus. "He that overcometh, I will grant to sit down with Me in My throne, even as I also overcame, and am sat down with My Father in His throne" (Rev. 3:21). SHL 123

≈ When a man is born from above, he does not need to pretend to be a saint. He cannot help being one. SSM 30

≈ We do not need the grace of God to stand crises; human nature and our pride will do it. We can buck up and face the music of a crisis magnificently, but it does require the supernatural grace of God to live twenty-four hours of the day as a saint, to go through drudgery as a saint, to go through poverty as a saint, to go through an ordinary, unobtrusive, ignored existence as a saint, unnoted and unnoticeable. SSY 69

---

a. Or for; or *in*
b. Or *men who were marked out for condemnation*
c. Some early manuscripts *Jesus*

SUBJECT INDEX OF QUOTATIONS USED IN DAILY READINGS

Day Subject

397